# Math for All

# Math for All

Differentiating Instruction,
Grades 6–8

*Linda Dacey* & *Karen Gartland*

Math Solutions
Sausalito, California, USA

*With deep affection for the two people who mean the most to us:*
*John Dacey*
*Joe Gartland*

**Math Solutions**
One Harbor Drive, Suite 101
Sausalito, CA 94965
www.mathsolutions.com

**Library of Congress Cataloging-in-Publication Data**
Dacey, Linda Schulman, 1949–
  Math for all. Differentiating instruction, grades 6–8 / Linda Dacey & Karen Gartland.
    p. cm.
  Includes bibliographical references and index.
  ISBN 978-1-935099-00-0 (alk. paper)
  1. Mathematics—Study and teaching (Middle school)  I. Gartland, Karen. II. Title. III. Title: Differentiating instruction, grades 6–8.
  QA11.2.D3284 2008
  372.7'044–dc22
                              2009038879

Editor: Jamie Ann Cross
Production: Melissa L. Inglis-Elliott
Cover design: Jan Streitburger
Interior design: Joni Doherty Design
Composition: MPS Limited, a Macmillan Company

Printed in the United States of America on acid-free paper
13 12     AAP     4 5

# A Message from Math Solutions

We at Math Solutions believe that teaching math well calls for increasing our understanding of the math we teach, seeking deeper insights into how students learn mathematics, and refining our lessons to best promote students' learning.

Math Solutions shares classroom-tested lessons and teaching expertise from our faculty of professional development consultants as well as from other respected math educators. Our publications are part of the nationwide effort we've made since 1984 that now includes

- more than five hundred face-to-face professional development programs each year for teachers and administrators in districts across the country;
- professional development books that span all math topics taught in kindergarten through high school;
- videos for teachers and for parents that show math lessons taught in actual classrooms;
- on-site visits to schools to help refine teaching strategies and assess student learning; and
- free online support, including grade-level lessons, book reviews, inservice information, and district feedback, all in our Math Solutions Online Newsletter.

For information about all of the products and services we have available, please visit our website at *www.mathsolutions.com.* You can also contact us to discuss math professional development needs by calling (800) 868-9092 or by sending an email to *info@mathsolutions.com.*

We're always eager for your feedback and interested in learning about your particular needs. We look forward to hearing from you.

# Contents

## Chapter 9 Teaching with the Goal of Differentiation / 229
Ten Ways to Sustain Your Efforts / 230

## Reproducibles / 247

# Preface

$T$his book is the third in a three-book series. To most effectively reach teachers' specific grade-level needs, I wrote the first book for grades K–2, with coauthor Rebeka Eston Salemi, and the second book for grades 3–5, with coauthor Jayne Bamford Lynch. When Math Solutions approached me to write a book for grades 6–8, I immediately contacted Karen Gartland. A valued colleague for many years, Karen is a seasoned teacher, tutor, math coach, and consultant who brings great enthusiasm to her work. There is significant overlap between the three books, though each is tailored to its particular grade span. The classroom vignettes differ, of course, as well as many of the teacher reflections and some of the teaching strategies and techniques. Sometimes particular stories and reflections were relevant across the grade levels and we made only those changes necessary for the intended audience. Sometimes middle school teachers were so positive about a previous example or reflection that they adapted it for this level.

Trends and buzzwords come and go in education, but the need for differentiated instruction is constant. Our students deserve to have their individual learning needs met in their classrooms. Throughout the book we suggest that teaching this way is a career-long goal, one part of our professional journey. We know that this is true for us, and we are eager to share our current thinking with you.

—LINDA DACEY

# Acknowledgments

This book features stories and student work from a number of classrooms. Numerous colleagues, workshop participants, and students have informed our work. We are profoundly thankful for their time, insights, and contributions. We are particularly grateful to the Massachusetts students and teachers in public schools in Cambridge, Lincoln, Groton-Dunstable, Melrose, and Somerville.

Linda would like to acknowledge Lesley University for its support of her work and Karen is appreciative of the Groton-Dunstable Regional School District. Together, we would like to express our gratitude for Rebeka Eston Salemi and Jayne Bamford Lynch, who helped shape this work. Also, our families and our friends fuel our spirits and we are always thankful for their patience, flexibility, and love.

We thank our editor, Jamie Cross, for her interest and guidance in this project, Toby Gordon for her earlier support, and Marilyn Burns for her direction and vision. Thank you, too, to Joan Carlson and Melissa Inglis-Elliott and the many other talented people we have encountered at Math Solutions.

# Connections to NCTM's
## *Principles and Standards for School Mathematics* (2000)

| Page | Grade level* | Strand | Focus | Type of Activity |
|------|--------------|--------|-------|------------------|
| 6 | 7 | Number and Data | Interpret comparative statements involving ratios. | pre-assessment embedded in lesson |
| 10 | 8 | Measurement | Solve problems involving volume and proportional reasoning. | lesson connected to book *Counting on Frank* |
| 24 | 6 | Number | Multiply with decimals. | problem discussion |
| 28 | 8 | Algebra | Create and analyze linear equations to represent situations. | lesson tied to buying school lunches |
| 34 | 8 | Algebra | Model linear situations with tables, graphs, and equations. | lesson built on parking receipts |
| 40 | 8 | Algebra | Pose problems related to tables, graphs, or equations. | lesson focusing on posing problems |
| 54 | 6 | Geometry | Describe and classify polygons. | polygon-sorting activity |
| 56 | 6–8 | Number and Algebra | Demonstrate number sense. | interview questions |
| 59 | 6 | Number | Demonstrate understanding of meaning of percent. | open-ended tasks |

*(Continued)*

*Single-grade levels identify the grade where the lesson or task was implemented during the development of this book. Many of these ideas can be applied in other grades as well.

| Page | Grade level* | Strand | Focus | Type of Activity |
|---|---|---|---|---|
| 73 | 7 | Geometry | Identify attributes of similar triangles, including scale factors. | post-assessment idea |
| 82 | 8 | Measurement | Develop and use formulas to find area of complex polygons. | lesson using geoboards |
| 87 | 6–8 | Data and Algebra | Organize information and look for patterns. | problem-solving task: Barrel of Monkeys |
| 97 | 7 | Number | Compute with fractions, decimals, and percents to solve problems. | lesson involving number puzzles |
| 110 | 8 | Measurement and Geometry | Applying the Pythagorean theorem to find volumes and surface areas. | tiered logic problems |
| 111 | 6–8 | Data | Collect, display, and analyze data. | tiered survey tasks |
| 115 | 6–8 | Algebra | Represent, analyze, and generalize patterns. | tiered tasks involving visual patterns |
| 115 | 6–8 | Algebra and Number | Interpret information in a graph to solve problems. | tiered tasks related to a trip to an ice cream shop |
| 125 | 8 | Algebra | Find and generalize patterns in nonlinear data. | lesson involving the Tower of Hanoi |
| 135 | 6 | Measurement | Understand units of measure and convert within a measurement system. | activities to serve multiple intelligences |
| 158 | 7 | Geometry | Classify angles. | computer applet Angles |
| 161 | 7 | Number | Develop meaning for integers. | student posts real-world connections on a class website |
| 165 | 8 | Data | Relate basic concepts of probability. | student-created concept web lesson |

*Single-grade levels identify the grade where the lesson or task was implemented during the development of this book. Many of these ideas can be applied in other grades as well.

| Page | Grade level* | Strand | Focus | Type of Activity |
|---|---|---|---|---|
| 183 | 7 | Data | Find, use, and interpret measures of central tendency. | choices in math workshop |
| 187 | 8 | Algebra and Data | Recognize linear, quadratic, and exponential functions. | conducting experiments with bouncing balls |
| 190 | 6–8 | Number | Understand large numbers. | collecting a million pennies |
| 191 | 8 | Algebra | Use systems of linear equations. | choices on a menu board |
| 194 | 6 | Geometry | Examine symmetry. | choices on a menu list focused on symmetry and art |
| 195 | 6–8 | Number | Compute with fractions. | choices in a Think-Tac-Toe format |
| 196 | 7 | Data | Make real-world connections to ideas of probability. | choices in a RAFT format |
| 196 | 7 | Number | Use proportional reasoning. | choices within learning stations involving modeling |
| 200 | 8 | Algebra and Number | Explore patterns and make generalizations. | choices with learning stations involving Fibonacci numbers |
| 238 | 6–8 | Number | Compute with decimals, fractions, and percents. | math games |

*Single-grade levels identify the grade where the lesson or task was implemented during the development of this book. Many of these ideas can be applied in other grades as well.

# Chapter 1
# Thinking About Differentiation

*S*usan, a seventh-grade teacher, is concerned about one of her students who is fairly successful at computation with integers but does not seem to know how to apply these skills to solve problems. He always wants rules about what to do and in what order to do it. He becomes frustrated easily and sometimes it seems as if he gives up before he has even started. His parents often work with him at home and write out step-by-step procedures for him to follow. For the past few weeks, Susan has been using a graphic organizer to support his ability to solve problems and his work has shown considerable improvement. Now she's wondering about the number of practice problems she has been giving him and how similar they are. Perhaps he's just recognizing the problems and following the steps that he has associated with them. Susan would like to give him a more challenging, nontraditional problem, but she is concerned about frustrating him again.

Sixth-grade teacher Tom is concerned about one of his students who seems to be quite advanced. It is early in the school year and Tom is introducing a three-day investigation about the sums of the interior and exterior angles of polygons. The first day's work focuses on triangles and the class is investigating a series of activities that will allow the students to discover that the sum of the angles in a triangle is always 180 degrees. They are just beginning the first activity when this student announces that she knows a formula that will work with all polygons. Tom knows he can't allow this student to keep the other students from making their own discoveries, but if he keeps her from sharing her ideas, how can she feel part of her classroom community? Also, he is worried about how to challenge her. She seems to already know so much more than this year's curriculum offers.

Middle school teacher Margaret knows that students have come to her eighth-grade class with much previous knowledge about addition and subtraction of fractions. A small group of her students, however, still struggles to recall the rules for subtracting fractions with unlike denominators. One of these students is particularly adept at knowing when to add or subtract fractions in real-life situations but cannot follow the proper steps to find the answer. He is angry about having to learn the same thing over and over, and one day he says, "Why do you people keep making me do this? I hate math!" Margaret is wondering about the use of a calculator that allows students to enter fractions and then perform operations. She knows that this would help this student arrive at correct solutions to problems. Her colleagues and principal do not believe that this type of calculator should be used and that Margaret should continue to provide instruction and practice with this skill. Margaret still wonders about letting the student use the calculator for a few weeks to improve his disposition.

These three teachers are like most middle school teachers. They want to provide for the needs of all of their students. They want to recognize the unique gifts and readiness each student brings to the classroom. These teachers also realize that addressing the variety of abilities, interests, cultures, and learning styles in their classrooms is a challenging task. Variations in student learning have always existed in classrooms, but some have been given attention only recently. For example, our understanding of intelligence has broadened with Howard Gardner's (2000) theory of multiple intelligences. Teachers are now more conscious of some of the different strengths among students and find ways to tap into those strengths in the classroom.

## Habits of Mind

Brain research has given us further insight into the learning process; for example, it has shown us that there is an explicit link between our emotional state and our ability to learn (Jensen 2005; Sprenger 2002). Having a sense of control and being able to make choices typically contribute to increased interest and a positive attitude. So we can think of providing choice, and thus, control, as creating a healthier learning environment.

At the same time that we are gaining these insights, the diversity of learning needs in classrooms is growing. The number of English language learners (ELLs) in our schools is increasing dramatically. Classroom teachers need to know ways to help these students learn content while they are also learning English.

Different values and cultures create different learning patterns among children and different expectations for classroom interactions. Also, our inclusive classrooms contain a broader spectrum of special education needs, and the number of children with identified or perceived special learning needs is growing. On a regular basis, classroom teachers need to adapt plans to include and effectively instruct the range of student needs.

How can teachers meet the growing diversity of learning needs in their classrooms? Further, how do teachers meet this challenge in the midst of increasing pressures to ensure students master specified content? Differentiated instruction—instruction designed to meet differing learners' needs—is clearly required. By adapting classroom practices to help more students be successful, teachers are able to both honor individual students and increase the likelihood that their class will meet the required curricular outcomes.

This book takes the approach that differentiated mathematics instruction is most successful when teachers do the following:

---

### Habits of the Mind: Successful Differentiated Instruction

1. Believe that all students have the capacity to succeed at learning mathematics.

2. Recognize that multiple perspectives are necessary to build important mathematical ideas and that diverse thinking is an essential and valued resource in the classroom.

3. Know and understand mathematics and be confident in their abilities to teach mathematical ideas.

4. Be intentional about curricular choices; that is, think carefully about what students need to learn and how that learning will be best supported.

5. Develop strong mathematical learning communities in the classroom.

6. Focus assessment on gathering evidence that can inform instruction and provide a variety of ways for students to demonstrate what they know.

7. Support each other in their efforts to create and sustain this type of instruction.

---

We like to think about differentiation as a lens through which we can examine our teaching and our students' learning more closely, a way to become even more aware of how best to ensure that our students will be successful learners. Looking at differentiation through such a lens requires us to develop new skills and to become more adept at doing the following:

| Six Focal Points: Differentiated Instruction |
| --- |
| 1. Identify important mathematical skills and concepts. |
| 2. Assess what students know, what interests them, and how they learn best. |
| 3. Create diverse tasks through which students can build understanding and demonstrate what they know. |
| 4. Design tasks with appropriate accommodations and modifications to meet students' needs. |
| 5. Provide students with choices to make. |
| 6. Manage different activities taking place simultaneously. |

Many teachers believe that the best way to differentiate mathematics instruction in middle school is to track students according to their abilities. While we recognize that many teachers feel this way, there are important reasons to differentiate mathematics instruction in other ways. First and foremost, we need to be sure that all students have access to a rigorous curriculum. Also, even if homogeneous grouping is supported in your school, such groups still represent diverse learners. It is our responsibility to make other instructional adjustments before adjusting content.

## Content, Process, Product

There are several indications that we are not yet teaching mathematics in an effective manner, in a way designed to meet a variety of needs. Results of international tests show U.S. students do not perform as well as students in many other countries at a time when more mathematical skill is needed for professional success and economic security. There continues to be a gap in achievement for our African American, Native American, and Hispanic students. Finally, we are a country in which many people describe themselves as math phobic and others have no problem announcing publicly that they failed mathematics in high school.

In response to these indicators, educators continue to wrestle with the development and implementation of approaches for teaching mathematics more effectively. The scope of mandated standardized testing continues to broaden and deepen, though the National Council of Teachers of Mathematics (NTCM) through its document *Curriculum Focal Points for Prekindergarten Through Grade 8 Mathematics* (2006) suggests paying greater attention to fewer key ideas at each grade level. The way we teach math has changed, requiring students to communicate their mathematical thinking, to solve more complex problems, and to conceptually understand the mathematical procedures they perform. And, all of this is happening at a time when our national agenda is clear that no child should be left behind.

Even though teachers strive to reach all of their students, learners' needs are ever increasing and more complex to attend to in the multifaceted arenas of our classrooms. Considering the ways differentiation can assist us in meeting our goals is essential. Carol Tomlinson (1999, 2003), a leader in the field of differentiated instruction, identifies three areas in which teachers can adapt their curriculum: *content, process,* and *product.* Teachers must identify the content students need to learn and then judge its appropriateness to make initial decisions about differentiation. The first step in this task is to read the local, state, or national standards for mathematics. A more in-depth analysis helps teachers become aware of the "big ideas" in mathematics and then connect the identified standards to these ideas. Teachers should base any decision to adapt content on what they know about their students' learning styles, interests, and readiness. Because teachers need this information about each of their students, taking time to pre-assess students is essential to differentiated instruction. Based on this information, teachers can determine the best ways for students to engage with the content and to demonstrate what they have learned. They can also decide the level of content that students can investigate and the pace at which they can do so.

## Differentiation Within a Unit

Let's consider a class of seventh graders who are beginning a unit on ratios. Standards of this content area include that students be able to

- translate among fractions, ratios, and percents;
- analyze quantitative comparisons; and
- use ratios and proportions in the solution of problems.

The classroom teacher knows that making connections among concepts and representations is a big idea in mathematics. She wants all of her students to be able to make connections among various

*Lesson Idea!*

**Strand:** Number and Data

**Focus:** Ratios

**Context:** Interpreting comparative statements about watching baseball

Begin with pre-assessment.

Build on student interests.

representations of proportional data. She knows that proportional reasoning pervades middle school mathematics and she wants her students to be able to recognize its importance in number, algebra, measurement, geometry, and data analysis.

The teacher will incorporate these ideas throughout the year, but first, she wants to informally pre-assess her students to find out how they might interpret and create comparative statements. She wants to know whether they can readily identify different mathematical conclusions that can be inferred from mathematical data. In lieu of just giving them one statement and having the students conclude whether other related statements are true or false, she'll launch the unit with a more open activity. The task will allow her to get a feel for her students' common understanding and to identify students who may need more or less support in this area. She'll observe her students carefully as they brainstorm ideas and identify conclusions. She'll be able to use the data to inform the lessons that follow.

The teacher knows that many of her students are distracted this week by the World Series. Following a long playoff season and several late-night games, many of her students are just plain exhausted. Though she often wonders why games can't start earlier, she appreciates the students' interest and the fact that many of them watch the games with their families. Two nights ago the game went into overtime and many of her students admitted that they fell asleep before the game was over. As baseball is on their minds, she decides to incorporate it into their work. She begins by asking the students, "How many of you stayed up to watch the game last night?" When fifteen of the twenty students raise their hands, she writes the following statement on the board: *Among the students in your math class, 15 stayed up late to watch the baseball game and 5 did not.*

She then says, "I want to know what you think this statement tells you. Jot down your ideas in your journal. I want everyone to have some time to think on their own, so don't share until we are ready." As she says this, she turns over the two-minute timer. The teacher finds the timer helpful when she wants students to brainstorm independently. They practiced this technique every day during the first week of school, when she asked a question such as "how many different things can you name that are circular in shape?" Since then, she has used it about once a month. The visual image of the timer seems to help students remain quiet as well as gain a sense of how much time is left.

As soon as the timer runs out, Brad says, "It means most of us watched the game and so most of us are tired!"

To establish the expectation that students identify different ways of expressing the same idea, the teacher acknowledges his response and then asks for other ways they could say that most of them watched the game. Sheila offers, "The majority of us stayed up to watch the game."

Lamar builds on Sheila's statement with his suggestion: "The minority did not watch the game."

"Hmm, interesting," says the teacher. "Did anyone write a statement using a number?"

Jeri responds, "Seventy-five percent of us watched the game."

Max then chimes in, "Oh, that means that twenty-five percent of us didn't watch the game."

Already, the teacher has heard students build on each other's ideas. She asks them to draw a line under what they have written so far and then turn to talk to their neighbors. She directs them to share their statements and to work together to determine other ways to communicate the same ideas. She also tells them to take notes about new ideas that arise in their conversations.

As the students share their work, the teacher hears a variety of mathematical ideas. Haley introduces fractions to her group with the comment that one-quarter of the students did not watch the game. Danny quickly adds, "That means three-quarters of us watched the game."

Some students continue to offer statements that do not contain numbers, such as Neil, who says, "The majority of the kids that watched the game probably follow the team or one of the teams."

Luke then adds, "That's me. I'm a real fan."

As the teacher walks around the room, she often reminds students to record the new ideas in their journals. Sometimes she also asks a student to restate what a partner has said or to communicate the same idea in a different way. She does hear a few students refer to ratios.

For example, Paul suggests, "The ratio of students who watched the game to those who did not was three to one."

Samantha then adds, "Seventy-five percent is the probability of us staying up late again."

The teacher is most struck by Jackie's statement that "one-third of the number of kids that stayed up late went to bed early."

When lulls in the conversations begin to occur, the teacher calls for the students' attention. Once again they share ideas. After each statement is offered, the teacher gives time for other students to ask questions or to build on the idea. Sometimes she asks a question herself, if she believes students need further clarification.

As the session ends, she asks students to comment on what they have learned. Chris replies, "When you get one way, like one-fourth, just get the rest, like three-fourths."

Ben suggests, "Or if you have a fraction, you can say the same thing with a percent."

Anna says, "I didn't know there were so many different ways to say things in math. It's just like English."

Brad concludes, "There are lots of ways to say it, but most of us are still tired."

While not formalized, this pre-assessment task embedded in the lesson gives the teacher some important information that she can use to further plan the unit on ratios and comparative statements. She can determine students' willingness to think divergently, to come up with different possibilities for the same statement. She has an initial indication of their understanding and comfort level with different types of comparative statements. She observes that the students did not refer to decimals in this exchange. With students' written work, she can determine the ideas they included prior to working with others. She can also gather evidence as to whether the students' notes are accurate, complete, and contain their own additional ideas.

Take Action!

Meet various levels of readiness.

From this information she can decide how to adapt her *content* for different students. The complexity of ideas can vary. Some students can reinforce ideas introduced through this activity, while others can investigate additional concepts such as the likelihood of events and related odds. She can have some students explore ideas that will allow them to complete or create if-then statements such as *If 6 out of 7 of the students like watching basketball, then _____% do not like watching basketball.* Students can further explore the relationships among fractions, decimals, and percents and how these relationships can be used to solve problems. Proportional reasoning can be used to solve a variety of problems, and relationships can be generalized through algebraic equations.

Take Action!

Meet various learning styles.

She can vary *process*, or the ways in which the content is considered. Some students can represent the relationships among the fractions, decimals, and percents by using physical manipulatives such as Fraction Tower Equivalency Cubes, manipulative models that show equivalent fractions, decimals, and percents on towers that are proportional to one. For example, the tower that is half as tall as the tower for one has $\frac{1}{2}$ on one side, 0.50 on another, 50% on a third side, and a blank fourth side. Others might choose to draw their own visual representations of such relationships.

The teacher can create some packets of logic problems, such as the one that follows, that require students to identify one number based on a series of clues involving rational numbers and ratios:

*What score did I get on my test?*
- *I missed fewer than 5 of the 25 questions.*
- *I got less than 92% of the questions correct.*
- *The ratio 21:4 does not compare the questions I answered correctly to those I answered incorrectly.*

*My score is _____%.*

She might create another packet including brainteasers that require proportional reasoning and translations among fractions and percents:

*On a bus that is three-fourths full, 30% of the passengers are young girls, 20% are young boys, and two-fifths of the passengers are women. There are also 9 men on the bus. How many people would be on the bus if it were full?*

Some students can explore ratios that compare the speed of toy cars on ramps. Other students can write short poems such as acrostics to help them remember how to represent a ratio as a fraction, as a decimal, or as a percent. Others can play memory games that help them remember common fraction, decimal, and percent relationships, such as $\frac{1}{8} = 0.125 = 12.5\%$. Students can focus on how these relationships are used to represent sports statistics, finances for their school, or other contexts based on their own interests. The teacher might think about pairs of students who will work well together during this unit and identify subsets of students that she wants to bring together for some focused instruction.

Then the teacher must think about *product*—how her students can demonstrate their ability to use and apply their knowledge of rational number relationships at the end of the unit. For example, students might use scale factors to build replicas of buildings from an era they are studying in social studies, visit a local grocery store and create a video to advertise best buys, create a card game that involves matching and ordering rational numbers presented in various forms, make a collage with visual representations of financial issues related to their school, or create their own problem booklet.

It's not necessary, or even possible, to always differentiate these three aspects of curriculum, but thinking about differentiating content, process, and products prompts teachers to

- identify the mathematical skills and abilities that students should gain and connect them to big ideas;
- pre-assess readiness levels to determine specific mathematical strengths and weaknesses;

*Take Action!*

Provide different ways for students to demonstrate their learning.

- develop mathematical ideas through a variety of learning modalities and preferences;
- provide choices for students to make during mathematical instruction;
- make connections among mathematics, other subject areas, and students' interests; and
- provide a variety of ways in which students can demonstrate their understanding of mathematical concepts and acquisition of mathematical skills.

It is also not likely that all attempts to differentiate will be successful, but keeping differentiation in mind as we plan and reflect on our mathematics instruction is important and can transform teaching in fundamental ways. It reminds us of the constant need to fine-tune, adjust, redirect, and evaluate learning in our classrooms.

## Differentiation Within a Lesson

**Lesson Idea!**

**Strand:** Measurement

**Focus:** Volume and proportional reasoning

**Context:** Counting peas, inspired by the book *Counting on Frank*

Consider the following vignette from an eighth-grade classroom. Having just taken a workshop on differentiated instruction, the teacher wants to try something different in her classroom. Her students have been studying volume and she would like to incorporate that concept within a bigger problem than she would normally consider trying. In the past, she has always had everyone do the same thing at the same time, but now she wants to provide more choice, be more open to variations in student thinking, and have a variety of materials available for the students to use. She feels that she is a novice in this teaching approach and is unsure of where these changes will lead her and whether students can stay engaged in a broader problem-solving task for an entire double period.

The teacher believes that she needs to motivate the students to think about different ways to solve problems. She decides to use one of her children's favorite books. She begins the class by introducing the students to *Counting on Frank*, written by Rod Clement (1991). She knows that this quasi–picture book might be seen as too juvenile by her eighth-grade students, so she addresses this issue directly. She holds the book up and says, "You might think that this book is too young for you, but I think that you will find the story line interestingly wacky and that we can find some intriguing math problems in the story, too." As one of the students asks who Frank is, several other students chime in that they think that Frank is the boy in the story. The teacher believes that she has now captured their attention, so she begins to read.

As the story unfolds, it turns out that Frank is the boy's dog. The boy has a keen interest in solving math problems with everyday objects, including studying how long pens will write before they run out, how many whales will fit in his living room, and how long it will take to fill his bathroom with water. The students now seem less concerned with the fact that this is a picture book and more interested in the humorous drawings and unusual story line. The teacher asks the students if they have ever been interested in thinking about everyday objects in this way and the students respond eagerly.

Jodi tells a story about the time her guinea pig crawled into the refrigerator and offers the question "How many guinea pigs could you fit into a refrigerator?"

Many students have questions related to the technology they use regularly; for example, Raj suggests, "How long can we use our iPods before the batteries run out?"

The teacher, returning to the story, reads about how the boy relates the growth rate of a tree in his backyard to his own growth rate. Then he compares the sound of a mosquito buzzing in his ear with the buzz he would hear if the mosquito were the size of an airplane. The teacher is interested in these descriptions in which ratios and proportions are embedded. Her students studied these topics extensively in seventh grade, yet she believes that they need a review of this material in eighth grade. She is hoping that this activity will allow students to review a previously learned concept in conjunction with one just studied. She believes this ability to apply several different mathematics skills within one situation will make her students stronger learners and users of mathematics and that it will strengthen their ability to solve multistep, multidimensional problems.

Once she has read the story to the end, the teacher asks students to choose a situation within the book that makes them wonder about the mathematical relationships. Margaret comments that she is interested in figuring out how the boy knows that there are a certain number of jelly beans in a jar. She asks if that is always true. This sparks a conversation about how the sizes of jars could differ and Lydia comments that it also depends upon the size of the jelly beans.

Priya raises her hand to say, "I think it is interesting that a toaster, increased by a certain scale, could send toast into the air and endanger low-flying aircraft." She isn't sure that this is possible and, to clarify her thinking, asks how high airplanes fly. The teacher asks if any of the students have toasters that send the toast into the air.

John says, "My brother and I sometimes try to make the toast go into the air by pushing the button really fast." He adds, "I think that the toast goes only about a foot in the air, so I'm not sure that it is possible to make a toaster that would shoot toast that high even if it is a lot bigger."

The teacher is confident that students are engaged in the story line and are thinking, albeit informally, about scale and proportional reasoning. She asks them to refer to the situation in which the boy is so disappointed that his mother serves peas every night that he tosses the peas on the floor instead of eating them. The story states that he tosses fifteen peas on the floor every night. How many peas would that be over time?

At this point the teacher gives students different durations to consider. Some students have to determine the number of peas tossed in one week and two weeks; some, one month and one year; and some, one year and eight years (the time mentioned in the story). The students naturally work in pairs or small groups. As the teacher listens to conversations, she hears Dakota, who is trying to find the number of peas at the end of one year, suggest that it makes a difference as to whether or not they consider leap years. Connor wants to know if they have to figure out how many peas will fall in one week before they figure out a year. The teacher is pleased to see that students are thinking about different ways to solve the problems. Occasionally she is tempted to jump into the conversations to offer a hint or to comment on a suggestion, but she reminds herself to let the students explore their own strategies.

Next she hears Leslie suggest, "Well, I think that we should take how many peas he drops in one day and then just multiply by seven."

Carlos responds, "OK, we can do that, but are we going to use days or weeks to figure out how many he drops in two weeks?"

Another pair of students is using calculators to find out how many days there are in twelve months.

When most of the students have arrived at an answer, the teacher invites students to come back together to share their conclusions. She gives each pair or small group an opportunity to first state its answer and then comment on how the students arrived at that conclusion. She also asks groups to comment on similarities and differences among their solution strategies.

She begins with the students who worked with one week and two weeks. The students note that doubling the one-week data or multiplying fifteen times the fourteen days yields the same answer. Then a few students report on how they determined the number of peas at the end of one month and one year. These results

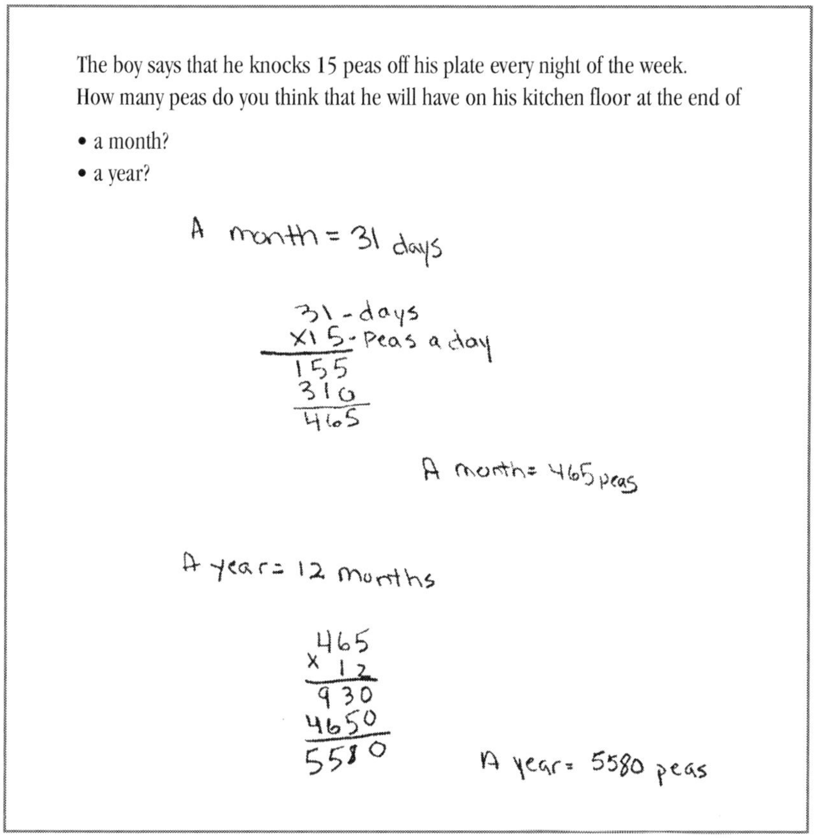

The boy says that he knocks 15 peas off his plate every night of the week.
How many peas do you think that he will have on his kitchen floor at the end of

- a month?
- a year?

A month = 31 days

$$
\begin{array}{r}
31 - \text{days} \\
\times 15 - \text{Peas a day} \\
\hline
155 \\
310 \\
\hline
465
\end{array}
$$

A month = 465 peas

A year = 12 months

$$
\begin{array}{r}
465 \\
\times 12 \\
\hline
930 \\
4650 \\
\hline
5580
\end{array}
$$

A year = 5580 peas

Figure 1–1 *Marta assumed there were thirty-one days in each month to solve the problems.*

differ because some students decided that a month has thirty days while others used thirty-one days. Marta worked with thirty-one days and found that that there would be 5,580 peas at the end of the year. (See Figure 1–1.)

Next the class considers one year and eight years. The first pair of students determined that there would be 5,475 peas at the end of one year, using 365 days for a year. (See Figure 1–2.) This total is not the same number as Marta found, but the class seems satisfied that the number of days in a month changes and depending on which is used, you get different answers. The students decide the numbers are "close enough." One of the student pairs includes two leap-year dates in their thinking because it was a period of eight years. Dustin reports that there are really 365.25 days in a year and Clint explains that the four quarter days add up to one more day every four years.

The class becomes interested in this thinking and decides that $6 \times 365 + 2 \times 366$ is the best way to find the number of days in eight years. They then multiply this number by 15 to confirm

The boy says that he knocks 15 peas off his plate every night of the week. How many peas do you think that he will have on his kitchen floor at the end of

- a year?
- 8 years?

ONE Year = 365 days

```
  365
x  15
 1825
 3650
 5475
```

ONE YEAR = 5,475 peas

```
eight years =  365
            x    8
             2,920 days
```

```
  2920
x   15
 14600
 29200
 43800
```

eight years = 43,800 peas

Figure 1–2  *These students assumed there were 365 days in a year.*

that there would be 43,830 peas at the end of eight years. The teacher notes that more students than she expected do not remember how many days there are in a year.

Then the teacher states that this problem is an introduction to another question and reads the following task:

> *The boy decides to build a container that will hold all of the peas that fall off his plate every night. How big of a container would be needed to hold all of the peas that fell off his plate at the end of a week? A month? A year? Eight years?*

She queries, "What will you have to consider to answer these questions?" Students provide several possibilities such as the size of the peas, the shape of the container they will use, and whether or not they should try to fill all of the space inside the container. One of the students asks if the peas can be squished, which leads to a discussion of what the peas would look like at the end of eight years. The teacher is happy when the class decides to think about the peas in their normal state.

Usually, this teacher would assign her students to answer all of these questions and tell them to begin by determining the size

**Take Action!**

Provide students with choices.

of the container needed to hold one week's worth of peas. This time, though, she explains that they may choose the question(s) they would like to answer. Her hope is that students will choose a time frame for the problem that suits them best academically.

To identify students interested in working on the same problem, she posts four signs in different quadrants of the room, one for each of the time frames: one week, one month, one year, and eight years. She explains that students will go to the area of the room that matches their choice and encourages them to partner with one or two others who have chosen the same duration to investigate. She also tells them that they will have another choice as well: she has a number of different materials that they can use, including canned peas!

Several students gasp when she shows them a can of peas and a can opener. They immediately start talking about how much they can't stand the taste or smell of peas. When Robert says, "But if we really want to know the size of a pea, we have to open a can," the uproar subsides. The teacher lets the students know that they have other materials available to choose among as well: measuring cups, graph paper, regular paper, rulers and metersticks, measuring tapes, and calculators. Leslie, despite seeing the calculators on the table, asks if they can use calculators and the teacher assures her that this is an appropriate tool to use for this problem.

Amid the flurry of deciding which problem they will tackle and with whom they will work, the students also begin to think about the materials they will use. As Ben and Caitlyn meet in the same corner of the room, Caitlyn comments, "We want to do the one about eight years of peas, and the numbers are going to be really big. We'd better get a calculator."

The teacher is pleased that the students seem engaged in what they are doing. Several groups of students head to the table where the materials are, including the canned peas. More time is lost as students laugh about how bad the peas smell. Finally Clint realizes that his group needs to measure the peas. He notices that the peas are different sizes and decides to take several of them. Once he picks up some peas, others are willing to do so as well.

Back in his group, Clint talks with his partner, Carla, about how they should find the size of the pea. They put a pea on the inch side of the ruler and notice that the pea measures just a little less than a half inch. Not being particularly interested in finding out exactly what fraction of an inch this is, Carla suggests, "Why don't we measure with centimeters instead? I think that will be easier." To their relief, the pea lines up closely to the 1-centimeter mark. This news travels throughout the room quickly.

Shannon and Jodi are working on measuring the size of the peas as well. They notice that the peas that they took from the can are different sizes. Shannon comments, "I think that we need to measure a few. But then what should we do?"

Jodi quickly responds, "Do you think that if we measure three, that will be enough, and then we could find the average?" The teacher is pleased to hear students recognizing the need to measure more than one pea, even though three seems inadequate to her.

As she moves to the table where Jake and Louie are working, she overhears their debate over what they need to know about the size of a pea.

Louie argues, "We just need the distance across the pea, then we can then find the volume."

Neither student can remember how to find the volume of a sphere, however. The teacher decides that others may want to be reminded of this formula, so she encourages these two students to look it up in a math reference book that she has readily available and then put the formula on the board. Now knowing that the formula is $V = \frac{4}{3}\pi r^3$ and that they have found the distance across their pea to be 1 centimeter, these students are considering how to use the 1 in their formula. Jake wants to change the $\frac{4}{3}$ to a decimal so that they can use the calculator for the computation.

Louie suggests changing 0.5 (the radius) to $\frac{1}{2}$ because "multiplying the fractions won't be so bad." The teacher is pleased to see that the students are trying different ways to solve the problem and is interested in finding out how close their answers will be when they are finished.

Louisa and Meg have already determined the volume of a pea and are talking about what kind of container that they would use for the peas. Meg says, "We have to put them into a cylinder because that's the shape of the can that peas come in."

Louisa comments, "It doesn't say that it has to be a cylinder in the problem. Wouldn't it be easier to use a box? Maybe they can come from a big box of frozen peas."

Louisa responds, "Great idea; boxes are always easier."

The teacher notices that Dakota has not moved to one of the four designated areas, though she does appear to be working. When the teacher approaches her, she says that she doesn't have a partner and that she's interested in solving a different problem anyway. The teacher encourages Dakota to talk about her interest. She tells the teacher that the story in the book talks about the peas falling on the floor and being level with the tabletop at the end of eight years. Dakota doesn't think that this is possible. She asks,

"Wouldn't I still have to think about how many peas fell on the floor but then figure out if they can fit in the room?"

The teacher is glad that the situation has intrigued Dakota. At times when she is working with other students, she appears disengaged and lets her group do most of the work. The teacher is encouraged by her interest and tells her that she may follow it. Her final product is shown in Figure 1–3. Note that she includes a drawing of the room with the table in the center. She then uses her measurements to find the volume of the room up to the height of the table, to find out how much space there would be for peas.

Figure 1–3    *Note the multistep process and the size of the room in Dakota's final product.*

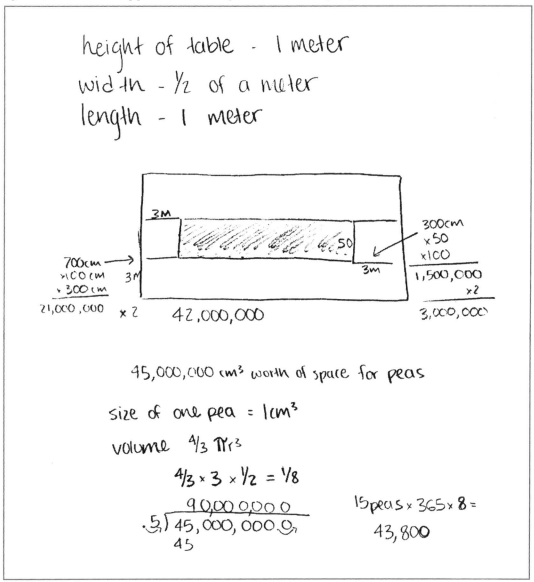

Dakota chooses to use a diameter of 1 centimeter for the size of a pea. She calculates, using the formula for the volume of a sphere, that the volume of this pea will be 0.5 cubic centimeters and remembers from the beginning of the class period that the number of peas collected over eight years was about 43,800. The teacher is concerned that Dakota has designated quite large dimensions for the room, extending it by 3 meters on either side of the table, but, knowing that raising this concern to her could derail her thinking, is willing to let Dakota continue her work.

Dakota breaks the volume of the area around the table into distinct parts and then determines the total volume of the room to be 45,000,000 cm$^3$. Based on her calculation that 0.5 cm$^3$ is the volume of a pea, she then determines how many peas can fit into the volume of the room. Her calculations show that there is room for ninety million peas. She is pleased to announce to the teacher that she has found out there is room for many, many more peas than the author suggests. The teacher notes that though Dakota made several errors, such as in the scale of her drawing and in the recording of the equation, she also did many things correctly. She wishes Dakota had been willing to work with someone else because a conversation would probably have helped her discover how she could have improved her drawing and how to record her equation in two steps: $(\frac{1}{2})^3 = \frac{1}{8}$ and $\frac{4}{3} \times 3 \times \frac{1}{8} = \frac{1}{2}$.

Next the teacher moves to Brad and Doug, who are talking about the volume of the peas that the boy would drop in a month and what size container they will need to hold them. They already know, from the earlier whole-group conversation, that there will be 450 peas dropped in a month (based on thirty days per month). They agree that multiplying their volume for 1 pea by thirty will give them the volume of the peas dropped in a month but are wondering about whether or not to include room for the juice in a can of peas. The teacher decides that she will not tell them what to do. She merely encourages them to provide a rationale for whatever they decide to include.

Joe and his partner, Chloé, are also working on the volume of a container that will fit a month's worth of dropped peas. They decide to use 0.5 centimeter for the radius of a pea. Now they want to find the size of a cylinder that would hold these peas. Chloé looks in the reference book for the formula for the volume of a cylinder. Finding that it is $V = \pi r^2 h$, Joe comments that it might be easier to just leave the volume of the pea with the pi symbol in it, rather than find the exact answer, and then they can do the same with the volume for the cylinder. (See Figure 1–4.)

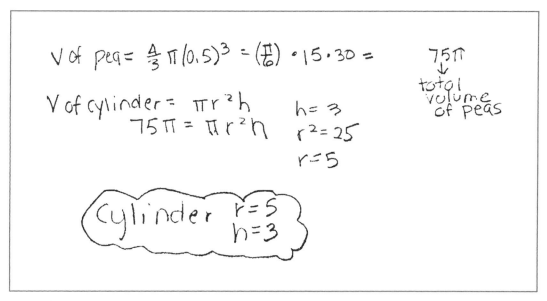

Figure 1–4 *Joe and Chloé found a unique way to simplify the computation.*

The teacher is rather amazed that these students are finding ways to make the problem easier to solve by manipulating the components of the equations. She knows she didn't think of this solution strategy, though she also notes that their answer does not indicate their unit of measure. When she sees their work, she notices the incorrect use of the equal sign. Finding the volume of the pea should be computed distinctly from the calculation of the volume of a month's worth of peas. She believes that the students' recording skills have regressed in the solution of this multifaceted problem and that they do understand that calculations on each side of an equal sign must actually be equal. She needs to follow up to be sure, though, and is reminded of the importance of having students investigate complex problems on a regular basis.

Once the teacher is satisfied that all of the groups have explored these tasks long enough to really understand them, the students come together to discuss their findings. As students share their answers to the problem involving a month's worth of peas, another pair comments that they did the same procedure but used the number for the peas that fell on the floor for eight years. Realizing that the questions involved basically the same structure, but with varying amounts of peas, seems to assure some of the students that their methods were appropriate.

Clint is excited to share the findings of his group. After finding the volume of eight years of peas, they thought about the size of a room that would hold these peas. He tells the class, "There is no way that there will be enough peas dropped on the floor to reach the table."

They have determined that the volume of 43,830 peas will be 22,271.6 cubic centimeters. He then explains how they chose dimensions for the room and the height of the table to find a volume of 3,000,000 cubic centimeters. Clint's classmates seem to be impressed that Clint's group figured this out.

Figure 1–5 *Clint concluded that there would not be enough peas to fill the room up to the table.*

Number of peas in eight yrs.
$365 \times 15 = 43,800$ peas
$+30$ for last 2 leap yrs
$= 42,830$

Volume of one pea    if each pea is 1cm across
$V = 4/30 \, pi \, r^3 = 4/3 \, pi$
$(.5)^3$

Volume of eight yrs worth of peas $.52 \times 43,830 =$
$22271.6$

Volume of room up to the tabletop
hit of tabletop $= .75m$
width of room $= 2m$
length " " $= 2m$

changed to cm
$200 \times 200 \times 75 = 3,000,000$

Volume of room compared to volume of eight yrs worth of peas $= 22,271.6$ cubic cm
For peas
$3,000,000$ cub cm
For room

Volume of one pea    $.52$ cubic cm

Volume of room    $3,000,000$ cubic cm

Volume of room ÷ vol of 1 pea
$= ?$ total peas needed to fill room up to tabletop
$3,000,000 / .52$cm
$= 5,769,230$

compare to number of peas in 8 yrs    $43,830$ compared to $5,769,230$

I wasn't very happy when at first I found out that there wouldn't really be enough peas to reach the top of the table. But, then I realized that the author was just eggsajerating to make the story funnier.

Figure 1–5 (*Continued*)

After finding that most students agree that this is "way more peas than what he drops," Carol adds, "It's worse—all of the peas would have dried up by then and gotten smaller."

Clint's recording, in Figure 1–5, shows that the group also determined, as did Dakota, the number of peas that would be needed to fill this space and concluded that the author exaggerated the numbers to make the book more humorous.

Chris follows up on Carol's idea by suggesting, "Why don't we leave some of the peas out near the window and see how much smaller they get?"

Dakota comments that this would stink up the room but agrees once she realizes that they will not be near her desk. The teacher does hope that some students will return to this problem again soon.

This activity provided several different types of differentiation. The students warmed up by working with different time durations that led to different levels of computation. The teacher allowed students to choose which of the four time periods they wanted to investigate and gave permission for students to investigate something somewhat different within the same context. Students used a variety of materials in order to complete the tasks and produced different recordings to demonstrate understanding. Yet as the students had all been involved with the same context and problem, they were able to follow each other's thinking.

After the activity, the teacher reflected on what she learned.

At first I was nervous about using a picture book with eighth graders, but I thought it would motivate them. It really worked. I loved hearing Jodi talk about her guinea pig in the refrigerator. Those kinds of stories remind us that strange things happen to all of us. It's good for us to laugh together as a class.

I started with the first problem about the number of peas because I wanted to begin with something that everyone could understand. Although the problem only involved computation, it ignited students' interest. This was just what I wanted, to engage students in a problem that was not overly complicated, but that would encourage them to think about different solution strategies. But now I wonder if this work limited their thinking when they were investigating the size of the container. Students just found the volume of one pea and then multiplied to find the volume of all of the peas. Errors of measurement were then multiplied. I thought students would use the graph paper and spread peas out or use the liter cup to determine the number of peas in a 10-by-10-by-10-centimeter space. My students all talked about the peas drying up or getting squished but never addressed the fact that there would be spaces between the peas that their techniques did not consider. I am going to talk with their science teacher about how we could collaborate to have students explore similar problems and to learn ways to minimize errors of measurement.

> *I know there would have been times in the past when I would have insisted that she choose one of the four given tasks, but because I was thinking about choice, I was able to really listen to her interest in doing something different than I had planned.*

I didn't know how much my students disliked peas! I wonder if they really dislike them that much or if they thought it was the right way to act in front of their peers. At any rate, the peas were quite a distraction and they did smell more than I realized they would. Next time I think I might use dried peas, even though they're smaller.

Dakota really surprised me. I know there would have been times in the past when I would have insisted that she choose one of the four given tasks, but because I was thinking about choice, I was able to really listen to her interest in doing something different than I had planned. I agreed to her suggestion in part because I was trying to provide more choice and partly because I was so excited by the depth of her thinking. She had posed a question that had caught her attention. It wasn't until later that I realized how related her problem was to the tasks I had posed. She wanted to see if the room, up to the table, was the right size for eight years of peas. That space is really a container.

> Clint's group took the problem further than I ever imagined. I'm not ready to investigate big problems all of the time, but I was astounded by the range of my students' work, and they stayed involved throughout the double period.

This teacher was not as much of a differentiation novice as she thought. This is true of most teachers. Every day teachers are trying to meet students' needs without necessarily thinking about it as differentiated instruction. Seeing teaching and learning through the lens of differentiation, as this teacher found, helps us better meet students' needs and do so more consciously. Over time, teachers can develop the habits of the mind associated with differentiated instruction. It helps to remember and think about the following questions as you plan:

### Questions to Plan By: Differentiated Instruction

1. What is the mathematics that I want my students to learn?

2. What do my students already know? What is my evidence of this? How can I build on their thinking?

3. How can I expand access to this task or idea? Have I thought about interests, learning styles, uses of language, cultures, and readiness?

4. How can I ensure that each student experiences challenge?

5. How can I scaffold learning to increase the likelihood of success?

6. In what different ways can my students demonstrate their new understanding?

7. Are there choices students can make?

8. How prepared am I to take on these challenges?

## Connecting the Chapter to Your Practice

1. What concerns do you have about meeting your student's mathematical needs?

2. What ways have you found to integrate students' interests with mathematics instruction?

3. Which is easiest for you to differentiate in your instruction: content, process, or product? Why do you think so?

4. How do you decide when to interject yourself into student conversations?

# Chapter 2

# Changing Expectations

$S$ome people describe mathematics as a subject that requires you to learn how to follow a series of prescribed steps in order to find the one correct answer. Such a description reflects the way mathematics is sometimes taught, but not the subject itself. Instruction that emphasizes a rule-based approach to mathematics focuses on factual and procedural knowledge. It is the way most of today's teachers were taught. Traditionally, factual knowledge, such as vocabulary and basic facts, was stressed as well as specific algorithms for finding sums, differences, products, and quotients with whole numbers, fractions, decimals, and integers. Students were expected to learn facts through memorization and to perform the same algorithmic procedures regardless of the specific numerical examples. Algebra was then considered in the same manner. Specific rules were taught for manipulating equations to find solutions. No attempt was made to examine concepts within arithmetic that would provide students with a bridge to algebraic thinking.

## Procedural Rules Compared with Conceptual Development

A common outcome of rule-based instruction is that to find the product of 3 × 2.98, many students (and adults) mindlessly proceed with the algorithm that they were taught. They multiply the hundredths, the tenths, and the ones, regrouping as necessary. Let's consider a sixth-grade class of students that is finding this product as they determine the cost of renting three videos at $2.98

each. Most of the students are using the traditional algorithm. Jason comments, "I wish the videos were three dollars."

Melissa laughs and says, "But then we wouldn't be solving this problem."

Several students ask if they are allowed to use calculators. Their teacher responds, "Yes, if you think that is the most efficient way to solve the problem."

Artie and Madeline look uncertain but then reach for calculators. Once they do so, the students sitting near them get out their calculators as well.

"Wait," says Sabrina, "maybe we don't have to use the calculator. I mean, it's just like three dollars minus the pennies."

Joshua groans and says, "Maybe you don't, but it's much faster for me!"

Flexible thinkers such as Sabrina use a conceptual approach; they consider the numbers and values first and then determine the most sensible way to compute. In this case, a simple mental computation is all they need. Thinking of $2.98 as 2¢ less than $3.00, they simply find 3 × $3.00 = $9.00 and then subtract the extra cents (3 × 2¢ = 6¢) to determine the price of $8.94. There are several mathematical concepts embedded in this method, for example:

- Whole numbers are easier to work with, so it makes sense to round to the nearest whole number.
- 2¢ can also be written as $0.02.
- The decimal 2.98 is 0.02 away from 3.00.
- To find $(a \cdot b)$, you can increase the value of one of the factors as long as you then subtract the product of the number you added and the other factor, that is: $(a \cdot b) = a(b + c) - a \cdot c$.

Similar thinking can be applied to operations with fractions. Consider the example $\frac{3}{4} + \frac{7}{8} + \frac{1}{2}$. The traditional approach involves finding a common denominator and then identifying equivalent fractions using that denominator. Following the several steps of this process, we would transform the problem to $\frac{6}{8} + \frac{7}{8} + \frac{4}{8}$. Now we can apply the algorithm for addition with like denominators. The sum of 6 + 7 + 4 is 17, and the improper fraction $\frac{17}{8}$ results. Finally, we divide 17 by 8 to change the improper fraction to a mixed number and identify the sum as $2\frac{1}{8}$.

This procedural approach involves several steps that each must be performed in the appropriate sequence. But most of us

Lesson Idea!

Strand: Number

Focus: Multiply decimals.

Context: Problem discussion

are fairly familiar with eighths, fourths, and halves, allowing for more flexible, conceptual thinking. For example, one student used the following mental arithmetic approach:

> *I know that $\frac{1}{2}$ is equal to $\frac{4}{8}$ and that I can add the numbers in any order. So I'll use the eighths where I need them. I'll use two with $\frac{3}{4}$ to make 1 and I'll use one with $\frac{7}{8}$ to make another 1. There's one left over, so the sum is $2\frac{1}{8}$.*

Such rich mathematical thinking is cultivated by teachers who focus on mathematical reasoning and facilitate the development of students' ideas. As we differentiate learning activities, these priorities must remain in place for all of our students.

Along with the lack of flexible thinking, other difficulties arise when we teach facts and procedures as just rules, without conceptual frameworks. Some students begin to believe that mathematics is only a set of isolated rules that have no meaning, some lose interest in learning mathematics, and all students become underexposed to mathematical reasoning. Further, when rules and procedures are learned in isolation of concepts, misconceptions can emerge. For example, sometimes teachers provide rules in hopes of simplifying a procedure for sixth-grade students who continue to struggle with computation. When working with subtraction of positive numbers, you might hear a teacher say, "You can't subtract a bigger number from a smaller one, so you need to borrow." When the students are working with the traditional algorithm for subtraction, teachers sometimes give this direction to students as a reminder to regroup. When negative numbers are involved, however, the generalization no longer holds true. You *can* subtract, for example, $4 - 7$ and get $-3$. This new idea may confuse some students. Further, there are always students who remember only the first portion of this phrase and make the common error shown below:

$$\begin{array}{r} 38.2 \\ -\ 13.9 \\ \hline 25.7 \end{array}$$

Such work does not demonstrate an understanding of or a connection with the purpose of the procedure, that is, finding the difference between the two numbers. It is this concept that we need to emphasize, not a procedural rule that could later lead to a misconception.

Giving simplistic rules that apply only to certain sets of numbers or assumptions continues throughout the grade levels. Consider these examples:

- We say, "You can't divide 6 by 8," and yet we later expect students to know that $\frac{6}{8} = 0.75$.
- We say, "Negative one does not have a square root," and then later we introduce imaginary numbers.
- We say, "Always line up the numbers on the right to add them," and then we expect students to understand that this does not apply to decimals.
- We say, "Always line up the decimal points," and yet this applies only to addition and subtraction, not multiplication.

As teachers, we should get into the habit of asking ourselves: Is there a mathematical concept that will help students understand what to do, regardless of the type of numbers? Am I limiting my less prepared students' conceptual development by providing them with an oversimplified rule? Am I depriving these students of opportunities to develop mathematical concepts?

Take Action!

Identify sources of common misperceptions.

## Understanding Models and Representations: There's More than One Way

It's not that facts and procedures aren't important—they are—but we don't want to teach them in ways that keep students from developing the conceptual understanding that underpins their procedures and connects the facts that they know. Ideally, all three types of knowledge—*factual*, *procedural*, and *conceptual*—work together to build mathematical power.

Let's think about linear equations. Traditionally, the study of linear equations meant that students memorized $y = mx + b$ and were simply told that the $m$ represented the change in $y$ over the change in $x$. Students then memorized a procedure for finding the slope that involved two points. They subtracted to find the difference in the values of the $y$s and to put that number on top of what was traditionally thought of as a fraction. Next they found the difference in the $x$s and wrote that number below, as the denominator. Finally, they reduced. Students had no idea why this procedure worked and this lack of understanding often led to several common mistakes: students put the $x$s on top and the $y$s on the bottom; students subtracted in an order that made the subtraction easier, even though it separated the corresponding $x$s and $y$s; or students found the difference between the $x$ and $y$ values of one point and placed that over the difference between the $x$ and $y$ values of the other point.

Today, teachers place more emphasis on the conceptual development of linear situations and their various representations before introducing formal terminology or developing algorithmic approaches. Let's consider an eighth-grade classroom early in the year. The teacher knows that in seventh grade the students explored the creation of linear equations to represent data in a table. He expects that most of them have retained that skill, especially when the problem setting is meaningful and the numbers are relatively simple. He is now interested in their ability to understand how a linear situation can be represented as a table of data, as a graph, and as an equation in the form of $y = mx + b$. He is also interested in knowing more about the students' understanding of how these different representations relate. In order to learn more about how the students think about linear situations, he poses the following problem:

> *Philip has brought in $50 to put on his lunch ticket. At his school, lunch costs $2.50 each day. Find a way to show how much money Philip has on his lunch ticket, given the number of lunches he has bought.*

The students are used to working in small groups and begin talking about the problem right away. The teacher walks around, observing and listening to the students at work. He hears Collin suggest, "Let's just say he starts with two dollars and fifty cents."

Bernie replies, "But he starts with fifty dollars on his lunch card. That's what we need to think about first."

Collin looks up and off to the right and then says, "Oh, you're right. I guess fifty has to come first in our equation."

Now Bernie is not convinced and asks, "Does it matter if we think about two fifty first or the fifty first?" The teacher is pleased that the students are thinking about alternative approaches.

As the teacher passes by another table, Maria asks, "Do we need to find an equation?" The teacher is tempted to simply respond, "No," but remembers it's Maria's responsibility to figure this out. He pauses for a moment and then Maria adds, "Is it all right if I do? It's easier for me to find the answer that way." He nods and moves on, glad that he did not answer first. It seems that Maria is following a procedure with which she is comfortable right now. She prefers to begin with finding an equation as this representation makes the most sense to her. As their work continues, the teacher believes Maria will be more willing to consider other ways to represent linear situations.

**Lesson Idea!**

**Strand:** Algebra

**Focus:** Create and analyze linear equations.

**Context:** How much lunch money is left

**Take Action!**

Support alternative strategies.

Next the teacher checks in with Roberto, who explains, "Our group is making a table. We are starting with twenty days." The teacher probes as to why the students have chosen to begin with twenty days.

Roberto responds, "Well, that's how many days he can buy lunches for with fifty dollars."

Tammy, who is sitting next to Roberto, adds, "We know that we need to make an equation to represent the situation. We need to find the amount of money that he will spend each day. That's the two dollars and fifty cents. But we need to figure out how to put the twenty days into our equation."

The teacher is delighted to see that this student has related the phrase *each day* with rate of change but realizes that the students have some work to do to connect the situation to the equation. As the teacher listens to the students' small-group conversations, he also hears them discussing the various ways that an equation can be written. He notes how much more complex this idea is than these students recognize.

After each group has come to some consensus, the teacher facilitates a whole-class discussion about what they have learned. First, the groups share the various ways that they represented the situation. Many of the students want to share the equations they developed. The teacher calls on a volunteer to record her equation on the board and directs that student to choose the next volunteer. He does not agree or disagree with their representations, but rather encourages them to make a list of different equations and expressions. He also asks students to briefly explain their equations.

The students' work on the board is summarized below. Their explanations are provided in parentheses.

**Janelle:** $-2.50\,\text{L} + 50$ (You subtract two dollars and fifty cents for each lunch and get a negative number. When you add this to the fifty, you know what's left.)

**Deidre:** $50 - (20 - \text{L} \times 2.50)$ (There are twenty lunches, minus the number of lunches you buy that each cost two dollars and fifty cents.)

**Raoul:** $50 - 2.50 \times \text{D}$ (You start with fifty dollars and subtract two dollars and fifty cents for each day you buy lunch.)

**Ari:** $\text{N} - 2.50 = \$$ (*N* is the amount of money on the lunch card. You subtract two dollars and fifty cents to find out how much money is left.)

Marissa:    *50 + −2.5*L (You have fifty and subtract two fifty for each lunch.)

Sam:    $\frac{50}{2.50} = 20$  $20 - L = y$  $y \times 2.50 = z$ (You divide and find that you can buy twenty lunches with fifty dollars. Twenty minus the number of lunches you bought tells you how many lunches you have left. That number times two dollars and fifty cents tells you how much money is left.)

The teacher asks the students to comment on the various equations and expressions and to focus comments on how they are the same and how they are different. Carina suggests that Raoul's and Marissa's techniques are almost the same except for the negative sign.

Carina states, "That's OK because you're adding a negative number instead of subtracting. That's the same." She is clearly quite proud of her response. The students have just completed a unit on operations with integers and she is pleased to show what she knows.

Maria notes, "We all used different letters for our variables, like *L*, *X*, *D*, and *N*. I like the letters that mean something specific, like *L* for lunch."

Bryn asks, "Does it matter what we use?"

The teacher refrains from answering and after waiting a bit, Maria replies, "Maybe so it makes sense to us, but the math works either way."

Alex comments, "Deidre's and Sam's ways have some things that are the same about them. They are both long and I'm not sure that they answer the question." The teacher probes further and Alex goes on to say, "I guess they eventually find how much money is left. They just sort of go about it the long way."

Janelle suggests, "Ari's equation is correct for one day, but maybe that's all."

Roberto builds on her idea by saying, "It works if you are just subtracting one lunch."

The teacher commends the students for their various expressions and equations and then asks if any group has represented the situation in a way other than an equation. One group explains that it decided to use a table. Two students from the group come up to the board to show their work. They draw a two-column table, label the first column *Days*, and proceed to enter the numbers 1–20 in the column. They label the second column *Money Left* and write *$47.50* as the first entry, followed by *$45.00, $42.50,* . . . all the way to *$0.00*, with each number being $2.50 less than the number above it.

The teacher takes this opportunity to draw students' attention to what the table shows that the equation does not by asking, "Do the equation and the table tell us the same information?"

Maria responds, "Sort of, but with the table I can see right away how much money is left on any day without having to compute any numbers." Heads nod in agreement and the teacher asks if they can think of any other way to show this situation.

Lisa offers, "Well, I thought of making a graph, but I wasn't sure what to put on it."

The teacher hopes that more than a few students will begin to understand that there are different representations for linear situations. He wants them to recognize the differences among words, tables, graphs, and equations, as well as to be able to relate one to another. Today, however, he wanted the students to begin with their own thinking and with their own representations.

## Teacher Reflection

I find it fascinating to watch my students work and to listen to their explanations. In years past I would have just showed them how to form an equation or directed them to make a table. Now I realize that it's best to start with determining how they think about representing a linear situation. When I was in school, there was really only one way to solve a problem. My students use several different approaches. It's important that I honor their ways of thinking.

I wanted to start this unit with a problem context that students could relate to immediately. We use lunch cards at my school and the lunches cost $2.50. I knew that all of my students would understand the problem and be able to offer something to their groups.

*I want students to see the similarities as well as the differences in their work. I think this helps them identify critical mathematical concepts.*

I was pleased to hear Bernie ask about whether to start with $50.00 or $2.50. This is a common question for students, especially when they are learning the general equation for linear situations using the slope-intercept form of $y = mx + b$. They often think that writing it as $y = b + mx$ is not acceptable, that the equation must be written in the opposite order. Yet several students wanted to record the $50 first because it represented the money Philip had in the beginning, before he bought any lunches. I want my students to be flexible thinkers, to be able to vary the things that can change without impacting the essence of

*(Continued)*

the mathematics. I've also learned the importance of revisiting the basic properties of arithmetic as we explore algebraic notation so that the students recognize that the commutative property of addition still holds.

When I first began encouraging students to create their own representations of linear situations, I was so impressed with their different thinking. I just wanted them to share their work. I wanted to respect their individual ideas and learning preferences while helping them become aware of the different ways we can think about rates of change. I'm still always impressed with the different equations students create, but now I want more than sharing. I want students to see the similarities as well as the differences in their work. I think this helps them identify critical mathematical concepts. This is a new idea for me and I am still working on it, but it feels like the next step in my voyage as a teacher.

This teacher's words help us think about teaching as a journey. For many, it is a continuous growing process through which we develop new ideas and teaching strategies to address current concerns. Over time, these strategies lead to the discovery of new questions and the further adaptation of classroom practices.

## Addressing the Differences We Discover

Recent reforms in mathematics education emphasize that learning mathematics is an active process, one that involves students in exploring ideas, making and investigating conjectures, discovering relationships, representing ideas, and justifying thinking. Such activity often results when students pursue real mathematical problems or explore open-ended tasks, that is, problems for which they don't already recognize a procedure that will lead them to a solution or tasks that can be completed in a variety of ways. When exploring these types of problems, students wrestle with ideas and are less likely to all follow the same solution paths. Allowing for different approaches to mathematical tasks can lead to rich discussions that help students establish and agree on facts, construct and utilize procedures, and develop and solidify concepts. This way of teaching has two advantages: it supports deeper mathematical thinking as well as alternative learning preferences.

Teaching with this mind-set is part of our changing expectations of mathematics instruction. Teachers facilitate mathematical discourse rather than delineate specific steps and demonstrate how to follow these prescribed procedures. Teachers focus on questions such as "Why do you think so?" "What are you thinking?" and

"How do you know?" When teachers engage in this approach, they often are surprised at the range of their students' thinking. Teachers come to recognize differences in readiness levels; in approaches to tasks; in the ways students describe their work; in the connections students make among ideas; and in the ways students model, represent, and describe their thinking.

In fact, many teachers who begin to teach in ways that allow these differences to surface are truly amazed at what they see and hear. Teachers recognize that they have uncovered information about their students that they had never known before. Focusing on the development of mathematical ideas and on making links among factual, procedural, and conceptual knowledge is a significant transformation in the teaching of mathematics, and it has raised two essential questions:

1. Once we reveal the wonderfully different ways our students think about mathematics, what do we do with what we learn?
2. How do we support differentiated thinking about mathematics while still focusing on unified mathematical ideas?

Let's return to the eighth-grade classroom, where students continue to explore ways to represent linear situations. It is important that students are able to move freely from one representation to another. Each student should be able to link real-world situations, equations, graphs, and tables and be able to create the other three representations when given any one of the four models.

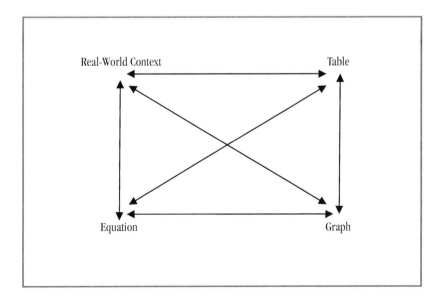

This teacher is particularly interested in having students connect the geometric model of a function (graph) with its algebraic representation (equation). Development of visual models of linear relations is vital. Studies have indicated the importance of the visual cortex in mathematical thinking (Sousa 2007). Activities that explicitly help students further develop their visual perceptions of algebraic relationships provide students with additional visual models to use when encountering new problems. Students can refer to, manipulate, and think about these models when grappling with new ideas. This teacher wants the students to eventually be able to look at the graphs of two equations and know which one has a greater rate of change and be able to imagine how a change in one of the $y$-intercepts would or would not change that comparison. He knows that this will take time, though, and that first students need to focus on understanding that the situation can inform how they can best represent the data.

Most of the students used an expression or an equation to represent the lunch problem. Only a handful of students used a table to represent it, but some students who developed expressions or equations did seem to understand that the table provided more accessible, explicit data for the given points. The teacher is fairly sure, though, that they did not also understand the limitations of the table, that it wouldn't have been as helpful if the problem had begun with enough money for an entire year of lunches. None of the students used a graph and the teacher is concerned that the students weren't sure how they would make one. He doubts they realized that for this situation, the graph should show only the points in the table because the data are not continuous. He also wonders if the students can construct the line graph for the equation itself. In the past, the students have had difficulty with determining the dependent and independent variables within a situation and perhaps these students are just not sure of what points to use to make a graph.

He thinks it is time to look more closely at the students' developing abilities with respect to varied representations. In order to encourage the use of representations other than expressions and equations and to probe students' thinking about how they are finding their equations, he provides students with copies of a variety of parking receipts along with the following problem:

*Ms. Perez has been volunteering at an animal shelter in the city. The shelter will reimburse her for parking, but she (and you!) want to know what the fee per hour is at Pete's Parking Place. Consider what representations you can use to determine the fee.*

**Lesson Idea!**

**Strand:** Algebra

**Focus:** Model linear situations with tables, graphs, and equations.

**Context:** Making generalizations from parking receipts

The parking receipts are from various times that Ms. Perez stayed in the garage and indicate the times she arrived and departed along with the fees she was charged. The teacher has purposely scattered them and let some bleed off the page to accurately portray the copies most people make when requesting reimbursements. (See Figure 2–1.) As students begin to consider the situation, the teacher circulates to see what representation each group or individual student chooses first. He is also attentive to representations that might be causing the students difficulty.

This task generates much conversation about how to interpret and use the information students have. The teacher hears "Usually parking fees decrease as the number of hours goes up" and "Let's see if the pattern is that it gets cheaper as you get further up." Without necessarily being aware, students are grappling with whether or not the situation is linear. A few students are readily organizing the data in a table.

Figure 2–1 *Receipts from Pete's Parking Place.*

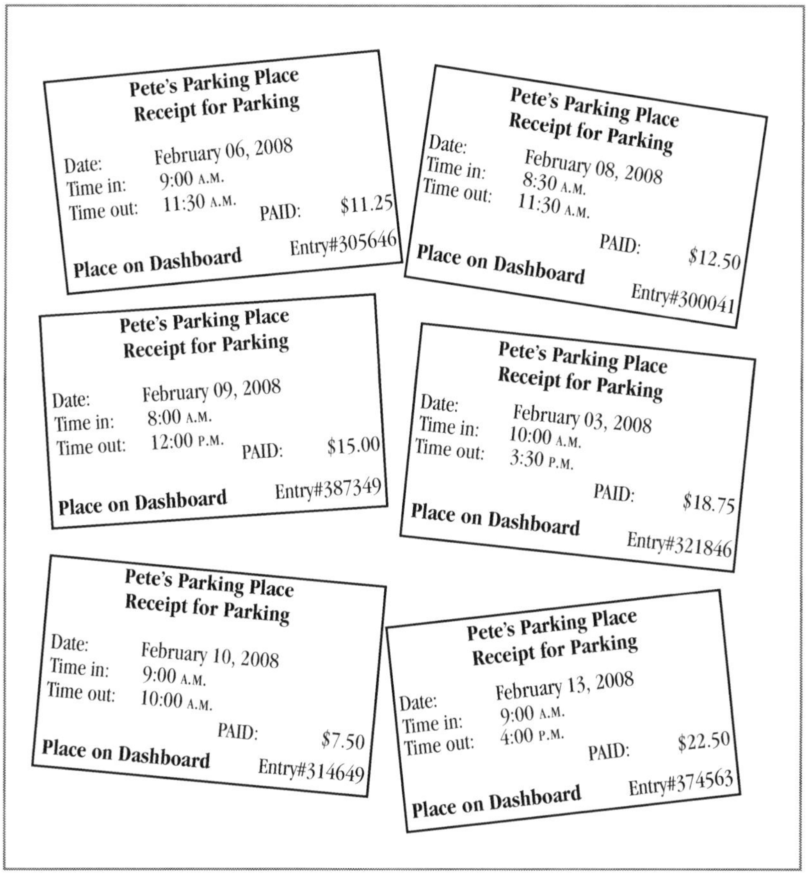
**Pete's Parking Place**
**Receipt for Parking**
Date: February 06, 2008
Time in: 9:00 A.M.
Time out: 11:30 A.M.
PAID: $11.25
**Place on Dashboard** Entry#305646

**Pete's Parking Place**
**Receipt for Parking**
Date: February 08, 2008
Time in: 8:30 A.M.
Time out: 11:30 A.M.
PAID: $12.50
**Place on Dashboard** Entry#300041

**Pete's Parking Place**
**Receipt for Parking**
Date: February 09, 2008
Time in: 8:00 A.M.
Time out: 12:00 P.M.
PAID: $15.00
**Place on Dashboard** Entry#387349

**Pete's Parking Place**
**Receipt for Parking**
Date: February 03, 2008
Time in: 10:00 A.M.
Time out: 3:30 P.M.
PAID: $18.75
**Place on Dashboard** Entry#321846

**Pete's Parking Place**
**Receipt for Parking**
Date: February 10, 2008
Time in: 9:00 A.M.
Time out: 10:00 A.M.
PAID: $7.50
**Place on Dashboard** Entry#314649

**Pete's Parking Place**
**Receipt for Parking**
Date: February 13, 2008
Time in: 9:00 A.M.
Time out: 4:00 P.M.
PAID: $22.50
**Place on Dashboard** Entry#374563

The teacher checks in with another group and asks about their thinking.

Tonya responds, "We found the hourly rate for each receipt. We tried using proportions, but that didn't really work." (See Figure 2–2.)

The teacher encourages the students to consider what the data show over time and what they can learn from the information. As he leaves the group, they are beginning to reorganize their data into lists.

Another group is focusing on the fact that when Ms. Perez went into the parking garage at 9:00 A.M. and came out at 10:00 A.M., her fee was $7.50. Jay concludes, "So, when she is only in the garage for an hour, it costs seven dollars and fifty cents, so that must be the hourly rate."

Raul protests, "But it doesn't work here. When she is in the garage for three hours, it should cost twenty-two dollars and fifty cents."

Figure 2–2  *These students tried using proportions to determine the hourly rate.*

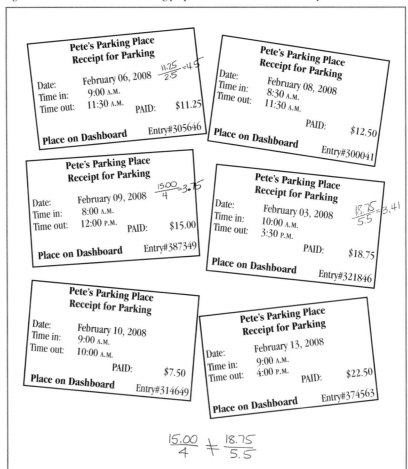

Paula asks, "How did you get twenty-two fifty? I see in the chart that it only costs twelve fifty for three hours, so it can't be seven fifty per hour."

These students are beginning to realize that they cannot just use one of the receipts in order to determine the hourly rate. Janelle suggests that they put the information in a table.

As the teacher circulates, he notes that other groups are creating tables as well. Some tables are horizontal and some are vertical. The teacher wonders if students who use a horizontal format will find it more difficult to determine the differences between the costs and how they relate to the numbers of hours parked. (See Figure 2–3.)

Nick and Clarke have made two separate lists, one for the number of hours parked and one for the cost of each use of the garage. (See Figure 2–4.) Note that the numbers of hours are listed without use of fractions or decimals, so that $2\frac{1}{2}$ hours is listed as 2:30. The students then find the average cost per hour of parking. This solution gives the teacher pause because it is the average cost of parking for *these* receipts but would not likely generalize to another set of receipts. He wonders how to help the students recognize that important difference.

Next the teacher joins a group that has jotted down a couple of data points and then created the equation $M = 2.50H + 5$, when one member of the group, Josie, asks, "What about a graph?"

Ronan gets up to get a couple of pieces of graph paper from the tray on the teacher's desk. Peter notes the relevant information from each receipt and marks these points on the graph paper, but reverses the $x$s and $y$s as he does so. A couple of the other students follow his lead. Ronan also plots the points inferred from the receipts but does so correctly.

Randy says, "Oh yeah, now just draw the line."

Ronan pauses and looks at the teacher. When the teacher asks what she's wondering about, Ronan replies, "It doesn't

Figure 2–3 *These students created a table in a horizontal format.*

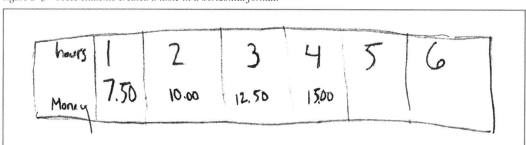

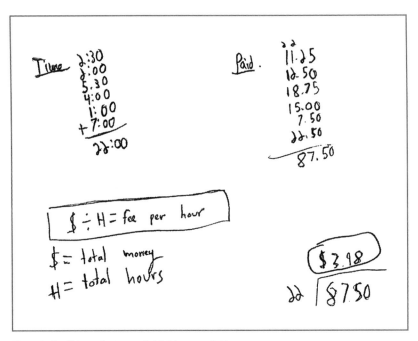

Figure 2–4  *This student recorded 2.5 hours as* 2:30.

keep going up, really. I mean, isn't there usually a maximum charge?"

The teacher leaves, gratified to learn that some of his students are thinking about the difference between graphing an equation and using a graph to represent a particular situation. Ronan is correct—most garages have a maximum daily charge. He purposely created receipts that were to the half hour or hour to limit distractions. He now wonders what his students would do if he had also included receipts with parking stays such as 2 hours and 17 minutes, but with a charge the same as for $2\frac{1}{2}$ hours, indicating that the garage rounded up to the next half hour. Would his students still have recognized an equation with a more limited domain? Would they know how to read a step graph that would be used to represent that situation? The teacher is amazed at the opportunities for further investigation.

Once again, the teacher brings the students back together to discuss how they represented the situation. Several students share that there is a $5.00 "starting fee" and then it costs $2.50 per hour to park. A few others express this as "an expensive first hour and then it gets cheaper." When the teacher asks them to show how they arrived at this conclusion, many students state an expression or an equation.

Bryn asks, "Is it OK if our group used $C$ and $H$ or did we have to use $x$ and $y$?"

This question comes up often for Bryn, and a few others, even though the teacher repeatedly reminds the students that it doesn't matter what letters they use as long as they are able to remember what the variables represent. Some students still think that they have to use $x$ and $y$ for their final equations or get special permission not to do so. There is a precision to mathematics that some students tend to overgeneralize; that is, they are unable to recognize that a variety of processes can lead to the same exact idea.

The teacher prods the students to talk more about how they found the hourly rate. Roberto explains, "My group made a table to show the amounts of money that it costs depending on the time in the garage. We ordered them in our table. Then we saw, like Paula's group did, that it couldn't work for the parking fee to be seven dollars and fifty cents an hour. It didn't work every time."

Alex says, "I used my chart to see that between three hours and four hours, the cost went up by two dollars and fifty cents."

Paula calls out, "Oh, I see now, that's how Brett got that the starting fee is five dollars."

Ronan connects to the previous problem by suggesting, "In the last problem we multiplied the cost of a lunch and the number of days. This time you multiply the cost of parking an hour and the number of hours. Both ways it's a cost per time."

As the students leave for their next classes, the teacher thinks about the success of the lesson. He is encouraged that more of the students were able to create a table or, at the very least, to see the validity of a table in this situation. Yet a number of students still were only willing to consider writing an equation or an expression. This preference held in spite of the fact that the table was quite valuable for finding the key data necessary in the equation. He wonders if some of the students think that use of an algebraic equation is always the best approach. He also notes that more students were challenged by writing an equation this time, as the equation was not as obvious.

Up until this point, the students have been able to participate in the same activities by thinking about the mathematics in different ways. Many of the students appear comfortable with choosing one representation, primarily an expression, but several have chosen a table, and a few have tried to construct a graph. The teacher feels that it is now appropriate to begin differentiating the instruction by having students further explore various representations based on their individual needs.

**Strand:** Algebra

**Focus:** Pose problems related to tables, graphs, or equations.

**Context:** Small-group work

**Take Action!**

Create groups for differentiated instruction.

Knowing that his goal is to have the students explore multiple depictions of linear situations, the teacher considers where the students' strengths lie and what types of representations they need to explore further. As his thoughts about the day unfold, he recognizes three distinct groups of students. He has students who feel quite comfortable with creating and using equations and expressions and yet need to understand how to explain the data they place in those equations. A second group of students need further practice with creating or interpreting a table. There are also some students who attempted to make a graph of the previous situation yet struggled with how best to represent the various components. The challenges of considering the independent and dependent variables and what they represent in a situation need further exploration, but, because the students have attempted to make a graph, the teacher thinks that they are ready to explore this representation further.

Once he identifies the groups, the teacher thinks about partners that have working relationships. Though he encourages a classroom environment where everybody works together and greets each new partner with respect, he also knows that social relationships can be difficult at this age. When he differentiates work for the first time in a unit, he tries to balance that challenge with pairing students he knows work well together.

The next day, the teacher asks students to come together as a whole class briefly to listen to the plan for the day. He explains that he has prepared the groups based on observing their work over the past few days and that their small-group activities are intended to strengthen their understanding of different types of representations. The teacher reveals the list of student groups. The list also designates assigned partners. He directs the first group to go to the table in the back of the room and to consider the task in the green folder. These students will focus on the various components of an equation. They will need to write a situation to represent the equation $4p + 7 = a$. The teacher hopes the students will engage in discussions to help them better understand the meaning of $y = mx + b$ as they try to create a situation to which the equation would apply.

Lisa and Alex are trying to decide the differences between the role of the 4 and that of the 7 in the equation. Lisa suggests, "Seven is what we add at the end."

Maria is intrigued by the variables that have been chosen for the equation. She sees the teacher approaching the group and asks, "I don't know what the $p$ means. And, I don't know what the *a* is supposed to mean either." She looks to the teacher for clarification.

The teacher asks, "Have you discussed the possibilities with your partner?"

Other students in the group seem more willing to consider that the variables can mean anything that they choose. Maria is drawn back in by the conversation, which begins to focus on the possibility that the *p* could represent packs of candy.

Nick suggests that he and Clarke start with the 7. He says, "Let's buy seven pieces of candy right away."

Clarke replies, "OK, then we can buy more candy pieces that come in packs of four." The problem they created is shown in Figure 2–5.

The second group of students is working at the desks nearest to the board. The students read the task in the red folder located at one of the desks and begin to work together. The teacher believes some of these students will need further guidance. They did not choose a table to represent either of the previous problems and some of them had difficulty seeing how a table was useful even after their classmates explained how they used one. Other students in this group worked reasonably well with a table, but the teacher is not certain that they would if the set of points did not include a pair with adjacent *x*s, allowing the students to recognize the change in *y* with an increase of one in the *x* variable.

Figure 2–5   *Nick and Clarke's problem for the equation 4p + 7 = a.*

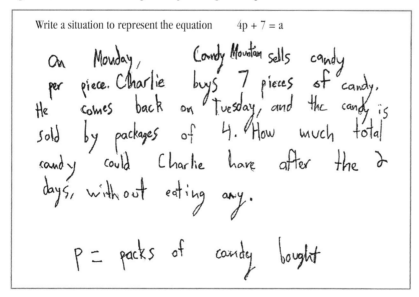

The teacher directs these students to write word problems that can be answered using the following table:

| A | C |
|---|---|
| 5 | 14 |
| 7 | 18 |
| 10 | 24 |
| 12 | 28 |
| 15 | 34 |

One set of partners lists the difference in the $y$ variables and notices that it is not a constant number.

Deidre states, "Let's see what the difference is on this side." They do notice that there is a pattern in the differences, but they have not yet figured out how to use the pattern to determine what the teacher knows as a rate of change.

As the teacher senses that this pair of students may soon become frustrated, he asks them to consider an alternative way of looking at the table. He refers the students back to the parking garage problem and asks them to think about what they learned from that problem that could help them in this situation.

Jay says, "Well, we had to figure out how much it costs an hour."

The teacher asks the students if they could use their knowledge of that situation to help them here. After making this connection, both Meg and Jim show renewed interest in discussing the problem and how to solve it. They are successful in creating a related story about babysitting.

The teacher moves to another set of partners, who have written the question *What is the cost per hour?* The teacher notes that in struggling to create a problem, the pair has reverted to something that they know. They may feel more comfortable writing about a parking garage, yet they appear uncertain about what the pattern in the table might reveal. The teacher asks these students to consider what the answer to their word problem might be. He knows that this will be a challenging question for these students but wants to direct them back to the mathematics in the table, rather than have them feel done because they have posed a question.

The teacher chuckles as he hears some of the students' problems. They all seem to write about items of interest or situations with which they are familiar. Their problems address the rate of change and the constant, but not always realistically. Note the inclusion of a constant tip, a meal for $2, and inexpensive babysitting fees among the problems shown in Figure 2–6. Also, the teacher notices that many of these problems don't include a question or can be solved

Figure 2–6  *A variety of student-created problems related to the table the teacher provided.*

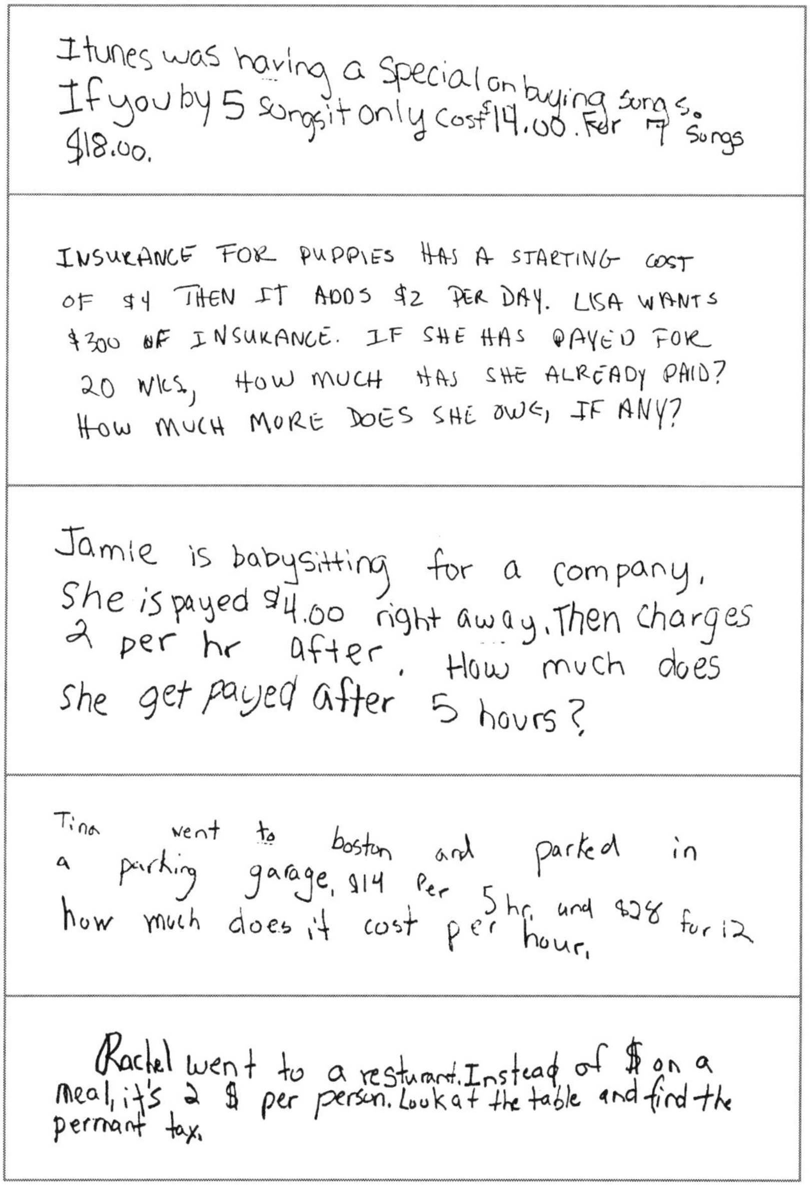

Itunes was having a special on buying songs. If you by 5 songs it only cost $14.00. For 7 songs $18.00.

INSURANCE FOR PUPPIES HAS A STARTING COST OF $4 THEN IT ADDS $2 PER DAY. LISA WANTS $300 OF INSURANCE. IF SHE HAS PAYED FOR 20 WKS, HOW MUCH HAS SHE ALREADY PAID? HOW MUCH MORE DOES SHE OWE, IF ANY?

Jamie is babysitting for a company. She is payed $4.00 right away. Then charges 2 per hr after. How much does she get payed after 5 hours?

Tina went to boston and parked in a parking garage. $14 Per 5 hr. and $28 for 12 how much does it cost per hour.

Rachel went to a resturant. Instead of $ on a meal, it's 2 $ per person. Look at the table and find the permant tax.

by just reading the table. Yet he is pleased that they are connecting situations to the table and invested in the problems they posed.

The third group of students is sitting at a cluster of desks in the middle of the room. The task in their blue folder is shown in Figure 2–7. The teacher knows that a few of these students (along with many others in the class) need to further explore how to make a graph, but he thinks they will be more successful at that task after they have spent some time interpreting a graph. As the given graph does not include a description of the dependent and independent variables or a scale, this is where the group's discussion begins.

Bernie is concerned with what the numbers on the scale should be.

Ronan responds to his concern by saying, "It doesn't matter. We don't even know what we want the numbers to mean."

Bernie explains, "Oh, I thought that the numbers on the bottom always meant time." Ronan pauses and nods her head yes, so Bernie proceeds to write the numbers *1–13* along the *x*-axis. He places his finger on the 1 and moves it up along that line of the graph paper until he reaches the line graph.

"Wait," he exclaims, "this isn't going to work. We need to land on a number."

Figure 2–7 *Task that requires students to write a story that relates to a line graph.*

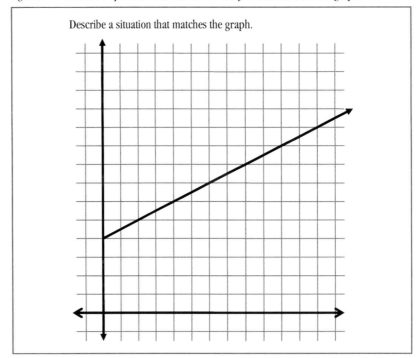

Describe a situation that matches the graph.

Ronan takes the graph to look at it more closely, and after pondering it for a moment, she says, "Look, the points are every other one. Let's number the bottom every other one, too. The middle ones will just be the halfway marks."

Bernie responds to her idea with an appreciative "Cool" and rewrites the numbers, which now show 0 through 6.

They then decide that the *y*-axis should be done the same way, but as Ronan explains, "In hundreds, because we'll make it about miles." Once the numbers are in place they decide to focus on spaceship travel and create a situation easily. (See Figure 2–8.)

As the teacher collects the students' work at the end of the period, he thinks about how having students work in various groups on different types of problems has allowed him to learn a good deal more about all of the students. He is pleased that they were mostly engaged in working on the tasks and that their responses have further revealed what they must work on next. He knows that he would like to have each group continue to work on these topics for another day. He wants them to reach success

Figure 2–8 *Bernie and Ronan created a problem about spaceship travel to match the graph.*

Describe a situation that matches the graph.

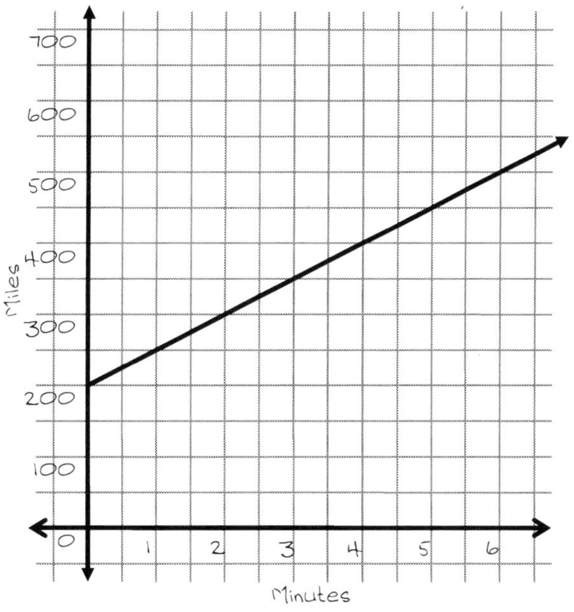

Eddie G. is on a spaceship 200 miles in the sky. It takes off. Where is he at any time you would like to know?

and gain confidence in their abilities to connect a real-world context to the representation they have been assigned. He also knows that it will be advantageous for the groups to eventually come together to see how all of these representations work as a whole. Tomorrow he will give each of the students representations that match the same data. That way, when they come together they can see how their separate work is really connected. He is excited about what lies ahead for the students.

## Teacher Reflection

After the first day, I realized my students were at many different levels of thinking about representations of linear equations. I decided I wanted to help them each work with one representation. I grouped the students so that all of them would be challenged while they deepened their understandings. When I can, I like to differentiate by having students involved in a very similar activity, but in a slightly different manner. This way, I can maintain my focus better while providing for individual differences. The fact that they were all presented data for which they had to pose problems really made them look at the data more closely.

Over time, I have become more respectful of the different ways my students think about mathematical ideas. A few years ago I would have just told them to make a table, graph, and equation from the same data. Now I realize that they have strong preferences for which representation they use and that I need to spend more time helping them connect the various representations they make.

*I am always amazed how my preconceived expectations can interfere with my ability to understand students' work.*

Many times the students take me in directions I would not have thought about. I was really surprised by the group who found the average price per hour for the parking problem. I was ready to tell them they were wrong and then I realized that they had actually found the hourly cost for these times that Ms. Perez paid for parking. I am always amazed how my preconceived expectations can interfere with my ability to understand students' work. Frequently, they are making more sense than I realize. I have begun to recognize that they may have solved a problem correctly, just not the one I had intended.

I always find it challenging to monitor and support three tasks simultaneously. Sometimes I just have two. Over the course of the year, my students get better at helping one another when I'm not available. That is my ultimate goal, to have a classroom of independent workers engaged in mathematical sense making!

# Attributes of a Worthwhile Task

The series of activities about linear situations led to a lively exploration of mathematical concepts. Students discovered, affirmed, or reaffirmed relationships, shared a variety of ideas, uncovered misconceptions, and connected symbolic notation to other representations. In addition, they were eager to explain their thinking. What type of task yields such results? While it is easier to recognize a specific task as worthwhile when explored with a specific group of students, there are five general attributes that indicate if a task will be worthwhile.

## Five Attributes of Worthwhile Tasks

### 1. It focuses on significant mathematical ideas.

The task should be connected to big ideas in mathematics and be problematic; that is, the solution should not be apparent immediately, or a variety of outcomes should be possible. In this case, algebraic thinking is the focus and connecting different representations to linear situations is the big idea. When instruction emphasizes significant ideas, students are more likely to make connections across mathematical strands or to pursue related ideas on their own.

### 2. It is developmentally appropriate.

For middle school students, a task is developmentally appropriate if the ideas are within reach both from a cognitive level and from an experiential one. The problem should encourage students to construct their own strategies or ideas and prod them to connect their intuition and natural language to their mathematical experiences. Concrete materials, visual models, and drawing materials should be available for use at all times to support their work. As the exchanges about the lunch data demonstrated, asking students to explain their ideas or make comparisons among representations—in this case, expressions and equations—often extends students' thinking. At this age, students should be encouraged to engage in deductive reasoning and to formalize their generalizations.

### 3. It is contextualized.

Presenting mathematical ideas in connection to literature (such as the problem involving peas in Chapter 1) or shared events can help students enter mathematical

(Continued)

activities. Situating mathematical tasks within everyday contexts, such as using their lunch cards, also captures students' interest and gives them insights on how to begin new tasks. Encouraging students to choose their own context, as when they pose problems, can be motivating and can deepen their understanding of mathematical connections to the real world.

**4. It offers an appropriate level of challenge.**
To be worthwhile, a task must offer a cognitive challenge that requires students to make decisions and explore new ideas, and yet not be so challenging as to feel overwhelming. Giving students the variety of parking receipts created a new challenge, but students readily understood the task. Even those who weren't able to immediately offer an idea about rate of change knew something about parking garages, or could determine the amount of time the car was parked on any given day. When a task has multiple entry points, it is possible to engage students with a broad range of readiness.

**5. It encourages multiple perspectives.**
An interesting task stimulates a variety of strategies, representations, and mathematical ideas and thus encourages students to engage in mathematical discourse in which they explain and justify their thinking. When the students explained their different equations and expressions related to the lunch money problem, other students were able to extend their views of the situation and to make connections among the representations shared.

Note that these characteristics of a worthwhile task serve two purposes. They build broader and deeper mathematical ideas and support differentiated instruction. That is, a task that is contextualized is developmentally appropriate, offers an appropriate level of challenge, encourages multiple perspectives, makes room for a variety of learners, and supports a variety of learning needs. While a variety of tasks are available in published materials, teachers often find that they are more successful with tasks they adapt or create themselves.

## Connecting the Chapter to Your Practice

1.  How much of your instructional time is allocated to the development of factual knowledge, procedural knowledge, and conceptual knowledge?

2.  How do you support students' use of multiple representations of mathematical ideas? What do you do when a student relies, almost exclusively, on one type of representation?

3.  What real-world contexts work best for your students?

# Chapter 3
# Getting to Know Our Students

*B*ack when we were in school, teachers assessed our mathematical work in the same way that our spelling tests were scored. We wrote our answers in a list and teachers marked them as either right or wrong. Then they wrote the number of correct answers at the top of the paper over the total number of items, for example, $\frac{15}{20}$. Teachers considered this ratio evidence of our learning and kept these grades in a record book for future reference. Feedback and assessment data were limited to these scores. Teachers gave little or no attention to analyzing our work and seldom valued process.

We're thankful this is no longer the status quo in most of today's middle school classrooms. As our expectations for teaching mathematics have changed, so have the ways in which we gather evidence of learning. In recent years, teachers have begun to examine their students' mathematical thinking more closely. They observe students as they work individually or in groups, use models, and tackle more complex tasks. They keep anecdotal records of these observations. They look closely at daily work, in which students are often expected to write or draw to explain and represent their mathematical ideas, and use it to assess students and inform instructional decisions. As well as correctness, teachers look at the work in relation to curriculum standards, developmental readiness, strategy choices, misconceptions, and conceptual thinking.

Some teachers give more focused assessment tasks at both the beginning and the end of units. Some keep portfolios that include samples of work completed during different times of the year and across mathematical strands. Some teachers have students include a piece of work they have revised in their portfolios. Roberts and Tayeh (2007) suggest that students submit metacognitive journals in which they include five problems of their choice considered over the semester. For each problem the students explain their solution strategies, reflect on their problem-solving processes and connections, and provide a rationale for including it in the journal.

These assessment techniques allow teachers to get to know their students as individual mathematical thinkers and thus more effectively match instructional practices to their students' various needs. As the teacher in the following reflection about the analysis of student work explains, these assessment practices require more time. But when teachers make the commitment to value their students' work, the results are informative and rewarding.

## Teacher Reflection

Sometimes I'm overwhelmed by my students' work. It can take a long time to analyze their recordings. I think about what the work is or isn't telling me about my students' understandings, their misconceptions, or their connections. When I think back to when it took very little time and effort to mark answers as correct or incorrect, I know I used to have a nagging feeling about this. On some level I realized that anyone could have corrected their work and that it didn't really tell me much about my students and their progress.

When I am not feeling overwhelmed, I do feel great joy while reflecting and commenting on their work. I see such possibility and get a sense of deep satisfaction about my role as a teacher. I look for patterns of thinking and use pieces of the work to help frame our next investigations. I try to give authentic, purposeful feedback, too. I want students to feel that I care about their thinking because I do! Each piece of work is evidence of learning.

> *I want students to feel that I care about their thinking because I do! Each piece of work is evidence of learning.*

This feeling is similar to how I feel when I listen to my students in class. I marvel at how students can communicate their ideas and how clever their thinking can be. I want them to feel the satisfaction that I feel, to take pride in their work and ideas.

It's challenging to write meaningful comments on work, given the number of students I have, but I do try to do so. Even short comments such as "Clear organization of data" or "Take a closer look at the patterns you found" let the students know that I considered their responses, that I didn't just look at an answer. My sister teaches elementary school and I used to envy the fact that she only needed to get to know one class of students, but she always reminds me that she has to do it for all of the subjects.

*(Continued)*

Though it certainly matters if an answer is incorrect, I try to see if I can figure out where any of the students got off track. For me, that's most important. If I can't make sense of their work, then I know that I need to spend more time with those students so they can help me understand what they were doing or thinking at that moment. When work is handed in that is incorrect or incomplete, I want to take the time to have students think about it again. I don't want students to feel as though their work is never finished, but at the same time, I don't want them to view each piece as a separate task that they can easily discard when they hand it in, saying, "Done!"

The students' work is interesting and informative. It has great value to me; it shows me what and how my students are learning. Isn't that the heart of the matter? I know that is not how I felt about my work in math class as a student, but it is how I want my students to feel now.

This teacher has captured many of the differences between assessment practices that were common when we were students and those she incorporates into her classroom. While other changes in assessment and evaluation of student learning have occurred during this time as well, such as the significant attention paid to high-stakes, mandated testing, the focus here is on those assessment practices and habits of mind that support differentiated instruction on a daily basis. Such practices include formal and informal techniques for collecting data, and most likely, many are already incorporated into your classroom. Through the lens of differentiation, however, the purposes of these data-gathering strategies become more focused and refined as do the assessment tasks you use with your students. Like this teacher, our sights should always be set on getting to know our students better and on understanding their ways of making sense of the mathematics they are learning. Our goals are to gather evidence of learning and to gain insights into best next steps.

## Pre-Assessment

To differentiate according to readiness, we need to determine what our students already know. Note that some of the earlier classroom scenarios began with an activity that allowed teachers to pre-assess their students' knowledge and level of familiarity or proficiency with the concept at hand. Many activities can serve this purpose if they include opportunities for discussion, group work, or recorded responses and explanations. It is the teachers' clarity of purpose and attention to students' work that allow such

Take Action!

Assess for readiness.

activities to become sources of pre-assessment data. Let's consider another teacher's words as she reflects on pre-assessment.

## Teacher Reflection

When I am thinking about pre-assessment, I know I am trying to identify students' zones of comfort and proficiency. I am looking for data that will help me answer questions such as, How familiar are my students with this new concept? What working knowledge, skills, and strategies do they have in place to support them in this, supposedly, new area of learning? What misconceptions might they have? How comfortable are they with the mathematical language associated with this topic?

I try hard not to make assumptions about my students anymore. Some of them come to middle school with a wealth of mathematical knowledge and experience. Other students come less prepared, and the range among them seems to be increasing each year. It's hard to find that place between where things are too hard and out of reach, and too easy and potentially uninteresting or not challenging, but I want all students to find math class worthwhile. So if a portion of the class already knows how to divide by a fraction, I don't want to spend two or three days with instructional activities designed to help them learn how to do it. I would rather find a way to challenge those who already know the concept, and a way to work with those students who need more time and assistance.

*When I spend time at the start of a unit by giving students a pre-assessment task, I can plan lessons based on what the students need to work on, not what I need to cover.*

I want to identify tasks and investigations that will be just right for my students, that will challenge their thinking without overwhelming them. And, I want to do this quickly, so that I begin to make adjustments as soon as they are needed. When I spend time at the start of a unit by giving students a pre-assessment task, I can plan lessons based on what the students need to work on, not what I need to cover. I also have a better sense of how to group students within the unit and how to keep track of the skills they are learning.

This teacher has identified many aspects of the importance of pre-assessment. So, just how soon in the year should we begin this pre-assessment process? To get a broad sense of students as a group and to begin to capture the range of their readiness levels and learning preferences, you should assess them immediately. Of course, teachers should also maintain a commitment to pre-assessment throughout the year as their classes consider new topics.

*Take Action!*

Gather data to inform differentiation.

# Anecdotal Records

From the first day of school, teachers have a myriad of ways to get acquainted with their new students. They are eager to learn about what their students know and their comfort levels with various mathematical ideas, social interactions, and working environments. For example, sixth-grade teachers might begin to collect anecdotal data about their students sometime during the first week by observing them sort a set of polygons according to the students' own criteria. As the students dive in, so do their teachers, who listen, watch, and often record what they see and hear.

During this activity one teacher observes that Shannon gathers all of the polygons and separates them into large and small shapes as Massie and Kim Su watch her work. She sees Peter and Sam compare the lengths of the shapes' sides and put the pieces in piles based on how many side lengths that they have in common. Peter refers to shapes by name. Sam uses gestures to indicate where polygons should be placed.

Kenny immediately picks up a trapezoid and asks his group, "Do you know what this is called?"

Willie starts to laugh and explains, "I had a second-grade teacher who knew I liked action guys. I used to always forget the name of this shape. So he told me a story about zoids and how we had to trap them. For a couple of days he called this a 'trap-a-zoid' and looked like a fierce fighter trying to trap something when he said it. I remember that and never forget the name anymore." Kenny, Willie, and Max strike a few fighter poses before returning to the task.

Deidre, Melissa, and Alexi begin to organize the polygons by number of sides. Then they further separate the quadrilaterals.

Deidre says, "Look, there are rectangles, squares, and just weird ones."

Alexi responds, "But if we organize these, we should do the triangles, too."

Melissa recommends, "Let's just separate each group of shapes into regular ones and weird ones."

Deidre suggests, "We can do that, but teachers really care about triangles and quadrilaterals. That's why there are all those special words for them, like *acute, scalene, parallelogram,* and *rhombus.* So we'll do all the polygons by regular and not regular, and then organize the three-sided and four-sided ones." Deidre looks up to see the other two girls nod, before assuming her idea is accepted.

The teacher does not try to record all of these details, but she does make notes in an attempt to capture what she's observing:

- *Shannon chose a simple characteristic and does all the sorting. Massie and Kim Su watch.*
- *Peter and Sam focus on common side measures. Sam's work is accurate—language?*
- *Kenny asks for shape name and Willie tells "trap-a-zoid" story. K, W, and M are playful together but able to get back to work without intervention.*
- *Deidre, Melissa, and Alexi discuss their plans. Deidre demonstrates leadership and strong vocabulary.*

Anecdotal notes like these help the teacher get a feel for students' engagement, learning style, and working knowledge. Over time, patterns of thinking or behavior might emerge for an individual as well as for the whole class that can help the teacher make more informed decisions for instruction. New information abounds during these first few days and weeks and teachers can sometimes feel besieged by it. Recording these simple observations can help us focus and remember what we have witnessed.

In today's world of mandated testing, students enter the classroom with considerable information in their files related to mathematical achievement. For many teachers, anecdotal records based on interactions in the classroom and standardized test scores are enough to get started. Other teachers do not want to consider test scores until they have gotten to know their students better or do not believe that such scores yield enough information. They sometimes conduct interviews in which they ask students to respond to a series of tasks or questions.

## Interviews

Early assessment interviews in sixth grade are usually designed to help the teacher learn relatively quickly about students' abilities in relation to number and operations (including whole numbers, decimals, fractions, and percents). In the seventh and eighth grades teachers also include questions related to patterns and variables. Often teachers construct their own interviews and use their state standards as a way to decide what kinds of questions to ask.

Given the brevity of the average mathematics class period at the middle school level, individual assessments of significant length are not usually practical. Middle school teachers have two other options: (1) brief questions that can be asked while other

**Strand:** Number and Algebra

**Focus:** Number sense and patterns

**Context:** Group interviews

students engage in individual work or (2) group interviews. Here are a few sample questions to ask a sixth-grade student:

- How can you use mental arithmetic to find 58 × 8?
- If you were dividing 98 students into 4 classes, how many students would there be in each class?
- Do you think that $\frac{1}{3}$ is closer to $\frac{1}{4}$ or $\frac{1}{2}$? Why?
- If you started at 4.7 and counted forward by tenths, what are the next four numbers you would say?

In addition to the previous questions, a seventh-grade teacher might consider:

- What is the next whole number that comes after 9.96?
- What are the next three numbers in this pattern: −26, −20, −14, −8?
- What benchmark fraction is close to 47%?
- How could you use mental arithmetic to solve $\frac{13}{4} + \frac{11}{2}$?

Eighth-grade teachers might include:

- What are the next three numbers in this pattern: 1, 4, 9, 16, 25?
- How can you estimate 32 ÷ 0.49?
- If you started at 156 and counted backward by thousandths, what two numbers would you say next?
- If $x + 5 = y - 5$, is $x$ or $y$ greater?
- What two whole numbers are closest to the square root of 5?

These questions are not comprehensive, but they do give the teacher an initial perspective on each student's understanding of number, operations, and patterns. Teachers can certainly adapt the questions during the course of the interview to make sure each student experiences some success.

We encourage teachers to use questions that might motivate some interesting discussion among participants in a group interview. It is worthwhile to observe students working together to arrive at responses and to note whether or not original ideas are transformed as the discussion ensues or if students are able to take a problem further because they are discussing it together, rather than solving it individually. Ideas for group interviews include the following:

- Create a word problem that requires you to find $34 \div \frac{3}{4}$ and round up the remainder to the nearest whole number.
- Make three different representations of +6 using black chips to represent positive numbers and red chips to represent negative numbers.

- Create two series of drawings that both fit the equation $y = 4x + 7$.
- What's different and the same about fractions and decimal numbers?
- How will a graph of $y = 2x + 6$ look different from a graph of $y = 4x + 6$?

Math coaches and special educators sometimes work together to collect more data about particular students identified as being at risk. While there are fewer individual assessment instruments available for use at the middle school level than the elementary level, some products do exist.

Developed for use in K–8 classrooms, First Steps in Mathematics (Willis et al. 2007) provides a framework that links instruction and assessment and is recommended for use with all students. Developed in Australia and validated in Canada, the program is now being used in the United States. Though it requires special training, it provides diagnostic tasks that allow teachers to assess whether students have acquired key understandings. The tasks are easily incorporated into classroom interactions and are linked to teaching suggestions.

Norm-referenced assessments are also available. KeyMath has been used for many years and has been substantially revised in its new edition. The KeyMath 3 Diagnostic Assessment (Connolly 2008a) covers mathematics content through ninth grade. Of particular interest to middle school teachers is that this diagnostic tool now includes content related to factoring and algebraic expressions. The student is interviewed individually for thirty to ninety minutes, so this assessment is used only for students who require this attention. Correlated instructional materials are also available (Connolly 2008b).

The norm-referenced Group Mathematics Assessment and Diagnostic Evaluation (GMADE) (Williams 2004) may be administered individually or in a group to determine proficiency with individual skills based on the National Council of Teachers of Mathematics standards. Test questions focus on concepts and communication, operations and computation, and process and application. Intervention instructional materials are provided that correlate to assessment results. Teachers can then use parallel test items to assess progress.

Another norm-referenced test, suitable for students from seven years old to seventeen years old, the Comprehensive Mathematical Abilities Test (CMAT) (Hresko et al. 2002), also aims to identify students particularly above or below grade level. It's divided into six core tests and six subtests, and teachers or schools may choose which of the twelve portions to administer.

You may already feel flooded with test data about all of your students and wonder why you would want any more information. Upon further thought, though, most teachers recognize that there are a few students in their classes about whom they would appreciate additional information. Whether by making tasks such as those suggested in First Steps in Mathematics (Willis et al. 2007) an integral part of your teaching or by reviewing data supplied through special tests, it is unlikely that we can be successful with struggling students without better understanding their key strengths and weaknesses.

Vygotsky (1978) defined the zone of proximal development as the difference between what learners can do independently and what they can do with support. Our job is to challenge students' comfort level and then help them find their next boundary. Through assessment, we try to identify evidence for what the student knows or has mastered, areas where she has formed initial ideas but needs additional experience, and those concepts and skills that require further scaffolding or additional readiness development. We also try to ascertain how successfully the student works alone and with others and what types of support seem to yield the best results.

It is becoming more commonplace for schools or school districts to require some initial assessment in mathematics. We are all being asked to be more accountable. In turn, each teacher needs to determine his or her own best way to use data gathered from an assessment, be it formal or informal. There was a time when such initial data were used only to determine ability groups in mathematics. Often referred to as *tracking*, these groups were thought to be homogenous in nature and tended to be a long-term assignment. That is not the goal assumed here.

We recognize that there is much pressure on middle school teachers and administrators to group students by ability levels. This pressure can become particularly forceful around algebraic readiness. Students who are not enrolled in algebra by eighth grade will not be able to take calculus in high school, assuming that they take one mathematics course each year. We encourage teachers to work with their colleagues to find ways to keep course levels from being rigid and exclusive. Try to find ways to support students in changing levels during the year. Also, remember to recognize the diversity among students assigned to the same level of coursework.

# Open-Ended Tasks

Along with interviews and anecdotal records as ways to collect information about what their students know and how they represent their ideas, some teachers find it useful to give every student an open-ended task or problem. One sixth-grade teacher asks her students to respond to the question *What do you know about 35%?* Mattie's response indicates that 35 percent is equal to 0.35 and $\frac{35}{100}$. (See Figure 3–1.) While recognizing that her first thought is 35 out of 100, she also acknowledges that the percentage may be applied to a total of 60 or 146 (though she does not explain the proportional relationship). Mattie identifies that 1, 3, 5, and 7 are factors of 35, without indicating why this might be relevant. She associates percents with statistical data and surveys. She also explains that 35 percent is not a benchmark percent as it does not go equally into 100 percent. Note that her response does not include any visual representations.

Charlie provides two visual models for 35 percent along with the conclusion that if 35 percent of a group ordered pizza, 65 percent ordered something else. (See Figure 3–2.) His work then focuses on a common elementary school task of finding several combinations of a particular number, in this case, thirty-five. Beginning with his fourth example, he provides a systematic listing of all of the ways to make thirty-five with two addends, appearing to end this pattern when he begins to repeat a combination previously

**Task Idea!**

**Strand:** Number

**Focus:** Percent

**Context:** Open-ended question

Figure 3–1  *Mattie's response to the open-ended assessment task.*

What do you know about 35%?

When I see 35% on a math problem, my mind automatically thinks of "35 out of 100", since % means "out of 100". But 35% could also have a lot of different meanings, like if it were 35% of 60 or 35% out of 146. I also immediately think about its factors — 1, 35, 5, and 7. I know that 35% is half of 70% and equal to .35 and $\frac{35}{100}$. I know that 35 could be talking about something less than a whole or something more than a whole — like 35% of a cookie or 35 out of 100 people. I also know that 35% could be used as a statistic — like about 35% of my juice is real juice — or in a survey, like my earlier example of 35 out of 100 people. Also, 35% does not go equally into 100%, so is not a benchmark percent.

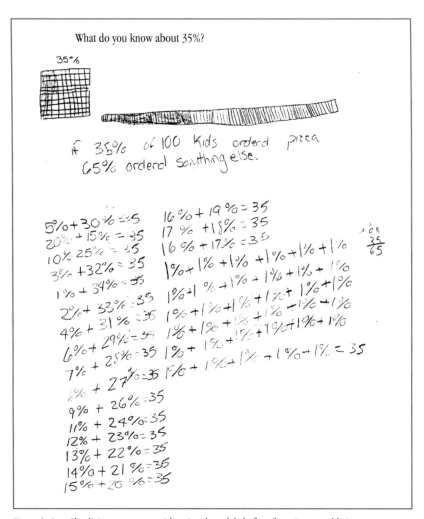

Figure 3–2    *Charlie's response provides visual models before focusing on addition.*

given in a different order. Such data, however, do not reveal his understanding of percent.

Many students write a decimal and a fraction equivalent to 35 percent. Holly expands on this idea by explaining that it could be written as 0.35, 0.350, or 0.3500, because *no matter how many zeros you put on the end of a decimal, the value is still the same.*

Margo includes a representation of what she identifies as a thermometer shaded to 35 percent, similar to what you might see for a fund-raising goal. In his response, Vic includes the misconception that 5% × 7% = 35%. Trevor correctly places 35 percent between $\frac{1}{2}$ and $\frac{1}{3}$ on a number line. Christo cites the familiar rule that to change from a percent to a decimal, you move the decimal point two places to the right.

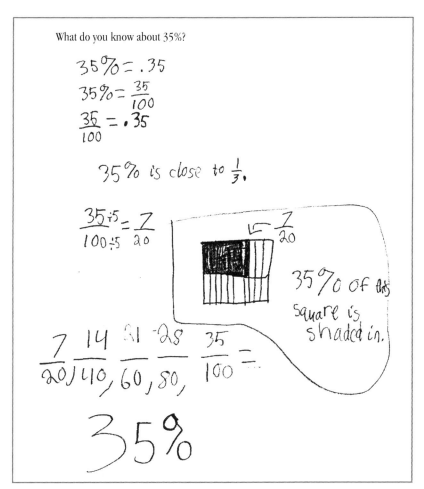

What do you know about 35%?

$$35\% = .35$$
$$35\% = \frac{35}{100}$$
$$\frac{35}{100} = .35$$

$35\%$ is close to $\frac{1}{3}$.

$$\frac{35 \div 5}{100 \div 5} = \frac{7}{20}$$

$\leftarrow \frac{1}{20}$

$35\%$ of this square is shaded in.

$$\frac{7}{20} \Big) \frac{14}{40}, \frac{21}{60}, \frac{28}{80}, \frac{35}{100} = \dots$$

35%

Figure 3–3   *Quinn made several connections with fractions.*

Quinn begins with writing 35 percent as a decimal and a fraction and then identifies it as close to $\frac{1}{3}$. (See Figure 3–3.) He divides 35 and 100 by 5 to find the equivalent fraction $\frac{7}{20}$, and draws a rectangle with 7 of 20 parts shaded. He writes, *35% of this square is shaded in*, next to this representation. He then writes five equivalent fractions equal to 35 percent.

## Teacher Reflection

I like to pose the question *What do you know about 35%?* to my students during the first week of school. It gives me a little window of insight into their mathematical thinking. This is a question that students generally feel comfortable answering, since most are familiar with

*(Continued)*

percent. I am always amazed at the variety of the students' responses. Some students just write lots about one idea, while others provide a greater range of concepts. I'm always saddened when a couple of students respond, "I don't know." It worries me that they are uncertain as to how to answer an open-ended mathematical question, even a fairly straightforward one.

While I encourage the use of representations, numbers, or words to describe their thinking, some students rely only on equations. I worry about whether or not these students are making connections between the mathematics they study at school and their own lives. Percents seem to be everywhere, but still, many students fail to identify a real-world application.

> *I want students to realize that I expect several ideas from them and that this year is not going to be about just giving an answer.*

I used to worry so much about finding the right assessment task when I first started using open-ended questions. Now I realize that a simple question such as this one gives me a quick look into students' thinking. Also, because this task is so open, it doesn't tend to intimidate them; they all have some way of responding. I also like giving my students only one question on the page. I want students to realize that I expect several ideas from them and that this year is not going to be about just giving an answer.

Though the range of responses to open questions is great, I don't want to read too much into them. After all, it's only one task and students sometimes need a week or two back in school before they really get going. But it is a place to begin and does help me develop some ideas about what my new students know. I don't have a specific response I am looking for, though I do look for accuracy, flexible thinking, and engagement. I also check to see if there is any evidence of a student looking uncomfortable during this work. It's just an initial task, but it really helps me get to know my students better.

This teacher reminds us of the balanced way we need to think about assessment tasks. No single task can be given too much attention and yet each appropriate task does provide us with some relevant data. It is particularly important to take a similarly balanced perspective on information that is passed from grade to grade. In many schools, teachers share data from one grade to another by way of lists of test scores and quarter and final grades. Many teachers receiving this information find it to be very helpful, while others prefer to begin to make their own judgments before reviewing any of the previous data. In either case it is important to remember the significance of gathering evidence from multiple sources.

While we have concentrated on early assessment tasks that address readiness, readiness cannot be the sole focus of mathematics teachers. We also want to differentiate instructional activities according to interests, preferred learning styles, intelligences, and mathematical dispositions. We can collect these data through observations, as indicated in the section on anecdotal records, and also through parent questionnaires, student input, and conversations with previous teachers. When we collect and use these data, we acknowledge that we expect our students to be different from one another and we show them (and their parents) that we care about getting to know students as individual learners.

## Questionnaires

Some teachers ask parents to complete questionnaires. Some middle school teachers send questionnaires home during the first week of classes. Others have parents complete a questionnaire at the fall open house. (See Figure 3–4 on page 65; see also Reproducibles.) Questions about hobbies, collections, and activity choices in and out of school provide insight into interests students have that may connect to mathematics. Collecting coins; playing cards, chess, or logic games on the computer; doing puzzles; having an interest in sports-generated statistics; and pursuing craft or woodworking projects often relate to skills that support and utilize mathematical thinking. Students' general interests are also relevant to mathematics as they allow us to position tasks in contexts that can help capture students' curiosity and illustrate the usefulness of what they are learning. Some teachers, aware of parents' busy lifestyles, prefer to use forms that do not require narrative responses. (See Figure 3–5 on page 66; see also Reproducibles.) The following reflection shows us how one teacher has gained respect for the information parents can provide.

## Teacher Reflection

When I first started teaching I thought my job was to teach adolescents, that only elementary teachers had to focus on families. I didn't give much thought to the parents of my students and what my relationship would be with them. How quickly I learned! Now in my fifth

*(Continued)*

year of teaching, I have made progress in finding ways to connect with my students' caregivers.

At the beginning of the year I send home a parent and guardian survey that asks questions about how their child learns and about their attitudes toward learning mathematics. I ask for these to be returned prior to the first open house at the end of September. I gather this information to use as a guide when I am addressing the parents or guardians. I am as surprised by the variety among the responses of the caregivers as I am by the variations in my students! I have parents who feel strongly that their role is to help their child with homework as well as parents who feel it is solely the student's responsibility. Likewise, I have many parents who support the recent changes in math education and several who think, "The way I was taught was fine. Why are we changing the rules?"

> *I have many parents who support the recent changes in math education and several who think, "The way I was taught was fine. Why are we changing the rules?"*

In addition to the survey, I share with each parent or guardian their own child's survey done in class. Often how a student answers the questions surprises the adult. One student wrote *Excellent* in response to the question, "How do you feel about your ability to solve problems about percents?" Her mother was shocked, but happy, and told me, "Last year my daughter always cried while doing her homework. I tried to help her, but I think she got more confused. She was not comfortable with me helping because she said I don't do percents the right way. I am glad to see that she is liking percents now." It's so easy for all of us to hang onto a perception that may no longer be true. It was important for Wanda's mother to realize that her daughter was now comfortable with percents. I think this knowledge will help her mother to treat her as someone who is successful in math, which will in turn reinforce that idea in Wanda.

When it comes to talking about math, parents or guardians frequently tell me that they were not successful in or didn't like math. Sometimes I worry that these parents don't hold high enough expectations for their children. Other parents tell me how much they excelled at math and how they want the same for their children. They tell stories of how their child has impressed them at an early age and identify family traits and interests they share: "We love to look at the football stats in the newspaper." "We play cards all the time and race to see who can add up the points first." "When they were young, I used to have them estimate when we had traveled a mile when we were on a long trip. Janney got really good at doing this, even when I changed the speed." These comments give me a perspective on how the families view mathematics and how mathematics is embedded in their daily lives. I can't believe how much more I learn about my students now that I have built family connections.

Dear Families:

I am always so excited about the start of the school year and a roomful of eager students. I am eager to get to know each and every one of them, as well as their families. As no one knows your child as well as you do, I am hoping that you will have the time to answer these few questions. There are no right or wrong answers, just responses that will help me meet the nee of your child when learning math.

I am very interested in helping students see that math is an important part of the world and thus exciting to learn. I believe by connecting the learning of math to other important aspects of your child's life, I can make it more relevant and exciting.

Please feel free to call me if you have any questions. Thank you.

Student's Name _____

Completed By _____

1. What are your child's favorite hobbies, interests, pastimes, books?

2. In what ways is mathematics part of your child's life at home?

3. What, if any, concerns do you have about your child's knowledge of mathematics?

4. What is a mathematical strength that you see in your child?

5. Describe your child's experience with math homework.

Figure 3–4 *Parent or guardian questionnaire.*

You can also use questionnaires to gather helpful data from students. See, for example, the general interest survey one teacher gives to seventh-grade students early in the fall. (See Figure 3–6 on page 68; see also Reproducibles.) Students can also tell us about how they learn best, for example, whether they like to work in groups or alone, the level of challenge they prefer, the noise level they find comfortable, the types of unit projects that interest them, and where they like to work in the classroom. Asking students about

Dear Parent or Guardian:

It's been a wonderful start to the school year. I am excited about getting to know each of my new students. I am hoping that you will help me by completing this questionnaire about mathematics. There are no right or wrong answers! Please feel free to call me if you have any questions. Thank you.

Student's Name _____

Completed By _____

1 = agree
2 = somewhat agree
3 = somewhat disagree
4 = disagree

| | | | | |
|---|---|---|---|---|
| My child will stick with a math problem, even when it is difficult. | 1 | 2 | 3 | 4 |
| My child lacks confidence in mathematics. | 1 | 2 | 3 | 4 |
| My child has strong computational skills. | 1 | 2 | 3 | 4 |
| My child's favorite subject is mathematics. | 1 | 2 | 3 | 4 |
| My child becomes frustrated when solving math problems. | 1 | 2 | 3 | 4 |
| My child does math homework independently. | 1 | 2 | 3 | 4 |
| As a parent, it is my job to help my child with math homework. | 1 | 2 | 3 | 4 |
| Math is talked about at home and is part of our everyday life. | 1 | 2 | 3 | 4 |
| I do not always understand the way my child thinks about math problems. | 1 | 2 | 3 | 4 |
| Math is taught better today than when I was in school. | 1 | 2 | 3 | 4 |

Comments:

Figure 3–5  *Parent or Guardian Survey.*

Photocopy It!
See Reproducible 3B

these preferences helps them realize that we care about how they learn best. It also allows them to reflect on their learning preferences. (See Figure 3–7 on page 69; see also Reproducibles.) As the following teacher's words suggest, knowing our students' interests and preferences can help us relate to them more deeply and better meet their needs.

I really like learning as much about my students as I can, as soon as possible. I like to know how they spend their time when they are not in school and who their favorite famous people are. With so many new students at once, written responses to questions really help me.

> With so many new students at once, written responses to questions really help me.

Yesterday I shared a baseball statistic with Melissa and asked Conrad to imagine what Oprah might do in a particular situation. I could tell that they were surprised I had remembered what they had written. September is such an exciting time of the year. It holds such promise as we all get to know each other and form our classroom communities. I love my summers, but this excitement and wonder really helps me make the transition to fall.

I have only recently asked my students to complete a questionnaire about their own learning preferences. When I first did so, I was surprised at how firm their opinions were. This year all of my students have communicated a preference for working alone or with a partner. I like to do a lot of group work. Maybe I should start with partner work and move a bit more slowly to small groups. I never would have thought about this if I hadn't collected these data.

It is also worthwhile to gain insight into students' mathematical dispositions, or their attitudes toward mathematics. As all teachers recognize, positive attitudes contribute greatly to successful learning. Ideally, all students enjoy mathematics, have positive mathematical learning experiences, think of themselves as successful learners and users of mathematics, and view mathematics as a useful tool in their lives. Simple observations, such as noting how a student sits or looks during mathematical activities, can often provide quite a bit of information. Does her body language suggest that she is tense? Do his eyes indicate that he is disinterested? Is the position of her shoulders a sign that she is confident? Is the angle of his upper body an implication of eager anticipation? We can often observe these behaviors during the first week of school and discover those students who might need closer attention.

Again, you can use questionnaires, such as a form used to collect data from sixth- through eighth-grade students about their mathematical dispositions. (See Figure 3–8 on page 70; see also Reproducibles.) Student responses suggest a variety of beliefs about

---

**General Interest Survey for Students:
What Interests You?**

Name: _____                          Date: _____

1. What activities do you like to do after school?

2. What are your favorite sports or games?

3. What music do you like best?

4. If you could plan a school field trip, where would the class go?

5. Who is your favorite character from a book or a video?

6. Which of these things do you like most? Put a **1** there.
   Which of these things do you like second best? Put a **2** there.

   ____ music                          ____ reading

   ____ sports                         ____ nature walks

   ____ acting                         ____ drawing or art projects

   ____ being with friends             ____ building things

   ____ science experiments            ____ field trips to historical places

---

*Photocopy It!
See Reproducible 3C*

Figure 3–6  *General Interest Survey for Students.*

mathematics. For example, when asked, "Why is math important to learn?" some students indicate its relevance to their daily lives with comments such as *You need angles to play basketball; When you get older you need math to take care of your life*; and *If you know it or not, every job uses math. I need it now to check my babysitting pay.* Other responses are school based; they contain expressions of concern about students' future education. Many eighth-grade students respond, *You need it for high school.* Some sixth-, seventh-, and eighth-grade students mention, *I want to get into a good college.*

Responses also reveal how students feel about math. Many students give short positive answers such as *really happy, smart, good,* and *fun.* Some students recognize differences in how they

Figure 3–7   *Learner Survey.*

feel about math based on the strand. For example, Jill wrote, *If it's algebra I feel good because it's like a puzzle.* Unfortunately, difficulties and ill feelings are also suggested with responses such as *frustrated, I will never be able to learn this stuff, stressed,* and *I want to be invisible so I won't get called on.* More than at the elementary level, the response *bored* also appears. When asked what they are good at, not good at, or want to learn more about, most students name an arithmetic operation. All of the students are able to identify something they are good at; *number math, working with numbers,* and *computing* are the most common responses. Yet

---

**Math Interest Inventory**

Name: _____          Date: _____

1. Math is important to learn because . . .



2. When I am learning math I feel . . .



3. One thing I am good at in math is . . .



4. One thing I am not good at yet in math is . . .



5. This year in math I want to learn about . . .

---

Figure 3–8  *Math Interest Inventory.*

either computation with fractions or computation with integers is identified frequently as something they are not yet good at. Teachers know that sixth- and seventh-grade students feel pressured to take algebra, often by the eighth grade, and are not surprised to find students commonly list *how to get into algebra* or *what I need for algebra* as what they want to learn about this year. Teachers are pleased when some of the students identify *word problems* or *working with my group* as their strength. Teachers also recognize that their students' responses suggest feelings that could potentially affect learning, both positively and negatively.

Some teachers ask their students to write their mathematical autobiographies, perhaps coordinating the assignment with an English teacher's lesson on personal narratives. A seventh-grade teacher, for example, offers a variety of questions in her assignment to help students brainstorm ideas and make connections, but she does not require them to respond to each question, as she thinks it might feel oppressive or repetitive to them. (See Figure 3–9; see also Reproducibles.)

**Mathematics Autobiography**

Name: _____          Date: _____

Directions: Write an autobiography that focuses on your experiences with mathematics. Use the following questions to guide your thinking. Be sure to explain your answers. You don't need to answer every question, but comment on at least five of them.

1. How do you feel about yourself in math classes?

2. What is your first memory of using mathematics?

3. What do you remember about learning to count or using numbers?

4. What kinds of things have your math teachers done to help you enjoy math?

5. What is your favorite topic in mathematics (geometry, computation, logic, algebra, problem solving . . . )?

6. What kind of math equipment, tools, or games do you like to use when learning mathematics and why?

7. What are two examples of when you have used math outside of school?

8. When solving problems, do you prefer working alone or in a group? Why?

9. What math topic is a strength for you?

10. What math topic do you find most challenging?

Figure 3–9   *Mathematics Autobiography.*

Lizzie responds briefly to each question. She discloses, *some of the time the material is tough for me.* (See Figure 3–10.) She also expresses appreciation for a teacher who involved students in math games and provided her with help so that she could understand.

Greg also notes his difficulties, explaining, *I find myself constantly struggling to grasp a question even though I made it into pre-algebra class.*

Some students are creative in their approaches to this assignment. Kaitlyn begins, *In a land far, far away there was a beautiful princess who lived among four brothers who taught her math when she was very young.*

Marco begins, *My first memory of using this unique art was when I was but a wee child.*

> 1) In math class I feel a little unsure of what is going on and at times may need more help. I sometimes understand but some of time the material is tough for me,
>
> 3) My memory of learning to count is probabley in 2nd grade, because I remember having to do flash cards every night and being quizzed on them
>
> 4) my math teacher that have helped me enjoy math class was ms. Glinka because we played math games and she gave extra help so I understood.
>
> 5) my favorite area in math is when we learn how to figure out problems that look like this (5+2)×6÷9=? I think those are fun
>
> 6) Math equitment that I have used are basicly just calculators
>
> 7) I have used math by going shopping or going on the computer
>
> 8) When working on problems I like being with partners (you get more done)
>
> 10) I find fractions and decimals most diffucult.

Figure 3–10 *Lizzie responded briefly to each question on the Mathematics Autobiography, Reproducible 3F.*

Many students present positive attitudes and experiences. Sherry begins, *I have almost always enjoyed math and feel pretty confident about my abilities.*

Denise expresses appreciation for her teacher who *gave [her] lots of ah-ha moments and gave [her] real-life problems to solve instead of made-up stories with no meaning.*

Desmond also begins with a positive tone when he states, *In math, I usually feel like things just come to me.* (See Figure 3–11.) He also says that he likes problem solving and finding other ways to solve problems.

Getting to know our students does not happen overnight, nor is it accomplished in the first few weeks of school. Most important, this information is not static; attitudes, interests, and readiness change throughout the year. Thus it is daily investigations and

## Arithmatic Life

In math, I usually feel like things just come to me. If a teacher tells us one way to do something, I like to find another way, or a patturn that will help me. I've been doing math since I was about 4 years oud. I used to count my toes to see how old I was! I remember learning to count in Kindergarden. I learned to count when my teacher told us to count the number of letters in our names. She showed us how to count to 100. It's pretty self explanitory after that. I liked to learn math because we always learned rymes or jokes, like 8 times 8 went to the store, to buy Nintendo 64. I like problem solving, because you have to find the equation. (x, ÷, -, +) I like flash cards because I like around the world. I had #5 and 3 items, and I had to find the sum to see if I could afford it. Another thing I tried was the penny doubling thing. (eventually you get like #1000) I like to work alone, because when I'm in a group, It gets too loud to think. My teachers really pushed my multiplication facts, so I really know those. I can't learn my division tables very well.

Figure 3–11 *Desmond presented a positive attitude on the Mathematics Autobiography, Reproducible 3F.*

interactions that provide teachers with the greatest source for assessment data for the greatest number of students. Teachers are always gathering data within their normal classroom activities and adjusting lessons accordingly. Probing questions ("How do you know?" "Can you tell me more?" "Can you restate what she just said?") allow teachers to gain a better understanding of what their students know and how they think about mathematical ideas. Asking students to record their thinking with words, numbers, and representations also provides mathematical artifacts that teachers can compare over time. Conversations we overhear as students enter or exit the classroom can update us on our students' current interests or concerns.

**Strand:** Geometry

**Focus:** Similar triangles

**Context:** Open-ended question

# Post-Assessment

You can also give open-ended problems or tasks as post-assessment tasks. At the conclusion of a geometry unit, one seventh-grade teacher poses this question: *What do you know about similar triangles? Write and draw to communicate your ideas.* Because of the open-ended nature of the task, students can control some of the difficulty level themselves, for example, by limiting their consideration to only a few concepts or by focusing exclusively on two right triangles. Also, students may choose to use drawings, charts, or diagrams to communicate their ideas or they may rely more on prose. This task gives the teacher an opportunity to discover what students choose to include, perhaps because it is what they know best, or what they believe is most important, or what they find most interesting. The teacher also can note what concepts students do not provide evidence for, or for which the evidence is incomplete or inaccurate.

Before setting the students off to work, the teacher talks with them about task expectations. Together with their teacher, the students create the following list to guide their work:

- Focus on similar triangles.
- Use words and drawings to explain what you know.
- Use correct vocabulary.
- Organize your ideas.
- Give several examples.
- Think about real-world connections.

Some of the students think for a minute or so before beginning to record their ideas, but most begin to write immediately. They submit a variety of responses to this post-assessment task. Janelle provides relatively minimal evidence of learning, for example. (See Figure 3–12.) She does recognize that side lengths and angle measures are relevant to the topic but doesn't demonstrate an explicit understanding of these ideas. In her opening statement she notes that similar triangles have similar side lengths, without describing what this means. She does draw an example of two triangles and identifies lengths that are proportional. She also states that the angles of these figures are *similar.* Her illustration indicates angle measures that are the same but that have been rotated in the second figure. This could indicate an understanding that similar triangles can be in different orientations from one another. The teacher notes that the angle measures Janelle has chosen suggest a misconception or lack of knowledge, as the sum of their degrees is 210.

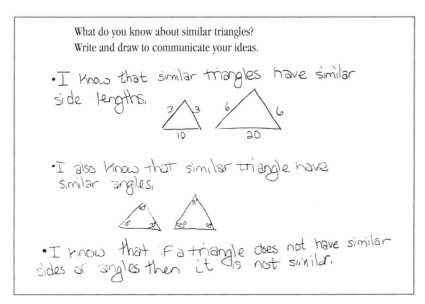

Within the figure box:

What do you know about similar triangles?
Write and draw to communicate your ideas.

- I know that similar triangles have similar side lengths.

- I also know that similar triangle have similar angles.

- I know that if a triangle does not have similar sides or angles then it is not similar.

Figure 3–12 *Janelle presented minimal evidence.*

Brian begins by stating that similar triangles have the same angles and that their measures sum to 180 degrees. (See Figure 3–13.) The representation that accompanies this statement relates to this

Figure 3–13 *Brian focused on triangles in general as well as similar triangles.*

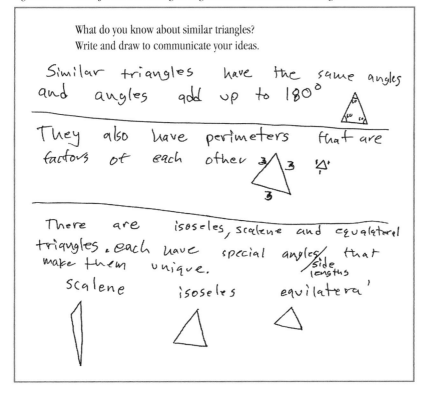

Within the figure box:

What do you know about similar triangles?
Write and draw to communicate your ideas.

Similar triangles have the same angles and angles add up to 180°

They also have perimeters that are factors of each other

There are isoseles, scalene and equalateral triangles. each have special angles / side lengths that make them unique.

scalene          isoseles          equilatera'

sum, as Brian shows one equilateral triangle with each 60-degree angle marked. He also notes a relationship between the perimeters of similar triangles, stating that they are factors of each other. He then shows two triangles, one with each side having a length of 1, and the other with lengths of 3. The teacher wishes Brian had actually found the perimeters of these triangles, because then he might have noticed that the number of units in one perimeter is a factor of the other, while in reverse, it is a multiple. Brian also focuses on triangles in general, identifying that there are isosceles, scalene, and equilateral triangles, and suggests that these categories are related to the triangles' lengths and angles. He provides a correct representation of each type of triangle though this information is not directly related to similarity.

Nicole organizes her response around ways similar triangles are the same and different. (See Figure 3–14.) She points out that similar triangles have the same angles, ratios, and shapes. She then

Figure 3–14 *Nicole focused on similarities and differences between similar triangles.*

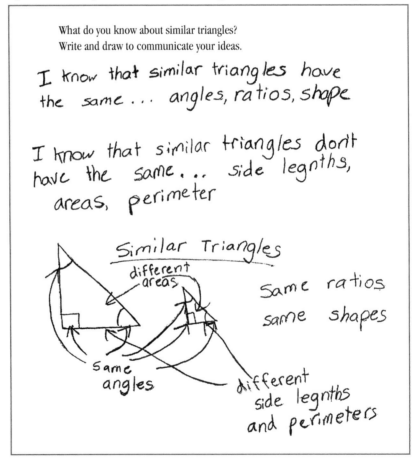

*Math for All: Differentiating Instruction, Grades 6-8*

notes that they don't have the same side lengths, areas, and perimeters. She summarizes these ideas in a drawing of two right isosceles triangles. Her teacher notices that Nicole has not attached any numbers to these diagrams, so he can't be certain what she means by *ratios*.

Lisa lists four ideas in her response. (See Figure 3–15.) She begins with the notion that similar triangles go by a rule. She then writes *2x*, *2y* and draws two similar triangles without any labels. The teacher believes that Lisa is referring to work in the unit that involved similar figures on a coordinate graph. Within that topic any coordinate point in one figure was identified as (*x, y*), and as the figures were related by a scale factor of two, the associated coordinate points in the other figure were identified as (*2x, 2y*). A few other students identified this "rule" as well.

The next point Lisa makes is that similar triangles can be found by a scale factor, but she provides no representation to further elaborate on this idea. Lisa also notes a relationship between the perimeters of similar triangles. She posits that this relationship is cubic, suggesting that if the perimeter of the first figure were 3 units

Figure 3–15  *Lisa overgeneralized an example of similar triangles.*

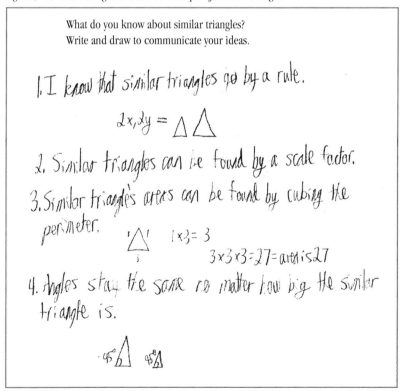

and the scale factor were three, then the perimeter of the other triangle would be 3 × 3 × 3, or 27 units. While inaccurate, Lisa is thinking about relationships among the areas and perimeters of similar triangles. Several emerging ideas and misconceptions may be involved in this statement and the teacher makes a note to follow up with Lisa.

Lisa's final claim is that angles in similar triangles stay the same, regardless of the sizes of the triangles. She illustrates this idea with two triangles, one large and one small, that both have an angle of 45 degrees.

Jay's first statement focuses on the importance of a scale factor. (See Figure 3–16.) The teacher notices that Jay is one of the few students who has included lengths that involve decimals. He also identifies the scale factor in both directions, 2 for scaling up, and 0.5 when scaling down. The unit gave attention to the fact that the scale factor is found by multiplying each side by the same number. This became quite complicated for some students, who

Figure 3–16 *Jay focused on the scale factor.*

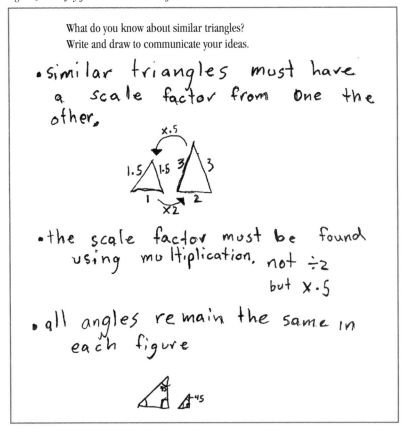

struggled to understand that dividing by two is the same as multiplying by one-half. Jay's next comment solidifies the importance of multiplication, stating that the scale factor must be found by multiplication. Just as Lisa did, Jay concludes by stating that angles in similar figures are the same.

Max's work is noteworthy because he is the only student who includes a real-life application, even though this was a goal identified before the task began. (See Figure 3–17.) His example of finding the height of the flagpole was considered at the end of the unit. The teacher is interested to see that Max has set up the proportional relationship correctly and found the correct missing number.

The teacher was generally pleased with the responses to this task. Many different ideas and skills had surfaced. The teacher also noted two concerns that he believed reflected on his teaching. Too many students suggested a misconception about a rule of $(2x, 2y)$ having importance. He wondered if he had overemphasized that example. He knew students can sometimes grab onto a simple rule

Figure 3–17   *Max provided a real-world application.*

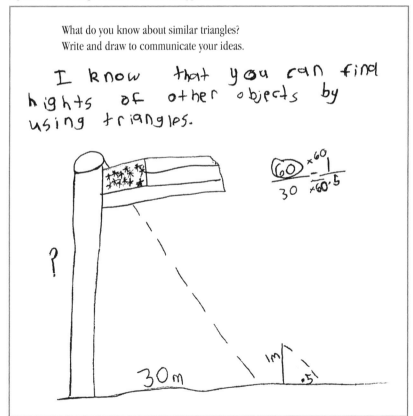

and he wanted to avoid this in the future. He also noticed that none of the students indicated a unit of measure when they referred to lengths, perimeters, or areas. He knew that when he showed multiple examples on the board he did not always include a unit and decided to attend more closely to this.

## A Note About What to Do with All the Data

Pre-assessments, post-assessments, interviews, questionnaires, and observations—what do we do with all these data? Many teachers comment that they can feel inundated with all of the information they collect. In a professional development course, one teacher bemoaned, "Sometimes I feel like I am drowning in paperwork. Every piece is important; I don't want to give it back to the student in case I need to refer to it in some way. It's all so interesting, but I'm beginning to want to find a way to figure out what I need to know versus just what is nice to know."

One recommended practice is to take a few minutes a day to write one or two items about what you know about five students in each class. The idea is to have focused on each student by the end of the week. Over time, teachers begin to see patterns among their students that can be useful to understanding developmental sequences. Furthermore, these notes can serve as summative statements of what teachers feel confident that their students understand. Or, the notes can provoke the next questions to guide instruction, such as "What do you mean by scale factor?" "When do we care about rates of change?" or "How could you test this conjecture?" Throughout this process, teachers are frequently asking themselves: What more do I need to know about my students to offer them an effective and engaging math program? Creating thoughtful rubrics and checklists can also help teachers assess student work in a more expedient manner. These tools can also, of course, provide helpful data for meetings with parents or for child study team and Individualized Education Program meetings.

## Teacher Collaborations

Sometimes teachers experience uncertainty or confusion with regard to particular students. No matter how much data they collect, they feel that they still have not gathered information that allows them to figure out how to best reach these students. Some teachers who face this situation have learned the benefit of turning to each other for assistance. Margaret, an experienced teacher, and Tom, a second-year teacher, both teach eighth grade and have begun to work together this year. Their school has recently established common planning time for teachers at the same grade level and these two teachers work closely during this time. Margaret appreciates Tom's fresh perspectives and his excitement about teaching. Tom is thankful for Margaret's experience and has nicknamed her Boss.

Together they meet weekly with their school's math coach to talk about the content and pacing of the unit, their homework assignments, what they think is important to test students on, and how their plans address their state's standards. The two teachers work together during their other planning periods as well and have found that they truly enjoy collaborating on their creation of lesson plans, quizzes, and tests and value time to talk about how to assist particular students in their individual classrooms.

Tom explained, "I was concerned when we first moved to common planning time. We were being asked to show how we used the time and the math coach wanted to meet with us, too. I felt I was losing control of my free time, of which there was very little! Now I realize how much I gain from our meetings and actually feel energized from them. I truly enjoy our conversations about how to assist students who are struggling with a particular concept. The ability to work together to formulate lessons and to discuss pitfalls is extremely helpful. In the long run, I think I get more free time at home because of how much I get done at school. As a new teacher, this saves my life."

Today Tom and Margaret are discussing a new unit they are about to begin that includes finding the area of a figure, square numbers, square roots, and investigating the Pythagorean theorem. They begin their conversation with recollections of strengths, challenges, and pitfalls from last year. They review notes they have written in their textbooks and talk about where in the unit they thought that the students would need extra practice, what was difficult for students, and how they might approach the material differently this year. Both find this discussion helps them feel more prepared for the new unit.

About a week into the unit, Tom expresses concern about a student who seems to sometimes just guess the areas of figures shown on dot paper. Tom is surprised because Luke is a bright student who generally performs well.

"I just can't figure out what he is thinking," Tom laments. He continues, "When I work with him he understands how to find the area of these less common shapes, but when I'm not right there, he seems to go back to guessing." Tom then shows Margaret an example of what he means. "We have been working with the figures composed of right triangles and squares and have just begun to include portions without right angles. The students worked in groups and discovered that they could use the outside space to help them, just liked we talked about. Luke was fine then; what happened?"

Though Margaret is obviously familiar with the unit, she knows it will help Tom to talk about it more, so she asks for an example. Tom pulls out a piece of dot paper and draws the triangle that follows. He shows her how Luke had been able to enclose the figure in an area of 12 square units, find the area of the two external right triangles and then subtract to find the remaining area of 3 square units.

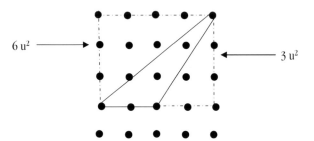

Tom continues, "Later in class, though, he was working on a more complex figure and just wrote the area in for the part that was somewhat like this one. When I asked him why he didn't use the same technique, he said he didn't need to—he could just see it. It's hard to have students like Luke making visual guesses rather then using mathematical reasoning."

Margaret and Tom have discussed that students often say things such as "Well, I just put this piece into this one with my eyes because it looks like they would go together and make a whole." Margaret has helped Tom see that the students are often correct but can't provide a geometric justification for their thinking. She has encouraged Tom to demand mathematical reasoning from his students and his teaching style has really changed. Margaret can see that Tom is frustrated and she wants to support him. She knows how easy it can sometimes be to just accept correct answers. She suggests that they ask the math coach to cover her class so that she can be in Tom's room and observe Luke. The coach agrees and the next day Margaret is in Tom's room.

The students know her and are used to others being in the room, so her presence doesn't disrupt them. She walks around the room, but makes sure to keep her eye on Luke. She quickly sees what Tom means. Luke writes the areas of portions of the figure quickly whether they are squares, right triangles, or other types of triangles. Margaret watches as he quickly divides a figure into two parts and labels the area of each correctly, as shown.

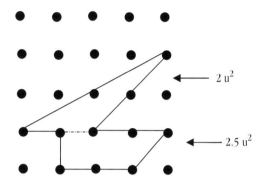

Margaret sits down to talk with Luke. She tells him that, as an eighth-grade teacher, she is really interested in all the ways students think about area and wonders if Luke can explain his thinking. Luke sighs but agrees to do so. He quickly identifies the area of 2.5 square units as the combination of two whole square units and one half square unit. Margaret nods to encourage him to continue.

Luke then says, "This one has to be two because it is just like the other one; I can just see it."

Margaret recognizes the familiar phrase "I can just see it" but wonders what Luke means by it being just like the other one and asks for further clarification. To Margaret's surprise, Luke's eyes light up and he appears excited.

Luke explains that yesterday they had investigated two figures, one after the other, that turned out to have the same exact areas. He draws the figures on dot paper for Margaret to see and shows that he can justify that the area of each figure is 1 square unit.

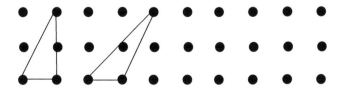

"That got me to wondering," explains Luke, "if that would always be true. So I tried some other figures to see if they would work, too. Look, I'll show you."

Margaret gets Tom's attention so that he is also there to observe Luke illustrate this idea with additional examples.

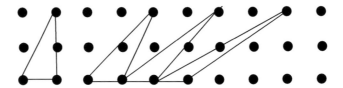

Luke finishes his explanation by saying, "As long as I don't change anything else, I can put this top vertex all the way down to the gym and as long as it's still one wide and two high, the area will be the same! So then I tried this with another group and it worked, too." Luke then draws another set of triangles that he found to all have an area of $1\frac{1}{2}$ square units. "So," he concludes, "if I just think about what the first one looks like, I can get them all."

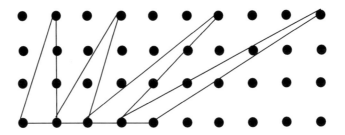

Margaret and Tom thank Luke for explaining his thinking and move on to work with other students. They don't want him to feel self-conscious about his thinking or other students to feel that their thinking isn't also interesting. During their next common planning period, the two teachers talk about Luke's work.

Tom admits he has never thought about the area of a triangle in this manner. They review it together and apply it to a few examples. They agree that Luke is developing a strong conceptual framework for the formula of the area of a triangle. So many students have trouble seeing the height of a triangle when the perpendicular line to the base is not one of the triangle's sides. The teachers are also impressed with Luke's creation of a conjecture and willingness to test it. Tom decides that some of the other students in the class are ready for this type of thinking and that he will have them work with Luke tomorrow.

Interesting, just when I thought I understood how to help students develop their own thinking, my students challenge me. At first, I didn't think Luke understood what he was doing; I thought he was just guessing. I was very close to insisting that he show more markings on his paper to indicate how he subtracted the outside area to find the area that remained. Only later did I realize that I was forcing my approach on his thinking.

> *Only later did I realize that I was forcing my approach on his thinking.*

I am so glad that Margaret was in the room. I don't know that I could have re-created his work to explain it to her. At first I was worried about whether this approach would always work. Trying it with some other sets of figures and having Margaret connect it to the formula helped me feel better about that. When I first taught this unit last year, I had seen $\frac{1}{2}bh$ in the right triangles immediately and was really excited that my students would be able to make this connection, too. I just never went beyond right triangles being half of related rectangles. Working with Margaret has gotten me so interested in how my students think.

This example reminds us to take the time to understand our students' thinking and not to assume that different is incorrect. It speaks to the importance of differentiating mathematical models within assessment tasks and instruction and to recognize that students can discover abstract ideas through concrete models and representations. It also reminds us to constantly adjust our lenses as we look for evidence of student understanding.

We believe that getting to know each student is at the heart of differentiation. By using a wider variety of assessment practices and specially designed data-gathering techniques, teachers can have a greater understanding of each student as a unique learner and, as a result, have a deeper and broader view of the learning trajectory for each student. Making decisions about for whom, why, and when to differentiate becomes clearer when it is based on what we know about our students and our curriculum. Information about students' readiness, learning preferences, and interests enables teachers to offer different ways for students to develop and to demonstrate their mathematical knowledge.

## Connecting the Chapter to Your Practice

1. How have you communicated with your students' parents to learn more about their children's learning preferences?

2. Sometimes students' self-assessments do not match what teachers have observed in the classroom. In general what do you think teachers should do when this happens?

3. Who are the colleagues who help you the most? What is it that they do that you find most helpful?

# Chapter 4

## Casting a Wider Net for Readiness

*T*hrough assessment we uncover many of the similarities and differences among our students' thinking. It offers us an opportunity to look for patterns in our students' learning, both as individuals and as a group. Inevitably, assessment data for any classroom reveal a range in students' experiences, interests, and readiness. In response to these differences, teachers work diligently to delineate standards for all learners, to build inclusive classroom environments, and to vary their teaching styles in order to address these differences. Yet, no matter how carefully they identify learning outcomes, develop habits to encourage community, or employ diverse instructional strategies, teachers remain most concerned about the range, great or narrow, of student readiness.

Consider the following words of this sixth-grade teacher.

**Problem Idea!**

**Strand:** Data and Algebra

**Focus:** Organize data and look for patterns.

**Context:** Barrel of monkeys

## Teacher Reflection

During the first week of school I focus on problem solving. Through problem investigations students learn how to work together and how my classroom works. I find that these activities help me learn a lot about my students quickly and help build the class's sense of community. Yesterday we worked with the game Barrel of Monkeys (a classic game with plastic monkeys in a container shaped like a barrel).

I had organized the monkeys so that in each container there was exactly one monkey of each color: blue, green, red, and yellow.

*(Continued)*

The question I posed was "If you made a chain using all of the monkeys in your barrel, how many different chains could you make?" Though it is likely that students in previous grade levels have explored simple permutations, they don't seem to connect that work to this problem. It's only when they see the patterns in their lists that they seem ready to make a generalization. Yet, though students at this age find this problem challenging, the monkeys provide a concrete model and students can each find a way to contribute to the solution.

There were six groups with three to four students. I told the students that I expected them to work together to find all the ways to arrange the monkeys. Patti didn't interact with her group. She seemed to think for about five seconds and then recorded something quickly. She turned her paper over, reached into her backpack, pulled out a novel, and started to read. I have to admit I was really surprised by her behavior. I'd never had a sixth-grade student do that before, and at first, I was unsure how to react. Did she understand the question? Why did she think she had the right to read a book during math class?

I asked to see her paper and saw that she had written the correct answer, twenty-four. When asked to explain her work, she merely responded, "I just know." I thought perhaps she had solved a problem similar to this one before, but she told me she had not, that she just figured it out by thinking about it. When I encouraged her to work with the group, she said, "I know my answer is right, I don't need help from anyone else, and I don't want to bother explaining my thinking."

> *When I encouraged her to work with the group, she said, "I know my answer is right, I don't need help from anyone else, and I don't want to bother explaining my thinking."*

I have to admit that I sometimes find it difficult to work with students who seem to walk in the door already knowing everything we're supposed to study this year, but Patti really concerned me. She didn't seem to have any interest in being a member of the class or have any sense that she could learn from interacting with her peers. How am I going to engage Patti in our work or entice her to want to work with others so that she will be better able to explain her thinking when the work becomes more challenging for her?

Not all students who seem to be ready for more challenging mathematics activities are disdainful of working with others. Consider Danielle, a sixth-grade student. This year her math class has allowed her to be more challenged and to work at her own level. Her comments indicate how much her classmates mean to her,

Before I was in my 6th grade math class, my previous math teachers would stand in front of the students and teach everybody the same thing. The problem with that approach, I realized this year, was that most of the time I had already learned the topics the teacher was teaching, and I was kept back from learning new things and demanding more from myself. When I was in those classes, I wasn't unhappy because I didn't know at the time that they could be different. But in my 6th grade math class, everyone is challenged, and at their own level.

Our math teacher gets this done during each class period by putting packets on a table of different math topics (algebra, SATs, fractions, logarithms, etc.) which he has created, and each of us chooses individually which packet we would like to work on that day. If any of us finds that the packet we have chosen is not interesting to us, we can pick another packet (knowing that the teacher will question us if we change packets more than one time in a class period). Each day, our teacher casually walks around the class and checks what each person is working on. The only time he will ask a student to change packets is if he knows that it is too easy for that person. Otherwise, he will let students decide what they want to learn. We work on problems in the packets by ourselves, and if we get stuck, we go up to our teacher who will give us just enough help to have us continue to learn by ourselves. Other times, he will ask another student who has already worked on that particular packet to teach the person just starting it (for about ten minutes). We are also allowed to go right to another student for help. Because of this system, we are all both students and teachers. (Our class has also taught math to second and third graders each week for half the year, during lunch or a free slot.)

I feel proud of myself and my classmates for being able to teach each other, and for the level of math that we have been able to reach. Because I know that having this special teacher is a privilege (because no other teacher helps us learn such complicated material in such a good way), I and most of my classmates work hard in class (and on homework).

I like this class because it is challenging and also because it is a comfortable place where you feel that you trust your classmates. This is probably because we have math each day and because we have learned to work well with each other as a group. It is a comfortable environment also because our teacher respects us all: there are no favorites in the class. I like my teacher a lot because he has set up this unique system and makes us better people by helping us to realize our own and each others' capabilities. He also makes us keep reaching for the time when we will be able to solve math problems by ourselves.

I go to math class almost every day with a sense of excitement, wondering which new packets will be on the table, and which math "mystery" I will need to solve.

Figure 4–1  *Danielle's reflection on her sixth-grade math class.*

even though they are most likely working on different tasks. (See Figure 4–1.)

On the other end of the spectrum, some of the students in our classes seem to be far less prepared for the curriculum. Consider the following reflection from an eighth-grade teacher.

# Teacher Reflection

One of my students, Joey, really concerns me. I still remember the second day of school when he looked like he was working quite hard. As I walked by casually I noted that though he didn't show work, he did seem to be recording an answer for each question. Before long he announced, "I'm done," and as all of the other students remained on task, I went over to look more closely at his answers to the five problems.

Every answer was wrong and in some cases, even the labels were incorrect. As I wondered whether he was making up the answers or whether he thought they were correct, I asked him to explain his thinking about the first problem. He looked embarrassed and muttered, "I just know it. That's the right answer," and when challenged that the answer is not correct, he often says, "This is stupid. I don't need to know this." Since then, I've tried to work with Joey alone a couple of times each week, but it seems as if we continually discover what I consider holes in his skills.

*What bothers me the most is that Joey used to be able to do this simple task. I review with him fairly often, but it never seems to be enough. I wish I knew how to help him hold onto his ideas.*

Yesterday was the end of our data analysis unit and we culminated with a Silly Olympics Day. There were a variety of workstations around the room at which students competed in such events as the cotton ball–throwing event and the pea-shooting contest. After its turn at a particular station, each group added its data to the class record sheet. After all of the stations were completed, each group was then given the data sheet from one of them and asked to represent the data in a graph and to determine the three measures of central tendency.

Joey and his partner, Pete, were trying to determine the mean distance for the cotton ball event. The event involved sitting at a table and, with one breath, blowing the cotton ball as far as possible. The distance was then measured in centimeters. Pete was reading the number of centimeters in each measure and Joey was entering those numbers into the calculator to find their sum. When Pete read the number 107, he noticed that Joey entered the number 17. Joey seemed comfortable with Pete correcting him, but shortly thereafter another error was made. Pete is very supportive of Joey and the boys play on a basketball team together. He suggested that they put the list on the table so that Joey could see the numbers and that they could both check them as they were entered into the calculator. Even though Joey could see the written numbers, Pete still detected an occasional error.

Though Pete had found a way to keep Joey involved, I was distressed to learn of his inability to read and enter three-digit numbers. Given his lack of computation skills, Joey often relies on the calculator. That won't help him much, though, if he can't enter the numbers correctly.

What bothers me the most is that Joey used to be able to do this simple task. I review with him fairly often, but it never seems to be enough. I wish I knew how to help him hold onto his ideas.

If I had an assistant in the classroom during math time, I could work with Joey more often. My friend who teaches English has a literary specialist in her room three times a week who works with the students who struggle the most. He tells me that this special time for them really makes a difference. I also need a wider range of materials in my classroom. It's not fair to make Joey use the same materials as everyone else. I'd like to have more materials available for him that allow him to work on similar tasks as his classmates but make the math more accessible to him.

Considering ways to manage and meet the range of readiness in our mathematics classes is no easy task. Most middle school teachers feel much as these teachers do. We can try to accommodate learners, that is, provide learning materials and assessment strategies matched to individual learner strengths, while keeping the content goals the same, but sometimes we need to modify the curriculum. We're often not sure how to challenge those students who are beyond grade level, and sometimes it feels as if the students who are less ready can slip easily through our grasps. At times, nothing feels just right or appropriate.

But how do we define *appropriate*? It is a word used frequently in the educational arena. Too often, we aim for the middle or average group and just hope the others will manage. Referring to Vygotsky's zone of proximal development helps us think more clearly about what is appropriate for each student. It is that area that provides challenge without going beyond the student's comfort zone or edges, that is, without being too easy or too hard. We can't possibly provide a separate curriculum for each of our students, nor would that be advisable. The social interaction and exchange of ideas among students is too important a component of learning. So how do we expand our curriculum so that it is appropriate for students whose grasp of mathematics differs greatly from that of the majority of students?

## Transforming Tasks

Choosing mathematical tasks is one of the most important decisions that we make as teachers. While it is difficult to find or create one task that is appropriate for all learners, we can transform most tasks to be more inclusive, to allow a greater number of students access, and to provide additional students with possibilities for more expansive thinking. When we do this, we are casting a wider net that can

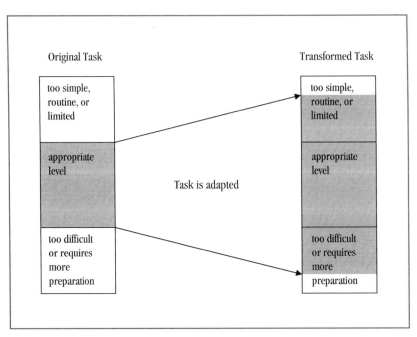

Figure 4–2 *Transforming tasks to meet a wider range of readiness.*

catch a broader range of students. Our goal then is to transform or modify tasks to meet a wider range of readiness. (See Figure 4–2.) Note that the range of learners does not change nor the field that is deemed *appropriate*; rather, the tasks themselves are stretched to be better aligned with our students' needs. To do this, we begin with the tasks in our curriculum and consider how we can modify them.

Teachers have discovered a variety of ways in which to modify tasks to accommodate different levels of readiness. One adaptation a teacher can make is to allow students to have some control over the difficulty level. You can do this, for example, with word problems. Instead of the standard format where all the numbers are provided, write a word problem without numbers and ask the students to provide them. For example, you could ask students to insert numbers in the following word problem so that it makes sense:

> *Ms. Marston took out a one-year loan for $_____.*
> *The interest rate on the loan is _____%, which is equal to $_____ in interest for one year. She will make twelve payments to the nearest penny, with the last payment adjusted as necessary. So she will make eleven payments of $_____ and one payment of $_____, for a total of $_____.*

Students can choose numbers according to their comfort levels; one student might choose an interest rate of 1 percent, while another

Take Action!

Provide choice.

might choose a rate of 3.25 percent. Still, both students *must* recognize the mathematical relationships among other numbers in the problem and their chosen rates. This is an important point. Whenever we expand tasks in order to allow more access, we never want to do so in ways that undermine the integrity of the mathematical challenge. All students must have access to tasks that require mathematical thinking, not just rote learning or less complicated thinking.

Students can also make choices within simple practice assignments. Imagine a standard list of ten fraction division examples. By changing the original directions, *Complete exercises 1–10*, we can encourage students to make choices according to their readiness. Consider the following alternatives:

> *Pick five of these examples that have a quotient that is less than ten and tell how you know that will be so.*

> *Pick one example and write four different fraction division expressions that will have the same quotient.*

> *Pick one example and find the quotient. Then write a word problem that could be solved with this computation.*

Another approach is to open up a problem so that there is more than one answer. Problems with more than one answer allow room for expansion of ideas. Some students will be quite satisfied with finding one answer and it may take them some time to do so. Other students may find one solution quickly but be able and interested to find more possibilities. By removing information or by creating a greater number of choices, we can adapt many problems to allow for multiple answers. Examples of such problems include the following:

*How might you shade 37.5% of this figure?*

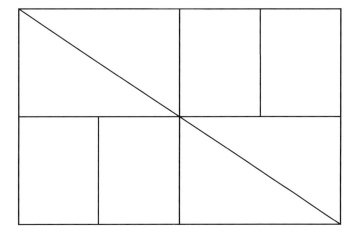

*Jacob has some thank-you notes to write. He wants to write the same number of notes each day. If he writes two, three, or four notes each day, there will be one note left to write. He has more than 14 and fewer than 54 notes to write. How many notes do you think Jacob has to write?*

*Use graph paper. Draw six different triangles with an area of 4 square units.*

We can also transform standard tasks by providing students with a number story and with answers, then asking them to create questions within the given context that will yield the answers provided. Students can make choices about which questions they provide; they may also identify more than one question for some of the answers. (See Figure 4–3 for an example of such a problem, along with possible questions.)

Some tasks have multiple solutions in that there are a variety of ways to respond to them. The problem in Chapter 3 that required students to describe what they knew about 35 percent is an example of such a task. Teachers usually create these tasks by thinking about the topic and identifying a broad question that taps

Figure 4–3 *Example of* What's the Question? *task.*

Here are the answers: 35, 2.5, 245, 7.35[*]
What could be the questions?

**Number Story:**
Sabina and Mike ran each day this week. Each day Sabina ran 3.5 miles in 28 minutes. Mike ran 6 miles in 63 minutes every day.

**Possible responses:** (Students may provide one or more questions for one or more answers.)

35: At this rate, how many miles would Sabina run in ten weeks?
How many more minutes did Mike run than Sabina each day?
How many fewer minutes did Sabina run than Mike each day?

2.5: On average, how many more minutes does it take Mike to run a mile than Sabina?
On average, how many fewer minutes does it take Sabina to run a mile than Mike?

245: How many more minutes did Mike run than Sabina this week?
How many fewer minutes did Sabina run than Mike this week?

7.35: How many hours did Mike run this week?

*[*]Other choices for answers are possible, but it is usually best to limit the list to four or five possibilities.*

into what students know, see, or recognize. Following are some examples of open-ended probes:

*Write and draw to tell about percents.*

*Your friend divided $8\frac{1}{3}$ by $\frac{1}{2}$ and got the answer $4\frac{1}{6}$. What would you write and draw to show your friend what is wrong with this answer?*

*How would you describe a tetrahedron to someone who has never seen one?*

*What are some linear situations that you can describe in relation to the world of sports or games?*

*How might we write numbers if we didn't have zeros?*

*How is measurement used in your home?*

## Using Mathematical Models

Teachers have long recognized that students operate on a variety of levels in terms of their need for concrete models. Therefore, the types of materials available may make the difference as to whether a problem is accessible. Consider the problem that follows:

*You cooked some popcorn and ate half of it, saving the rest for your friend. Your friend was late and by the time she arrived you had eaten $\frac{1}{3}$ of what you had saved for her. Your friend said she was not too hungry and evenly split the rest of the popcorn with you. What fraction of the popcorn did you eat?*

Teachers can make a variety of materials available to students when solving this problem, including drawing materials, Cuisenaire rods, fraction strips, pattern blocks, and a laminated picture of a bowl cut into sixths. This is not to say that all students would choose to use these materials; many students might prefer abstract thinking.

As teachers, we need to think carefully about the manipulatives in our classrooms. We must make sure that the materials we use embody important mathematical relationships or ideas. Roberts (2007) also reminds us to be sure that materials minimize the potential for inaccurate ideas to develop. We believe that misconceptions form when students work with models that are too limited, that is, do not vary enough to represent all of the mathematical possibilities. This notion of the importance of mathematical variability was suggested by Zoltan Dienes in his seminal work, *Building Up Mathematics* (1960). For example, most students and adults are surprised to find that a cylinder does not have to have faces that are circles and that it can be tilted. We would be less likely to eliminate these possibilities for cylinders if our models did not always portray the same shapes. So though use of manipulatives does not guarantee successful learning, as we learn from the following teacher's reflection, having a range of materials available can provide more students with access to more sophisticated mathematical thinking.

## Teacher Reflection

When I first began teaching at this level three years ago I thought my students would no longer need to use manipulative materials. I started my teaching career at grade 1 and so, of course, I expected my students to use concrete materials at that level. Over the years I've come to recognize that mathematical models are important at any age. This really hit home when I was taking a professional development course. We were solving a problem about twenty-seven small cubes arranged in one larger 3-by-3-by-3 cube. The question was about how many of the small cubes had one, two, or three faces showing. I saw some people making drawings and some others apparently able to figure this out in their heads. There was no way I would be able to do that! I was so grateful for the small cubes that the professor had made available. At first I was embarrassed to need them, but then I saw other teachers starting to build with them, too. From that moment on I vowed that I would always have different kinds of materials available for student use.

During the past year I've tried to pay closer attention to which kinds of materials my students prefer. I noticed that some of them use the red and black chips when we are working with integers, while some find the number line model easier to use, and others prefer to draw their own pictures that often resemble thermometers. In the fall some of my students were reluctant to use materials of any kind. It seemed to me that my students thought that if I saw them using manipulatives I would think that they weren't smart.

> It seemed to me that my students thought that if I saw them using manipulatives I would think that they weren't smart.

I encouraged them to try using concrete models and kept a variety of manipulatives available. Last week one of my students was struggling with a decimal problem, but I knew he was a student who rarely sought out manipulatives. I just brought over a box of decimal squares and suggested we work together. He seemed pleased with his own success when he was able to solve the problem using the squares. Yesterday, he went and got them himself. I do try to only intervene when necessary. I want my students to realize that ultimately they are in charge of their own learning and responsible for making choices that help them succeed.

# Tiered Activities

Sometimes tasks need to be tiered in order to be successful with a wide range of student readiness. Such activities allow students to focus on the same general concept or skill, but to do so according to their levels of readiness. Consider the following example from a seventh-grade classroom.

The teacher begins the lesson by asking, "Do you like to solve mysteries?" With most of the students nodding "yes," she asks them what they need to solve a mystery and they respond with ideas about how investigators collect and study evidence and clues. She draws upon their responses to connect their conversation to the idea that they will be solving a mathematical mystery. Number puzzles that include clues to find a mystery number can be used to reinforce students' recognition of classes of numbers and familiarity with the associated mathematical terms. They also provide opportunities for students to strengthen their problem-solving abilities to reason deductively, make an organized list, eliminate possibilities, and make inferences.

The teacher shares one clue at a time with the students in order to capture their attention and better assess their thinking. Here's the entire number puzzle:

**Strand:** Number

**Focus:** Fractions, decimals, and percents

**Context:** Solving secret number puzzles

> *What Could Be My Secret Code?*
>
> *The number is between 400 and 410.*
> *The tenths digit is one-third the hundredths digit.*
> *All of the digits are different.*
> *The tenths digit is one-half the ones digit.*
> *There are five places in the number.*

The teacher asks students to think about what numbers are possible when she gives the first clue: *It is between 400 and 410.* Students are beginning to write lists of numbers when Trevor asks, "Should I include four hundred and four hundred ten in my list?"

The teacher responds by asking the students their definition of the word *between*.

Emily says, "It means that you don't include the numbers on either side."

Trevor says, "OK, so that means that I'm not going to put four hundred and four hundred ten in my list."

The teacher notes that all of the students are writing the numbers *401–409*, rather than simply generalizing that a 4 must be in the hundredths place and a 0 must be in the tens place. She knows that for many students, identifying all of the potential candidates makes the problem-solving process more concrete, but she thought a few students might be willing to simplify this recording process by just leaving the ones place empty for now.

Ben remarks, "I think the list is not complete because you can also have decimal numbers that are between four hundred and four hundred ten."

The teacher is impressed with his comment because they have not talked about decimals for a while. However, she chooses not to respond, but rather to leave room for other students to react to Ben's idea. At first it appears as if no one heard Ben's conjecture.

Then Amy calls out, "Wait, Ben's right. I mean, there are a whole lot of decimal numbers between four hundred and four hundred ten."

The teacher is struck by Amy's reference to *a whole lot* of numbers and decides to ask, "Do we know how many?"

Tammy remarks, "Those numbers go on forever because I can have lots of places after the decimal point."

Oliver says, "Oh, yeah, I can have four hundred and three-millionths, right?"

Some students are beginning to feel that the task is enormous. Vanna groans, "This will take forever."

Greg, often interested in negotiation, asks, "Can you tell us if there are any places after the decimal point?"

In response, the teacher unveils the second clue, which states, "The tenths digit is one-third the hundredths digit."

Patia asks, "So, does this mean that I have to put all of the numbers in between four hundred and four hundred ten with the tenths and hundredths numbers?"

Ben suggests that that this would still mean a lot of numbers. He asks, "Would it be OK if I just put lines to show the places where the numbers for tenths and hundredths will go and then add ideas as we figure it out?"

Reggie says that he thinks that's a good idea because then he knows that he won't need to go past the hundredths place. Students readily agree to this plan and begin to draw places for the digits in the code number. Most students record:

———— ———— ———— · ———— ————

The teacher notices that Miranda is not writing anything on her paper and is looking like she might want to ask a question. The teacher decides to probe by asking, "Do you have something to say, Miranda?"

Miranda appears hesitant at first, but the teacher and the students give her some time to clarify her thoughts. Timidly she asks, "How do we know there aren't thousandths?"

The teacher turns to the class in a way that lets students know she is not going to respond to Miranda's query and she expects them to give it some thought. When no one responds, she suggests that they talk in their groups about how to answer Miranda's question. Soon the room comes alive with small-group conversations.

After a couple of minutes, the noise level lessens and the teacher asks the groups to report back to the class. She calls on the groups in a purposeful order, based on the conversations she heard as she walked around the room.

The first two groups report that they don't need to think about anything more than hundredths, because "that's all the clue says."

The next two groups suggest that they assume the number has only hundredths, "unless another clue tells us something about the thousandths place."

Then Miranda's group proposes that "until we get a clue that says otherwise, there could still be lots of places. We don't know for sure."

The teacher decides that she will leave this conversation open for the time being and directs students' attention back to the clue: the digit in the tenths place is one-third of the digit in the hundredths place. She asks, "What does the clue tell us about the possibilities for these two places?"

One student responds, "You have to be able to multiply the number in the tenths place by three to get the number in the hundredths place."

The teacher asks the class if someone would like to state what Nathan said in his or her own words.

Yoshi says, "Well, I thought of it the other way. I think that you should take the number that is in the hundredths place and divide it by three to get the number in the tenths place."

The class then discusses whether or not both students are correct and how the two ideas relate. The teacher is pleased that this simple clue has provided an opportunity for them to apply ideas related to the inverse relation between multiplication and division.

The teacher unveils the next clue and asks students to consider what they might learn from knowing that all of the digits are different. Students talk about knowing that the first two digits in the code are 4 and 0, so 4 and 0 can't be repeated anywhere else.

The students are now eager for the last two clues: *The tenths digit is one-half the ones digit* and *There are five places in the number.* The students begin to talk about these clues as the teacher checks from table to table. Yoshi's group has identified 402.13 as the code, while Patia's group believes the code to be 406.39. Ben claims that the code could be 402.13, 404.26, or 406.39. Liza reminds him that they can't repeat the 4. After the groups report, the students agree that both 402.13 and 406.39 could be the code. A few grumble about there being more than one possibility, but they all agree that both numbers fit all of the clues. Several students ask if it's OK that there is more than one answer.

The teacher responds, "Do you all agree that both of these answers will work?"

One student offers, "Yeah, we know that they both work, so I guess that both codes are OK. This problem must have more than one answer." The teacher is pleased that the students have come to this conclusion themselves.

Believing that the students are now ready to investigate similar problems on their own, the teacher shows the class a chart that lists the students' names in three groups. Within each group the students are free to form partnerships or to work alone. Each group is color-coded to correspond to the folder in which students will find copies of a code problem tailor-made for their group. Red is associated with the first level of the task, blue with the second, and green with the third—the most challenging level. (See Figure 4–4; see also Reproducibles for individual tasks identified by color.)

The students who have been assigned to do the red (first tier) task have some difficulty figuring out how to get started. As the teacher observes them, she notices that several students are looking at the written clues and several others are looking for pencils and a comfortable place to sit. The teacher knows that it will take this group a bit longer to get going, but that it will be worth it to have them determine how best to work together in order to accomplish their work. She knows that if she steps in too early, the students will not learn how to bring themselves to the table to work on their own. So, she waits until they are settled before checking in on them. Their task is similar to the one completed as a group, purposely repeating a clue that refers to one digit being one-third of another.

The teacher checks on the other two groups and once she observes that each group is engaged in solving its number puzzle, she moves back to the red group, which has now settled into

**Take Action!**

Manage group assignments.

**What's the Secret Code?**

Name: _____          Date: _____

**Red Group**

1. Use the clues to find the code number.
   - The code number is between 3,600 and 3,800.
   - There are six places in the number.
   - All of the digits are odd numbers.
   - The number is 0.41 less than a whole number.
   - The digit in the tens place is one-third the digit in the hundredths place.
   - The digit in the tenths place is four more than the digit in the ones place.

2. What's the code number?

3. Pick two clues and explain how they helped you find the code.

**Blue Group**

1. Use the clues to find the code number.
   - No digit is used more than once.
   - It is between 6,600 and 6,800.
   - When multiplied by 4, the result is a whole number.
   - The digit in the tenths place is one-fourth the digit in the ones place.
   - The sum of the digit in the hundredths place and the digit in the tens place is even.
   - There are six places in the number.

2. What code numbers fit these clues?

3. Pick two clues and explain how they helped you find these possibilities.

4. Write one more clue so that there is only one possible code number.

**Green Group**

1. Use the clues to find the code number.
   - It is between 8,500 and 8,800.
   - When multiplied by 8, the result is a whole number.
   - The digit in the hundredths place is $\frac{3}{4}$ the digit in the thousands place.
   - The sum of all the digits in the number is 26.
   - The digit in the hundredths place is 200% of the digit in the tenths place.
   - There are no zeros in the decimal places.

2. What code numbers fit these clues?

3. Explain how you used all of these clues to find these possibilities.

4. Write one more clue so that there is only one possible code number.

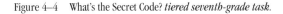

Figure 4–4    What's the Secret Code? *tiered seventh-grade task.*

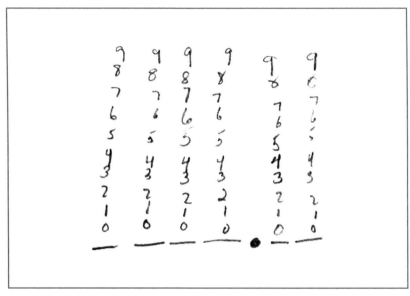

Figure 4–5  *Mark listed each digit as a possible choice for each of the six places.*

work. The second clue identifies the number of places in the code with hopes that it will help students organize the later clues. Mark immediately draws six blanks and writes the digits *0–9* above each blank as possible choices for each place, including the thousands place not recognizing immediately that the digit in the thousands place must be a 3. (See Figure 4–5.) The task is a bit simpler than the whole-class puzzle in that there is only one possible code number. Once they identify the code, students have to explain how two of the clues helped them find that solution.

Several of these students seem to be stuck on the clue that tells them that the number code is 0.41 less than a whole number. Tonya refers to the importance of thinking about zeros and Mark doesn't think there is any number that would fit all of the clues. The teacher listens for a while and then decides to ask the students how addition or subtraction might help them.

They seem a bit perplexed by this question until Mark says, "Maybe we could subtract from one, but the numbers won't line up."

Tonya then connects to this idea by saying, "Oh, that must have been why I was thinking about zeros; we need to do it like this," and writing *1.00 − 0.41.*

A couple of students complete the subtraction and once they do so, a few of the other students pay closer attention and appear to understand why this clue identifies the last two digits in the

**Take Action!**

Encourage further thinking.

number. When a few students in the group find the secret code, there is growing interest by the remaining students to find it as well. When they do so, they appear to believe that their work is completed. The teacher knows that it can be a challenge for some of these students to explain their thinking. She reminds them that they can work together. Each person can talk about how one clue was used and then they will each have two clues to explain. This idea seems to reenergize the students.

Ramie and Todd talk to each other about the first two clues and then write their responses separately. Ramie recognizes that the first two clues allowed her to determine the first two digits of the number, but does not explain how they do so. (See Figure 4–6.) Todd correctly recognizes that knowing the digits are all odd allows him to determine the hundredths digit. (See Figure 4–7.)

Figure 4–6  *Ramie explained how she used two of the clues.*

**What's the Secret Code?**

**Red Group**

1. Use the clues to find the code number.

- The code number is between 3,600 and 3,800.
- There are six places in the number.
- All of the digits are (odd) numbers.
- The number is 0.41 less than a whole number.
- The digit in the tens place is one-third the digit in the hundredths place.  $3 \times 3 = 9$
- The digit in the tenths place is four more than the digit in the ones place.  $5 - 4 = 1$

3600 - 3800

```
  1.00
- .41
_____
  .59
```

3 _ 3 1.5 9

2. What's the code number?

3731.59

3. Pick two clues and explain how they helped you find the code.

I used clues 1 + 3 to find 37.

**What's the Secret Code?**

**Red Group**

1. Use the clues to find the code number.

  - The code number is between 3,600 and 3,800.
  - There are six places in the number.
  - All of the digits are odd numbers. 37__ _
  - The number is 0.41 less than a whole number.
  - The digit in the tens place is one-third the digit in the hundredths place.
  - The digit in the tenths place is four more than the digit in the ones place.

$$1 - 0.41 = 0.59$$

$$3 \ 7 \ 3 \ 1 . 5 \ 9$$

2. What's the code number?

3731.59

3. Pick two clues and explain how they helped you to find the code.

Clue four helped me find 5 and 9 because 1 - 0.41 = 0.59. Clue 3 helped me because 7 is odd.

Figure 4–7 *Todd explained his use of two clues.*

The students working on the second-level task (blue) begin talking right away about the clues.

The teacher hears Liza say, "It can't be six thousand eight hundred because *between* means that it can't include that number."

Then Jason states, "The numbers in the thousands and hundreds places cannot both be six."

Together, they have determined that the first two digits are 6 and 7. The group is interested in writing down its ideas on paper and is willing to work through the clues together as a group once the students realize that they each have an idea to offer.

This code puzzle is more challenging. To use the clue *When multiplied by 4, the result is a whole number*, students may apply their knowledge about inverse operations as well as relationships between decimals and fractions. The clues result in three possible code numbers. Students then explain how two of the clues helped them solve the codes. Finally, students create an additional clue that eliminates all the possible code numbers but one.

Zak uses variables to represent the code number and to organize his data. His teacher is impressed that he recognizes that multiplying a number ending in 0.25, 0.5, or 0.75 by 4 would result in a whole number and then uses another clue to identify 0.25 as the only possibility. (See Figure 4–8.) The teacher notes that Zak may have been successful with the green task and wonders if she has underestimated his abilities.

As the teacher moves to the green group, she notices that some of these students are working alone. They appear to prefer to read the clues to themselves and to begin working on a solution without consulting their peers. It isn't until Lucy reads the clue *When multiplied by 8, the result is a whole number* that the students begin to talk to each other more readily.

Lucy asks, "I think that we need to have an answer that ends in zero, right?"

When another student asks why, she responds, "Zero is the only number that you can multiply eight by to get zero for an answer." Other students disagree and encourage her to think about other possibilities.

To determine the code, students must recognize that $0.125 \times 8$ will result in a whole number. Another clue requires students to recognize that 200 percent of a number is the same as twice that number. As with the blue task, students must write a final clue to identify exactly one code number, but these students are expected to explain their entire solution process and are not directly told the number of places in the number.

The teacher notices that unlike many of the students in the other groups, these students read all of the clues before using one of the clues to begin a list. Nick thinks about the clue he will write before he even starts to use the clues that are given. He remarks, "There are already a lot of clues about finding the sum of the digits. I think that we should write something else for our last clue."

Alicia misses the ending *ths* in the fifth clue and is confused by how it would be possible to have two different pieces of information about the same place. Her peers quickly remind her that hundreds is different from hundredths. The teacher notes how

Figure 4–8 *Zak used variables to represent the code and show his conclusions from the clues.*

those able to work through the mathematics quickly can, at times, miss important details. She is pleased that it really matters how well they read the components of this problem.

Ericka's response demonstrates many common aspects of the written work within this group. She is comfortable using the clues out of order, uses letters to represents digits, creates equations, and provides a complete explanation. (See Figure 4–9.)

Although the student groups have worked on different code problems, the teacher believes that it is important to have the class

**Take Action!**

Support a sense of community.

**What's the Secret Code?**

**Green Group**

1. Use the clues to find the code number.
    - It is between 8,500 and 8,800.
    - When multiplied by 8, the result is a whole number.
    - The digit in the hundredths place is $\frac{3}{4}$ the digit in the thousands place.  $\frac{3}{4}$ A = B
    - The sum of all the digits in the number is 26.
    - The digit in the hundredths place is 200% of the digit in the tenths place.  200% E = F
    - There are no zeros in the decimal places.

$$8x = 0 \quad so \quad x = 0.25,\ 0.5,\ 0.75,\ or\ 0.125$$
$$2 \times 1 = 2 \quad so \quad 0.125$$

$$\frac{8}{A}\ \frac{6}{B}\ \frac{}{C}\ \frac{}{D}\ .\ \frac{1}{E}\ \frac{2}{F}\ \frac{5}{G}$$

$$8 + 6 + 1 + 2 + 5 = 22$$

2. What code numbers fit these clues?

8604.125    8613.125    8622.125    8631.125    8640.125

3. Explain how you used all of these clues to find these possibilities.

1. I knew it was 0.25, 0.5, 0.75 or 0.125. It had to be 125 because of the 200%.

2. I knew 8 because 8500–8800. $\frac{3}{4}$ 8 = 6 so it's in the 8600s.

4. The sum is 26, but A + B + E + F + G = 22, so I need 4 more. 0 + 4, 1 + 3, 2 + 2, 3 + 1, 4 + 0

5. Last clue means there's no zero in the ten-thousands or later or like .50

4. Write one more clue so that there is only one possible code number.

The digit in the ones place is half the digit in the thousands place.

8604.125

Figure 4–9   *Erika's work is typical of students in this group.*

come back together to discuss their work. Talking about the different tasks takes the mystery out of what each group was doing and reveals the similarity among the tasks. Also, sharing ideas and experiences helps maintain their sense of community as a class.

The red group explains its work first. The teacher has displayed the clues to this task at the front of the room so that presenters can point to the clues as needed and the rest of the class will have access to the puzzle. As soon as the clues are revealed, several students who were in the other groups begin to work on the puzzle. The teacher, wanting to maximize the time spent in whole-group conversations, advises, "You may spend two minutes getting to know this puzzle, but be prepared to stop at that time and listen to the reporters. Your job is to ask questions as they present their work."

Mark begins the report by saying, "We thought that this puzzle was going to be really difficult to solve, but once we got going, it was easier than we thought."

Liza, a member of the blue group, says, "That's what happened to us, too."

When the blue group reports, the teacher notes that members of the red group are staying engaged. Ramie asks, "How did you know that four times one-fourth would get to a whole number?"

Liza thinks for a few seconds and then responds, "I thought of quarters. If you get four of them, you get a whole dollar." Ramie appears satisfied with this response.

When Zak reports, "At first, we were not happy that our clues didn't get us to one answer," Lucy, a student from the green group pipes in, "Yeah, us too!"

The teacher is particularly pleased that students remain engaged during the green group's explanation. She knows the other students can't necessarily complete this version of the task, but being familiar with the format allows them to feel comfortable to ask questions such as "How did you use the third clue?"

Finally, the teacher asks all of the students to identify problem-solving strategies they used to find these codes. As they brainstorm, the teacher records the ideas for all to see:

- *Read carefully to see if there is* ths *at the end.*
- *Make lists.*
- *Think about easier numbers to understand a clue.*
- *Talk together and share ideas.*
- *Make lines for the number to show where the digits can go.*
- *Decide the best clue to use first.*

As the students exit this seventh-grade classroom, several make positive comments about today's work. Tonya says, "I liked trying to find the code, even though it was hard to solve the puzzle."

Nick asks the teacher, "Do you have any more puzzles like these? We liked doing them."

Cameron, who was a member of the blue group, asks, "Can I get a copy of the puzzles the other groups got, so that I can solve them at home?"

## Teacher Reflection

The math consultant for my district encouraged me to try this problem with my students. I have done a few tiered assignments before, but usually for homework or for just part of a class period, and then we didn't discuss them. I was reluctant to devote an entire class to this.

My biggest surprise was that the first-tier (red group) students stayed so involved in the class discussion. I think they were really boosted by the fact that the other students wanted to try their task. I had not planned for this, but it makes sense to me now. I guess I underestimated how much students would enjoy these puzzles.

It was wonderful to observe how well the students stayed on task once everyone got to work. The red group didn't want to write much at first, but they were happier when I reminded them that they could work together. As well, once one of the students in the group had a sense of where to start and shared it with others, they were more willing to attempt the problem. Students in the green group often complain when they are asked to write complete explanations. This time they seemed eager to share their thoughts and final clues. Maybe they didn't mind doing some writing in math class because it was about their own ways of using the clues and their own new clue, not just what the teacher wanted them to write. This time I could really see the power of tiered tasks. The students were able to work so well because they were challenged at just the right level. Too often some of my students who have difficulty give up too easily and some of my better students just rush through things.

> *This time I could really see the power of tiered tasks. The students were able to work so well because they were challenged at just the right level.*

Also, it didn't feel as if I had to teach three different lessons at the same time. I was somewhat nervous about supporting all of this at once, but it really felt quite natural because, really, everyone was doing the same activity.

The story from this seventh-grade classroom demonstrates the effectiveness of tiered assignments. This is usually the case when the teacher has a clear rationale for creating the assignment and makes sure that the activities include mathematical ideas at varying complexities so all students can be challenged appropriately. Simultaneously, the teacher made sure that the task could be completed alone or with others and that students could begin with the clue that made the most sense to them. Finding the right combination of accessibility and challenge is the goal of a tiered approach.

So how do we create tiered assignments? As always, the first step is to identify the important mathematical ideas. Consider eighth graders studying geometry and measurement, focusing on applying the Pythagorean theorem within the context of finding the volume and surface area of rectangular and triangular prisms. Teachers can use logic tasks to reinforce these content goals while also providing students with opportunities for deductive reasoning and making inferences. *Who Won What?* problems require students to determine the prize money each contestant received based on clues related to the boxes in which the prizes were hidden. It often helps to begin with the middle level, focusing on what you would expect most of your students to be able to do. (We call this level, or tier, blue.) Teachers can begin by developing a *Who Won What?* problem for that audience. (See Figure 4–10; see also Reproducibles.)

The figures for this level include two rectangular prisms and two triangular prisms. Two of the clues are negative statements, including *Fredrika did not choose a box with a volume of 120 cm³*. Students will need to find ways to organize this information. The fourth clue is the only single clue sufficient to identify the choice of one of the contestants. Students must recognize the Pythagorean triplets 3, 4, and 5 and 6, 8, and 10 or apply the Pythagorean theorem.

Two other tiers can then be developed by adjusting the middle tier. For example, in a less complicated version (red), all of the boxes are rectangular prisms, including one cube. (See Figure 4–11 on page 112; see also Reproducibles.) All of the clues are positive statements. The solution can be found using the clues in the order they are presented.

In a more complex version (green), the figures include two rectangular prisms, a triangular prism, and a cylinder. (See Figure 4–12 on page 113; see also Reproducibles.) None of the clue statements can be used independently to identify a contestant's choice, two of the clues are negative statements, and one of the clues involves a ratio.

**Tiered Task Idea!**

**Strand:** Measurement and Geometry

**Focus:** Pythagorean theorem, surface area, and volume

**Context:** Solving logic puzzles

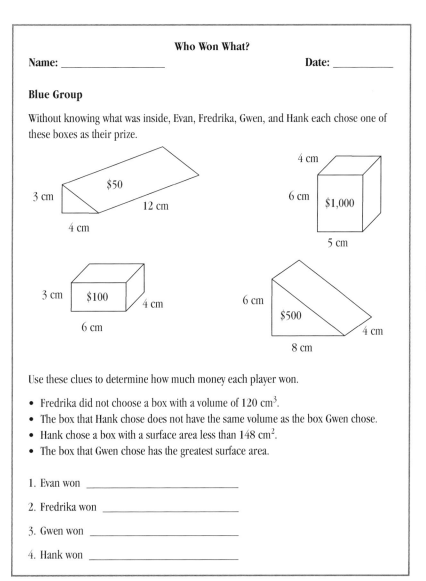

**Who Won What?**

Name: _____          Date: _____

**Blue Group**

Without knowing what was inside, Evan, Fredrika, Gwen, and Hank each chose one of these boxes as their prize.

Use these clues to determine how much money each player won.

- Fredrika did not choose a box with a volume of 120 cm$^3$.
- The box that Hank chose does not have the same volume as the box Gwen chose.
- Hank chose a box with a surface area less than 148 cm$^2$.
- The box that Gwen chose has the greatest surface area.

1. Evan won _____

2. Fredrika won _____

3. Gwen won _____

4. Hank won _____

Figure 4–10    Who Won What? *task for blue group.*

As noted by Pierce and Adams (2005), the number of tiers does not have to be three, nor does the number of students in each group need to be the same. The goal is to create groups according to the students' needs. We focus on three groups here, as teachers often find it the easiest way to think about making tiers to address readiness. Note that you can also make variations to address interests and learning styles.

A tiered task for data collection and analysis requires students to conduct a survey, represent and interpret results, and compute costs related to the data. (See Figure 4–13 on page 114; see also Reproducibles.) In the less complex tier (red group),

**Strand:** Data

**Focus:** Collect, display, and analyze data.

**Context:** Design, conduct, and interpret a survey

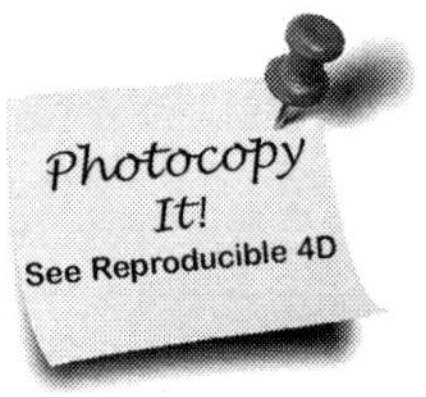
Photocopy
It!
See Reproducible 4D

**Who Won What?**

**Name:** ________________ **Date:** __________

**Red Group**

Without knowing what was inside, Abe, Belinda, Carlos, and Dani each chose one of these boxes as their prize.

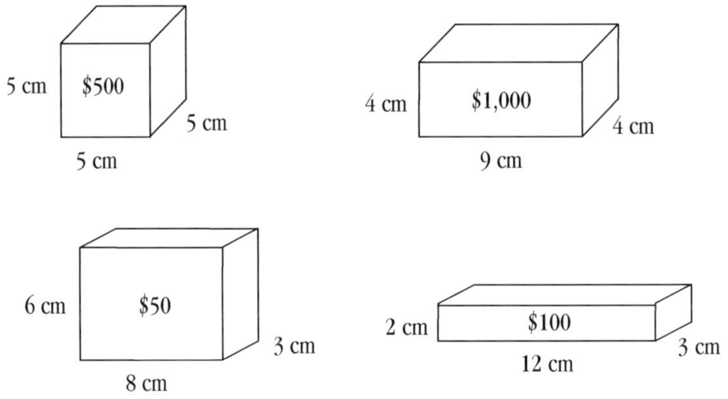
5 cm
$500
5 cm
5 cm
4 cm
$1,000
4 cm
9 cm
6 cm
$50
3 cm
8 cm
2 cm
$100
3 cm
12 cm

Use these clues to determine how much money each player won.

- The boys chose boxes with the same volumes.
- Belinda chose the box with a surface area of 132 $cm^2$.
- The box Carlos chose has a surface area greater than the surface area of the box Abe chose.

1. Abe won ______________________
2. Belinda won ______________________
3. Carlos won ______________________
4. Dani won ______________________

Figure 4–11 Who Won What? *task for red group.*

students plan a class trip. Four choices are provided for the trip in order to make the data more manageable. The computation is fairly straightforward and students are told which of the statistical representations of the data that they must include. The next tier (blue group) requires students to collect data to make recommendations to a clothing store about hat preferences. It does not restrict the data about the attributes of the hats and the computation is also more complex, perhaps necessitating finding averages. As well, students are given choices about what visual representations they will provide in their report and they must make inferences about these

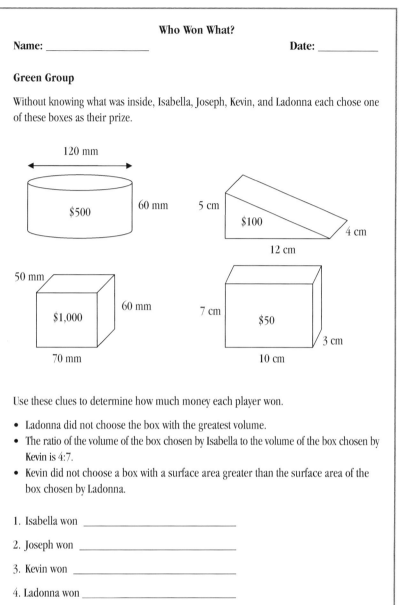

**Who Won What?**

Name: _____    Date: _____

**Green Group**

Without knowing what was inside, Isabella, Joseph, Kevin, and Ladonna each chose one of these boxes as their prize.

120 mm

$500    60 mm

5 cm    $100    4 cm    12 cm

50 mm    $1,000    60 mm    70 mm

7 cm    $50    3 cm    10 cm

photocopy It! See Reproducible 4F

Use these clues to determine how much money each player won.

- Ladonna did not choose the box with the greatest volume.
- The ratio of the volume of the box chosen by Isabella to the volume of the box chosen by Kevin is 4:7.
- Kevin did not choose a box with a surface area greater than the surface area of the box chosen by Ladonna.

1. Isabella won _____

2. Joseph won _____

3. Kevin won _____

4. Ladonna won _____

Figure 4–12   Who Won What? *task for green group.*

data in order to make recommendations. The most challenging tier (green group) asks students to prepare a report about fund-raising opportunities in their school. There are no limitations placed on what data they will collect or how to analyze the data, although students are asked to provide a more complex form of statistical representation: a box-and-whisker plot. These students are also asked to determine the purpose of such a plot in this report. Lastly,

**Data Collection and Analysis**

Name: _____     Date: _____

**Red Group**

*Plan a Visit to the Capital City*

You are going to plan a place to visit in your state's capital city.

My state's capital city is _____.

1. Survey your classmates to find out the type of place that they would like to visit. The choices are a museum, a historic place, a memorial, or an aquarium.

2. Prepare a report of what your classmates have chosen. You should include the following in your report:
   - the selections that your classmates made, shown in a frequency table
   - a circle graph of your data
   - your recommendation for the place to visit with an explanation as to how you analyzed the data to help you decide

3. Consider what it would cost to visit the place that you chose. You should plan to:
   - brainstorm possible costs
   - collect the data about cost by researching online the place that you have chosen
   - find the total cost based on the number of students and chaperones who will attend

**Blue Group**

*Become a Business Consultant*

The local clothing store wants to know more about students' preferences for hats. The owners are interested in learning more about the types of hats that they should keep in stock. You are to collect the data for our classroom and prepare a report to give to the clothing store owners.

1. Discuss the attributes of hats that you would like to know about before you collect data.

2. Make sure to include the data you collect in a frequency table as well as to display the data in an appropriate graph. Include in your report your recommendations with a thorough explanation as to why you made the recommendations that you did.

3. Investigate the prices of hats. Based on the data that you collect, how much do you think that your classmates will spend on hats this year?

**Green Group**

*Make a Fund-Raising Plan for a New Fitness Center*

As the president of the student council at your middle school, you have been asked to make a plan for raising money for a new fitness center at your school.

1. Collect data about possible fund-raising opportunities. Make sure to include the data you collect as well as graphical representations of the data in your report. You should give a detailed explanation of why you chose the fund-raisers you are recommending. At least one of your graphical representations should be a box-and-whisker plot.

2. Report on how much money you would like to raise and how you will allocate the monies. Use references, such as catalogs and websites, to estimate the cost of the equipment that you would like to purchase.

3. Make a plan as to how you will implement your fund-raisers. Include information about how each class in the school will be involved and how you will keep records of how much money is raised.

Figure 4–13    Data Collection and Analysis: *tiered activity.*

these students are asked to plan for the implementation of their fund-raiser(s).

A tiered task involving pattern finding and algebraic thinking shows how broad the tiers can be, reaching a wide range of readiness. All tiers involve the same growing pattern of quilts, for which the first three models are shown: Quilt 1, Quilt 2, and Quilt 3. In the first tier, students begin by making a sketch of Quilt 4. Then they generalize a one-to-one relationship between the number of dotted squares and the quilt number. They answer specific questions about Quilt 6 and Quilt 7 and then explain how they used patterns to determine the number of plain squares in Quilt 10. (See Figure 4–14 on page 116; see also Reproducibles.)

In the second tier, students move to generalizations right away. While sketching a quilt is a strategy they could use, students are not directed to do so. The task begins with questions about Quilt 10, Quilt 12, and Quilt 15. Then it asks students about Quilt 40. Finally, it directs students to create an equation for predicting the number of plain squares in a quilt, given the number of dotted squares. In the most challenging tier, students begin with a question about Quilt 40. They are then asked to create an equation for predicting the number of plain squares in a quilt, given the number of dotted squares. The next question asks them to reverse their thinking; that is, they are told the number of plain squares and asked to identify the number of dotted squares. The final question asks how students can see the equation they write in the quilts.

Interpreting graphical representations is an important part of the middle school mathematics curriculum. The next example of tiered tasks asks questions of varying levels of difficulty about the same graph. (See Figure 4–15 on page 117; see also Reproducibles.) In the red tier, the first three questions require students to look at only one line at a time on the graph. Next students must relate the lines of two people in the graph to respond to questions posed. Then students are asked to pose and answer their own question about the graph.

In the blue tier, students are asked several questions about speed, necessitating a deeper understanding of the relationships between the $x$- and $y$-variables. To answer a question such as *Which of the friends never goes to the ice-cream shop?* students must recognize the importance of the $y$-intercept. In the last task, students are asked to write a story that matches the graph for Liam's entire trip.

In the green tier, students are immediately asked to interpret relationships among the lines in the graph. Their answers may be

*Tiered Task Idea!*

Strand: Algebra

Focus: Represent and generalize patterns.

Context: Quilt patterns

*Tiered Task Idea!*

Strand: Algebra and Number

Focus: Interpret information in a graph to solve problems.

Context: Trip to an ice-cream shop

**Quilt Patterns**

Name: _____                               Date: _____

Look at these quilts.

Quilt 2 shows a total of 2 dotted squares and 13 plain squares.

Quilt 1                    Quilt 2                                Quilt 3

### Red Group

Assume the quilt pattern continues.

• Make a sketch of Quilt 4.

• How many dotted squares will there be in Quilt 6? _____
• How many plain squares will there be in Quilt 6? _____
• How many total squares will there be in Quilt 6? _____
• How many plain squares will there be in the top row of Quilt 7? _____
• How many plain squares will there be in Quilt 10? _____
• Explain your thinking.

### Blue Group

Assume the quilt pattern continues.

• How many squares will there be in Quilt 10? _____
• How many plain squares will there be in the top row of Quilt 12? _____
• How many plain squares will there be in Quilt 15? _____
• Explain your thinking.
• How many plain squares will there be in Quilt 40? _____
• Show your work.
• Write an equation for using the number of dotted squares in a quilt to find the number of plain squares.

   _____

### Green Group

Assume the quilt pattern continues.

• How many squares will there be in Quilt 40? _____
• Show your work.
• Write an equation for using the number of dotted squares in a quilt to find the plain squares. _____
• Explain how you can see this equation in the quilt figures.
• If a quilt pattern has 303 plain squares, how many dotted squares does it have? _____
• Write an equation for using the number of plain squares in a quilt to find the number of dotted squares. _____
• Explain how you can see this equation in the quilt figures.

Figure 4–14    Quilt Patterns: *tiered activity for algebraic thinking and pattern finding.*

different based on different interpretations. The question *What happens after about 3 seconds?* may lead to factual answers chosen from the graph itself or may lead to more creative responses that provide elaborate details about what happens to the individuals.

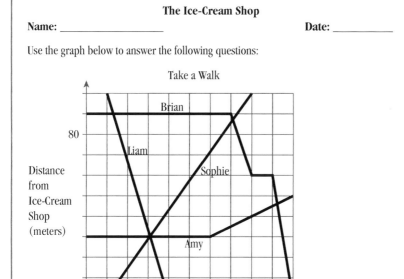

**The Ice-Cream Shop**

Name: _____     Date: _____

Use the graph below to answer the following questions:

Take a Walk

Brian

Liam

Sophie

Amy

80

Distance from Ice-Cream Shop (meters)

1  2  3  4  5  6  7  8  9  10

Time (seconds)

**Red Group**

1. Which of the four friends starts out at the ice-cream shop?
2. Which friend is the farthest away from the ice-cream shop when time = 0?
3. How long does it take Brian to get to the ice-cream shop?
4. Who got to the ice-cream shop first: Amy, Liam, or Brian?
5. How far away is Sophie from the ice-cream shop when Brian gets to the ice-cream shop?
6. Write and answer your own question about the graph.

**Blue Group**

1. What is Sophie's speed as she walks away from the ice-cream shop?
2. What is Liam's speed as he walks toward the ice-cream shop?
3. Which of the friends never goes to the ice-cream shop?
4. How far is Sophie from the ice-cream shop when Amy starts walking?
5. Whom does Brian meet along his way to the ice-cream shop?
6. Write a story about Liam's trip.

**Green Group**

1. What happens after about 3 seconds?
2. Who stayed in one place the longest? How do you know?
3. Write a verbal description of the story of the four friends and the ice-cream shop.

Figure 4–15   The Ice-Cream Shop: *tiered graph activity for algebraic thinking and number and operations.*

The last question asks students to write a story that describes the relationship among the trips of all four of the friends in relation to the ice-cream shop. As they write these interpretive stories, students must also justify their thinking.

# Compacting Curriculum

Along with designing tiered tasks, some teachers consider *compacting* content for more ready learners. This strategy recognizes that some content can be accelerated or eliminated for these learners. What remains is a more compact version of the standard curriculum. The process is similar to all models of differentiation: the teacher identifies key curricular ideas, pre-assesses students, and makes appropriate learning decisions based on that data.

Though compacting is often associated with better-prepared learners, it is important to remember that a variety of factors influence students' readiness. A student may have come from another school district or another country where the material was already considered. Students' interests or family culture may have already provided significant learning opportunities within a particular content area. For example, Joseph is a sixth-grade student who has been assisting with his family's farm stand for as long as he can remember. In this role he frequently computes with decimals and fractions and finds the percent of a number to figure out the tax that he must charge. Joseph's parents like him to do as much of this computation as possible without the use of a calculator, just as they did when they first started working on the farm. As a result of Joseph's experience at the stand, his mental arithmetic ability as well as paper-and-pencil computation skills with decimals and percents are strong. Though Joseph still has more to learn about rational numbers, the teacher can compact various aspects of this curriculum for him.

Though compacting can serve a variety of students, teachers are sometimes reluctant to actually eliminate content from the curriculum. As we learn from the following teacher's reflection, outside support for compacting can be helpful.

## Teacher Reflection

Jamie seemed to walk in the door already knowing everything covered in our curriculum. Fortunately, my school system has been holding workshops on differentiated instruction. In these workshops the presenter introduced me to the idea of compacting. I never thought about eliminating some of the lessons. The technique I had been using was to persistently find a way for Jamie to be more involved, primarily by helping others. This technique was not always successful, as Jamie often tired of being the teacher's helper. I was reluctant to try compacting but didn't know what else to do. I made an appointment with my principal and asked for her advice. She was supportive and encouraged me to try this approach.

Now Jamie and I hold a mini-conference at the beginning of each unit. After pre-assessment, we look at the list of the unit's lessons together. He sees me check the ones that he is still responsible for and cross some of the others out. Jamie knows that he will participate in some of the lessons with his classmates and at times be given the opportunity to be an independent learner. Together we identify projects that he can do in lieu of participating in the other lessons. The plan is also shared with his family. Jamie is so much happier now that we have begun to compact his learning. He now offers to help his classmates more readily and looks more engaged during our class discussions. It's as if a burden has been removed from both of us. We no longer have to just make the curriculum work; we can change it more than I realized.

> *In these workshops the presenter introduced me to the idea of compacting. I never thought about eliminating some of the lessons.*

## Additional Resources

Though the teacher in the previous reflection has been successful with the compacting strategy, it should be noted that the strategy requires teachers to closely monitor independent work and to have additional resources available. Also, unlike Jamie in that reflection, there are students who need not less, but more support. Teachers who use nontraditional textbooks feel this need in particular. Such textbooks tend to have fewer practice exercises and problems. In these situations, teachers can find help by participating in exchanges with other teachers, as well as exploring the wide world of online (Web) resources. The ultimate goal is to have built a library of multilevel mathematical materials equivalent to a library of multilevel reading materials.

Classroom libraries of multilevel mathematical materials can play a crucial role in providing for the broad spectrum of grades 6 through 8 readiness. One way to build such mathematical libraries is to have teachers purchase sets of supplementary materials specific to their grade level. Teachers can then redistribute the materials among themselves so that each class set contains tasks for additional grade levels. If purchasing is not an option, teachers can find problems in textbooks for each grade level. Problems can also be found in the menu featured in each issue of the magazine *Mathematics Teaching*

Take Action!

Design an individual plan of study.

Take Action!

Acquire multigrade resources.

*in the Middle School*, published by the National Council of Teachers of Mathematics. Problem-solving leagues such as Mathcounts (www.mathcounts.org) are a great resource for more challenging problems. Mathcounts fosters problem solving at the middle school level and offers a variety of problems at no cost.

One way teachers organize multilevel problems from various resources is to cut them out and paste them onto file cards. The challenge level of the problem could be indicated by the color of the file card. For example, red cards feature less challenging problems, whereas green cards feature the most challenging problems. Cards can also be further separated within their challenge levels by letters: Challenge Levels A, B, and so forth. Finally, cards are sorted by strand. Hence, for a geometry strand, a classroom library could have these groups:

basic problems below grade level (red A)

advanced problems below grade level (blue A)

basic problems at grade level (red B)

advanced problems at grade level (blue B)

basic problems above grade level (red C)

advanced problems above grade level (blue C)

This organizational approach allows students at all readiness levels to have access to all levels of problems. Students may self-select problems or teachers may assign particular cards. Though the initial creation of the decks is time-consuming, teachers find that such decks serve their students well and can be used over many years. Consider involving students in the creation of these decks as well; students are often very aware of which problems interest and challenge them.

Resources are also abundant via technology; if you have computers in your classroom, you can make available webquests, virtual manipulatives, applets, and practice games that meet a variety of readiness levels. A worthwhile site for learning more about webquests is http://school.discoveryeducation.com/schrockguide/webquest/webquest.html. Virtual manipulatives are available at http://nlvm.usu.edu/en/NAV/vlibrary.html and other websites. These unique manipulatives allow individual access to a variety of models, and because the manipulatives are virtual, they can be used wherever and whenever students have access to a computer (including home). Practice games on the computer provide different levels of challenge and can often be found for free on the Internet. **Note:** A game in which the focus is merely to practice should not be played for too long; once a skill is mastered, the student should move on from that game.

Each of these curriculum adaptations is a response to variation in readiness. Ways to provide for a range of student readiness are summarized in the following chart:

---

**Casting a Wider Net: Providing for Various Levels of Readiness**

1. Allow students some control over the difficulty level by having them
   - provide the numbers in the problem or
   - choose exercises to complete.

2. Transform problems so that they allow for
   - one or more solutions or
   - a wide range of responses and understandings.

3. Provide multiple models such as
   - students' own drawings and sketches,
   - different models of fractions, including number lines, Cuisenaire rods, fraction bars, pattern blocks, and Fraction Tower Cubes, and
   - different models of operations with integers such as red and black chips, number lines, and thermometers.

4. Vary the challenge offered students through
   - tiered tasks or
   - curriculum compacting.

5. Extend resources by
   - sharing materials with teachers at other grade levels and
   - using the Internet.

---

Decisions to make these kinds of adaptations or to provide differentiated learning opportunities are grounded in knowledge of our curriculum and our students. As we choose among modifications we must remember that all students deserve challenging, thought-provoking problems and tasks. Too often, in the spirit of helping, we provide students with simplistic tasks or rules that are not connected to conceptual understanding. Algorithmic steps such as *first, outside, inside, and last* do not help the learner understand the process for finding the product of $(x + 7)$ and $(x + 8)$. Similarly, the simplistic description of three-fourths as *three out of four* does not allow students to understand the variety of language or uses associated with fractions.

Knowing our students and our curriculum is an essential first step, but making decisions about what content and teaching strategies are appropriate is where we begin the hard work of providing all of our students with improved access to the curriculum. It is in the conscious act of matching our students' needs with what our curriculum and pedagogy have to offer that differentiation helps us most effectively meet our instructional goals. Readiness is only one piece of the puzzle, however. The goal of matching tasks to learners also has to encompass language, learning styles, and preferences.

## Connecting the Chapter to Your Practice

1. What do you find most challenging about meeting different levels of readiness?

2. What methods do you have for transforming tasks so that they are more inclusive?

3. What do you say if students ask why they are working on different tasks?

# Chapter 5
# Breaking Down Barriers to Learning

*T*he term *universal design* originated in the field of architecture. This philosophy of design is committed to providing inclusive environments that work better for everyone: for example, showers without curbs, door levers rather than knobs, and doors that open automatically. The idea is to build in an inclusive way right from the beginning, rather than to retrofit spaces when special circumstances arise. In this type of environment, barriers to independent living are removed at the design stage. Access for people with physical disabilities is considered from the inception and everyone benefits from these decisions.

Many of our students face learning barriers in our classrooms. Students' readiness levels are not always apparent, even when conscientious teachers observe their students closely and provide tasks designed to pre-assess learning. Sometimes there are barriers that keep students from accessing prior knowledge or from demonstrating what they have learned. When not attended to adequately and respectfully, language, learning styles, sensory preferences, and anxiety can keep students from reaching their full potential as successful mathematical doers and thinkers.

Educators have begun to think about a teaching philosophy that embraces universal design. What would our curriculum plans look like if we designed activities that worked for everyone right from the beginning rather than remediating or reteaching or, in architectural terms, retrofitting after original plans proved unsuccessful or inadequate?

# Understanding Language and English Language Learners

Consider this scenario from a sixth-grade class: The teacher begins the lesson by asking a student to remind everyone what they did yesterday. Johna volunteers, "We found percents of numbers, like twenty-five percent of fifty."

The teacher responds, "We are going to continue with this concept today as we solve problems. Work alone first and then check your answers with a neighbor." The teacher presents the following problem to students:

> *Using a $5 off coupon, Kate buys a pair of athletic shoes priced at $35.95. Melissa uses a 15% off coupon to buy the same shoes at another store with a price of $44.00. Who pays less for the shoes, Kate or Melissa?*

The teacher connects today's work to yesterday's lesson and uses student names in the problem. From the perspective of students who like to gather their thoughts first before interacting with others, this sequence may be viewed as positive. When we think about language, though, this scenario presents several challenges:

- In the United States athletic shoes are known by many names, including cross-trainers, gym shoes, high-tops, running shoes, sneakers, and tennis shoes. In other English-speaking countries they are also known as joggers or takkies. Sometimes students are told to wear their shoes to an important or formal event, and in this case, the term is intended to eliminate the choice of athletic shoes.
- The sentences in the problem are dense, containing several phrases and pieces of information.
- *Price(d)* is used as a noun and a verb.
- No real objects (realia such as store coupons), gestures (pointing to someone's athletic shoes), or dramatizations (shopping) are used to make the problem more comprehensible.
- When the teacher wants a combination of independent and collaborative work, and some students face language challenges, it is better to discuss the problem first. Then once understanding is assured, the students can complete the mathematical work alone.

As well as the general complexity of our English language, mathematical language becomes denser in middle school as the

*Take Action!*

Note the complex language associated with algebraic thinking.

concepts become more sophisticated. At this level, students are expected to symbolically represent statements such as *There are six times more cats than birds as pets*. Given our left-to-right orientation in reading, it is no wonder that many students, in error, express this relationship as $6C = B$. It takes considerable experience for students to become familiar with the importance of achieving balance in the creation of the algebraic representation of relationships.

Even a mathematical term that has been discussed for several days can still be challenging. Students build a deep understanding of mathematical language only through several approaches that develop concepts and connections. Sometimes when the nature of the activity changes, less than complete understanding is revealed. Sometimes partial understandings, built on everyday uses of a term that are less exact than that of a mathematical interpretation, can cause difficulties.

Consider this lesson in an eighth-grade classroom: The students are investigating the classic *Tower of Hanoi* problem that begins with six disks of increasing size stacked on the first of three poles. (See Figure 5–1 for a diagram of the tower with six disks.) The goal is for students to move the disks from the first pole to the third pole in as few moves as possible and without ever putting a larger disk on top of a smaller one. Only one disk may be moved at a time. Each time a disk is moved from one pole to another, it counts as a move. The teacher begins the lesson by telling the

**Lesson Idea!**

**Strand:** Algebra

**Focus:** Find and generalize patterns in nonlinear data.

**Context:** Tower of Hanoi

Figure 5–1    Tower of Hanoi *challenge with six disks.*

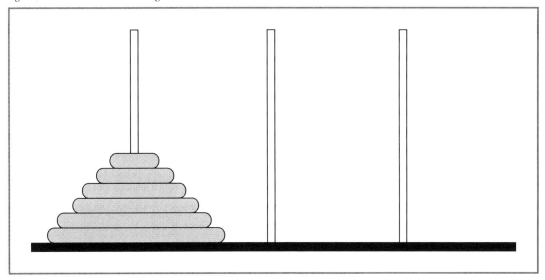

students the folklore associated with this task: "A group of monks in Vietnam are trying to move sixty-four disks according to certain rules. When they complete this puzzle, the world will end." The teacher ends the story with the questions How many moves are needed with sixty-four disks? If the monks are able to move the disks at the rate of one disk per second, how long after they begin this puzzle will the world end?

Disks are cut from file folders of different colors. Students organize themselves in pairs and each student gets six disks. Pairs mark three spaces on a piece of paper to signify where the poles would be. As the teacher walks around, she marvels at the number of different ways the pairs interact. Jordan and Eli work separately, each working with his own disks. Ronald and Maggie work together, using one set of disks. Ronald takes a turn and then Maggie does, and they confer with each other before making a move. As the teacher passes Ronald and Maggie, he hears Ronald say, "No, if you move there, we will have nowhere to go on our next turn."

Marco and Elvira speak quietly as they work. When Elvira asks Marco a question she does so in Spanish. Marco replies first in Spanish and then in English. Tran and Billy work closely together. Tran's English is limited, but they point and shake their heads until they agree, each making significant contributions to their solution.

Some students become quickly frustrated trying to move the six disks. A few students try the task using a lesser number of disks. Emily and Jared are successful at moving three disks in seven moves and immediately begin to explore four disks. Shortly thereafter students around them are working with three disks as well, then moving on to explore the task with four disks. Some students ask the teacher to check their work. Sometimes the teacher has to suggest that they try completing the task in fewer moves. Jared and Emily have moved four disks in fifteen moves but still find it too difficult to work with five disks.

Tran and Billy begin to make a table of the number of disks and the number of associated moves. The teacher is pleased to see them organize their data but wishes they would try even fewer disks so that the pattern would become more obvious.

Guy becomes frustrated with the puzzle and announces, "This is just too hard."

The teacher lets the frustration build a bit longer, in hopes that such emotions will encourage them to simplify more next time. Then he interjects, "When a problem is too difficult for us, what strategies can we try?"

*Take Action!*

Note the different ways students converse.

Glenda responds, "We can simplify, but we already did."

Glenda's partner, Ophelia, calls out, "Wait, we can make it easier—we can start with one." Soon all of the students are making tables and beginning with one disk. The teacher marvels at how often students need to relearn this important strategy.

When nearly all students have had success with one, two, and three disks, the teacher calls them together. He has built a stand with three dowels and is using plastic rings from a stacking toy. He now wants the students to build the table as a class. Each time he adds another disk on the first dowel, he asks the students to predict how many moves will be needed to complete the task. Then he asks a student to demonstrate the successful series of moves and to add the corresponding entry into the table. Tran, after several practices, proudly demonstrates the thirty-one moves necessary with five disks and the class has now created the following table:

| Number of Disks | Number of Moves |
|:---:|:---:|
| 1 | 1 |
| 2 | 3 |
| 3 | 7 |
| 4 | 15 |
| 5 | 31 |
| 6 | |

The class predicts that it will take sixty-three moves with six disks.

Maggie explains, "You just look at the difference. It goes plus two, plus four, plus eight, plus sixteen, so the next one has to be plus thirty-two."

Manny says, "I see it differently. It has to be sixty-three because thirty-one times two plus one equals sixty-three, and that works for all of the other numbers."

Cassie suggests that the function is growing exponentially.

Jared states firmly, "This can't be exponential. The numbers are too small."

**Take Action!**

Discuss confusing mathematical terms with everyday uses.

The teacher realizes that Jared associates exponential growth only with large numbers. It makes sense given that the term is often used to express largeness in everyday language.

Developing the exponential equation and seeing the recursive function within the moves will have to wait for tomorrow. The teacher knows that Jared will note the large growth when students realize that at a rate of one second per move, it would take about a billion years to move sixty-four disks! It's important, though, that Jared get a more complete understanding of an exponential function so he knows that, for example, it can grow smaller as well as larger.

Although Jared is an immigrant, he received considerable instruction in English before he came to the United States. He is a confident student, quite willing to express a difference of opinion. Students who are confident in their thinking are often more willing to expose their misconceptions and less concerned about having a different perspective. Clearly not every learner has that level of confidence. Misconceptions involving language are sometimes hidden. Learners may pretend to understand or be able to submit work that can be deemed correct in spite of their literal interpretations and misperceptions of the related mathematical terms. Students who are shy, have less developed English-speaking abilities, or have language difficulties may be reluctant to communicate their thinking.

Some students have weaknesses in their native languages as well as in English. This lack of proficiency in their primary language makes it even more difficult for students to be successful quickly. Consider the following reflection from a sixth-grade teacher.

## Teacher Reflection

Isabella arrived midyear with limited English proficiency. If you saw her on the playground, everything looked fine, though she never spoke in the classroom. By the second week, however, she was distracting other students. She often made faces to get students to laugh or played with manipulatives noisily. In preparation for statewide testing, students were asked to complete the assessment used the previous year. Isabella seemed to be reading each item carefully and recording something for each

> *Isabella arrived midyear with limited English proficiency. If you saw her on the playground, everything looked fine, though she never spoke in the classroom.*

question. I don't like to walk around when the students are taking a prep test as I know the motion can be distracting to some of them. So it wasn't until I collected the responses and had time to look at them during my free period that I learned that Isabella had recorded *nose* for each item after the first page.

I have to admit that my first response was to wonder if she was trying to be funny. I half expected to see *eyes* or *mouth* as the next response. I decided I needed another meeting with my district's ELL specialist. When I showed her the exam, she frowned, but then quickly recognized what Isabella was trying to communicate. She explained to me that in Spanish, *no sé* means "I do not know." The fact that Isabella did not include the accent mark or write the phrase as two words suggests that she has had little formal schooling in her own language.

I now see Isabella in a different light. She had sat quietly and responded to each item. Though schooling was indicated on her transcript, it may not have been a formal school with a strong curriculum. I need to advocate for her to receive additional services.

These classroom examples emphasize the important role of language in the teaching and learning of mathematics. For some students, talking about mathematical ideas can solidify concepts and further develop confidence. Occasionally, students such as Jared have a minor difficulty or misunderstanding that can be addressed easily. For others, language can be a significant barrier—one that keeps them from grasping new ideas or from demonstrating what they know.

It is common to hear teachers' concerns about students who are struggling to learn the language necessary to be successful in mathematics. The vocabulary of our mathematics classrooms has increased dramatically in recent years. Both teachers and students are challenged to use correct terms as they communicate their understanding of concepts. One seventh-grade teacher explained, "These students have so many mathematical words to learn. When I went to school I had never even heard of a box-and-whisker plot."

Take Action!

Use word walls.

Some teachers invest a great deal of time creating word walls in their classrooms so that students have constant access to the vocabulary related to current topics. At the beginning of the school year, one group of teachers began with words already posted on the wall, and as the year went on, they added more terms. Many of these teachers, however, found that several of their students did not refer to the word walls, even though doing so would have been beneficial. They came to believe that their word walls did not work because they were a teacher initiative that did not involve the students.

The following year these same teachers had their students participate in the creation of the word walls. Students chose words they wished to define and illustrate and then posted their work beside the word strips. This level of involvement made the word walls more meaningful, and students consulted them more regularly. Students may also feel further connected to word walls if they, too, are developing their own word banks in their notebooks or with vocabulary flip books.

Sometimes it is difficult to separate language difficulties from mathematical ones. For example, Brenda was being interviewed by her teacher in the late spring.

The teacher asked her, "What is one-tenth of twenty?"

Brenda replied, "Two hundred."

The teacher asked a related question, "What is one-tenth of ten?"

In response, Brenda replied, "One hundred."

The teacher, knowing that he had fish crackers in his desk drawer, asked, "If you have ten fish in your fish tank and one out of ten of them is a goldfish, how many of them are goldfish?" As he asked her this question, he got the bag and laid out ten fish crackers on his desk.

Brenda took one fish cracker and responded, "One." When the teacher asked about one-tenth of twenty in the same manner, Brenda was able, with some assistance as she attempted to break the twenty fish crackers into two groups of ten, to correctly identify that the answer would be two. The teacher was not sure if Brenda needed the real-world model or the gestures to understand what to do or if she just didn't understand the phrase *one-tenth of.*

The teacher wondered why Brenda's first response was to multiply by ten rather than divide by ten and decided to emphasize the language by saying, "Yes, one-tenth of twenty is two."

Brenda looked up at him a bit perplexed, but then her eyes widened and she said, "Oh, when you wanted to know one-tenth, you meant smaller parts, not bigger. I get it now." The teacher knew Brenda had made an important connection.

We need to be sensitive to language issues. According to the National Clearinghouse for English Language Acquisition (2007) the school population has grown 3.66 percent since 1995, while the number of limited English proficient students has increased by 57.17 percent. Before you ask students to complete mathematical tasks, make sure that they can understand the language of the task. Consider using this checklist when preparing tasks:

| How to Support Students' Understanding of the Language of a Mathematical Task |
| --- |
| ☐ Preview vocabulary at the beginning of a lesson, using realia whenever possible. |
| ☐ Encourage students to dramatize word problems. |
| ☐ Ask students to summarize the task in their own words. |
| ☐ Have vocabulary lists available when students write about their ideas. |
| ☐ Use accurate mathematical terms, rather than simpler everyday terms that will need to be relearned later; for example, use *rhombus* rather than *diamond* (Lee and Herner-Patnode 2007). |
| ☐ Use pictures, models, and gestures to clarify ideas whenever possible. |
| ☐ Have students try out their thinking in pairs or small groups before speaking in front of the whole class. |
| ☐ Map symbolic notation carefully onto everyday situations and concrete models. |
| ☐ Speak slowly and avoid idioms and contractions. |
| ☐ Pose problems in familiar contexts that students will recognize. |

We also need to pay attention to particular terms that may be problematic. For example, many mathematical terms, such as *face*, *plot*, and *similar*, have a different meaning in everyday usage. (Please see the following page for examples of words found in the middle school curriculum that have different everyday and mathematical meanings as well as examples of mathematical words that have everyday homophones.)

*Homophones*—words that sound the same but have different spellings and meanings—can be similarly problematic. Again, teachers should give special attention to these terms (humorous examples can be helpful). One teacher tells her students about the following conversation and asks them to figure out what happened.

> *Two people leave a doctor's office when one says, "What was your weight?"*
> *The other replies, "Five minutes."*
> *"Oh," says the first. "Mine was one hundred thirty pounds."*

| Words with Different Meanings in Everyday Life Than in Math Class | | |
| --- | --- | --- |
| acute | intercept | real |
| altitude | mass | ruler |
| center | mean | reflection |
| cylinder | median | rotation |
| degree | mode | set |
| edge | net | side |
| expression | odd | similar |
| face | origin | table |
| fair | plot | turn |
| factor | point | volume |
| graduated | power | yard |
| identity | range | |

| Mathematical Words That Have Everyday Homophones | |
| --- | --- |
| cents/scents | pi/pie |
| complement/compliment | sum/some |
| fair/fare | symbol/cymbal |
| eight/ate | week/weak |
| hour/our | weight/wait |
| one/won | whole/hole |
| plane/plain | |

Some everyday words sound similar to mathematical terms, including *sense* (*cents*), *have* (*half*), *court* (*quart*), and *spear* (*sphere*). And some math terms sound alike (e.g., *hundreds* and *hundredths*, *intercept* and *intersect*). Teachers should enunciate these words carefully, record them when they first introduce the words, and listen deliberately to students' pronunciation of them.

Rubenstein (2007) reminds us to also pay attention to those words that are often learned in pairs and thus confused. Examples include *factor* and *multiple*, *perimeter* and *area*, *permutation* and *combination*, and *power* and *exponent*. One strategy she suggests is having students learn one of the words in these pairs first and then introducing the second term and concept only after the first one is familiar.

*Take Action!*

Attend to confusing pairs of words.

As with universal design, attention to language will benefit all of our students. When we listen deliberately to our students and ourselves, and attend deliberately to the language used, students are better able to access their previous learning as well as to understand the tasks we ask them to perform. As with all language skills, learning the language of mathematics is an important goal for all students and can remove barriers to learning mathematical ideas.

Before closing this section on language, we want to add an important point about English language learners. These students also bring many strengths to our classrooms and it is important not to embrace a deficit model of their backgrounds. Students who have strong backgrounds in primary romance languages, along with prior study of English, may be more aware of root words, prefixes, and suffixes than some native speakers. They can bring informative connections to the classroom, such as seeing the commonality in the words *multiplication* and *duplication*. Great familiarity with the metric system is an asset and may suggest strong mental arithmetic with powers of ten. Alternative algorithms can provide stimulation for interesting conversations. Consider the following reflection, from a sixth-grade teacher.

---

## Teacher Reflection

I taught for eight years before I had an English language learner in my classroom. The district has changed over the years, though, and now about one-third of my students are ELLs. I was quite unprepared for this phenomenon and regret many of the things I did wrong, albeit unintentionally. Each summer my school system offers professional development related to this topic, but it never seems very relevant to mathematics teachers. Then last year we finally had a math specialist consult with us for three days. I learned some of the algorithms that are more common to other countries. It was amazing. I know I've had students who used some of these before, but I didn't recognize them at the time and didn't investigate them further. Instead I taught students to compute as I did.

I've had students from Brazil who used a different division algorithm. I remember wondering why they did it

*I've had students from Brazil who used a different division algorithm. I remember wondering why they did it backward, as if our way were the only right way.*

*(Continued)*

*backward,* as if our way were the only right way. At a workshop I learned to understand this algorithm and it really isn't very different from ours; it's just recorded differently. The workshop leader pointed out the translation from the written form 342 ÷ 2 is easier with this algorithm, as the numbers are written in the same order, while our algorithm reverses them.

I really regret many of my early decisions and would never make them now. These students have so much to learn; why make them relearn skills they already have? Also, it is interesting for the other students to try to figure out why the different algorithms work. Some students even begin to use them in lieu of their own techniques.

This teacher reminds us to embrace and celebrate our differences and that there is much we can learn when we do. Dionice, from Brazil, has provided us with an example of how she was taught to divide. If you are not familiar with it, we encourage you to look at Figure 5–2 and then see if you can apply the division algorithm to a new example.

## Addressing Multiple Intelligences

Along with language, students differ greatly in the ways they prefer to explore mathematical ideas. Howard Gardner emphasized the differences among students' thinking when he developed his theory of multiple intelligences. He has now identified eight intelligences: linguistic, logical-mathematical, spatial, bodily-kinesthetic, musical, interpersonal, intrapersonal, and naturalist (Gardner 2000). When lessons and activities do not tap into different ways of knowing, barriers result. Let's consider the goal of learning about measurement through the perspective of multiple intelligences.

Figure 5–2  *Dionice learned this division algorithm when she lived in Brazil.*

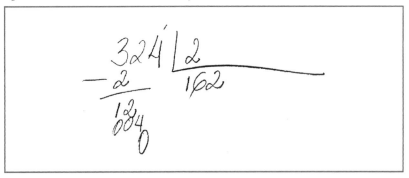

Trends in International Mathematics and Science Study (TIMMS) results indicate that students in the United States perform relatively poorly in the areas of measurement and geometry (Mullis, O'Martin, and Foy 2005). We ask middle school students to be proficient in both the metric system and the U.S. standard system of measurement, yet we attend inadequately to either system, often regulating much of the instruction to elementary or science classrooms. The result is that middle school students may

- compute inaccurately as they convert from one form of measurement to another;
- lack benchmark units and the spatial reasoning skills that, together with proportional reasoning, would allow them to estimate measures based on a visual sense of the relative sizes of various units;
- be unaware of the inverse relationship between the size of a unit and the number of units needed;
- lack familiarity with formulas for determining area and volume and for converting between units;
- choose inappropriate units; or
- be unsure of how to use tools that may be new to them, such as protractors, compasses, and angle rulers.

Middle school teachers are uncertain sometimes about what is the appropriate emphasis to place on conceptual understanding versus memorization of measurement skills. Similarly, teachers may struggle with the balance between the time they should give to abstract learning and the time they should give to hands-on measuring. Certainly there are aspects of our measurement system that need to be memorized, for example, the number of pints in a quart or the formula for determining the circumference of a circle. Yet too many classrooms focus solely on traditional methods that we know do not best suit all learners. (Please see the following page for a summary of possibilities for addressing students' multiple intelligences while they investigate measurement.)

Consider this sixth-grade classroom, where students are working with various forms of measurement: There are a number of different small groups working throughout the classroom, most of which have chosen their own activities to work on from a list of possibilities. One group is sitting at a table with various weights of measure, a triple-beam balance, items to weigh, and drawing materials. They estimate the weight of objects first and then measure to check. After their hands-on experiences they complete

**Lesson Idea!**

Strand: Measurement

Focus: Convert units of measure.

Context: Multiple intelligences activities

## Addressing the Eight Multiple Intelligences While Investigating Measurement

### Linguistic

- Read about Eratosthenes and how he determined the circumference of the earth.
- Hold a debate about whether the metric system should be the only system used in the United States.
- Read the poem "One Inch Tall," by Shel Silverstein (1974), and write one called "One Mile Tall."

### Logical-Mathematical

- Make a spreadsheet using formulas to convert one form of measurement to another.
- Solve logic problems that give measurement clues to identify objects.
- Make generalizations about which units of measurement should be used when.

### Spatial

- Design a poster to visually display various forms of measurement.
- Develop graphic organizers to remember measurement conversions.

### Bodily-Kinesthetic

- Conduct a kitchen scavenger hunt at home, looking for various measures.
- Design and build a birdhouse.
- Take a measurement trip to the outdoor basketball court.

### Musical

- Write song lyrics to practice area formulas.
- Choreograph dance moves (for a favorite song) that demonstrate measuring volume.

### Interpersonal

- Participate in a Silly Measurement Olympics Day.
- Conduct an experiment with a partner that involves measuring weight in grams.
- Brainstorm acts for a humorous one-act play that dramatizes measurement errors.

### Intrapersonal

- Conduct a webquest about measurement.
- Set personal goals for learning one new unit of measurement each day.

### Naturalist

- Find examples in nature that are best measured with various units.
- Categorize the use of measurement in various occupations.

an estimation sheet. The first two questions on the sheet are shown below:

*Best Measure*

1. *The weight of a feather is best measured with . . .*
   *pounds     ounces     grams     milligrams*

2. *The weight of bricks that will be used to make a patio is best measured with . . .*
   *pounds     tons     ounces     grams*

The last item on the sheet asks students to write a question in which they choose their own item to measure and identify an appropriate unit of measurement. As Peter has an Individualized Education Program (IEP) that suggests he have many experiences with manipulatives, he has already explored this activity this week. The teacher realizes that he has always chosen to write about pounds. She asks Peter to consider writing a question that involves ounces, and Peter is ready for the challenge. There is a new turtle in the science classroom that Peter will measure.

Mark and Oscar, along with some other teams, are writing a song about measuring. They are both very interested in rap music and are very excited to share their most recent creation. The lyrics they've written are

*My doctor says I'm 60 inches tall,*
*but how many feet is that all?*
*Well, my teacher says 12 inches in a foot*
*so take 60, divide by 12 and my work is done.*
*Guess I'm five feet tall, that was fun!*
*Now I want to know how much I weigh.*
*But my scale only measures ounces,*
*so much math in one day!*
*1600 oz. is my weight on the dot*
*but how many in a pound has got me caught!*
*My teacher says 16 so divide by that, and my weight*
*is 100 pounds—flat!*

The students are engaged in the lyrics as well as the beat of the rap. After the singing duo complete their composition, the teacher asks them to incorporate other forms of measurement to demonstrate their growing knowledge of units of measure for weight. As they excitedly consider new lyrics, the teacher moves to check on another group's progress.

Lindsey and Zari are among a group writing newsletter articles about measurement facts. This week they are the chief contributors to the math column of the school newspaper. They have chosen to write an advice column about learning various forms of measurement. One of their contributions is

*Q: I have been trying to measure the distance that I can throw a baseball, but every time I try to measure with centimeters, it gets too complicated. Can you help me to find another way?*

*A: We would suggest that you try using a meterstick. When you are measuring a longer distance, it is better to use a longer unit. By the way, 1 m is the same as 100 cm. If you can really throw a baseball very far, you might also consider using a really long tape measure, which often measures in centimeters and meters for very long distances.*

Allison and Brett are among the students who are creating activities for their school's family math night, to be held at a local grocery store. They are working on writing clues for a scavenger hunt that involves finding things that are measured in various units. Brett is certain that milk comes only in containers measured in "whole amounts" and Allison teases him that he must be thinking of buying whole milk. She reminds him that, although there is not a specific form of measurement called a half gallon, that it is the way that her family frequently buys its milk. She says, "My mother always says, 'Go over to the milk section and get a half gallon of milk.'"

Brett says, "When I go to the supermarket next, I'm going to check for sure."

Nick, Connor, and Ryan have always enjoyed playing the board games that the teacher puts out for use at the end of their double-period day. Recognizing their interest, the teacher has asked them to use an existing game board and—working together—make up their own rules for a game that will provide practice with formulas for area. They have chosen to include formulas for the area of a triangle, a square, a rectangle, a circle, and a trapezoid. They have written each term of the formulas on a separate card. As players move around the game board, they collect cards. The first person to find all of the terms of a particular formula wins that set. As they are creating the cards, Ryan remarks, "There are a lot of formulas that use base and height. I get why, though. It's because area is about two dimensions and for most figures that's the base and the height." (See Figure 5–3.)

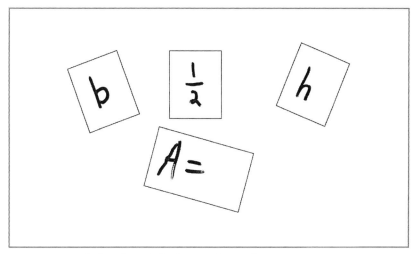

Figure 5–3    *Sample formula cards for the area of a triangle.*

Alexis and Hallie are also interested in using games as a way to practice their measurement facts. The teacher met with them the day before to prepare a list of several units of linear measurement that they need to master. She has asked them to write game cards for a game called *I Have, Who Has?* As they prepare the cards, they realize that they must be accurate with their computation as they move from one unit of measurement to another. Hallie remarks, "I think that we'd better double-check our computation before we try to play this game with the whole class." (See Figure 5–4.)

Figure 5–4    *Sample cards from the game* I Have, Who Has?

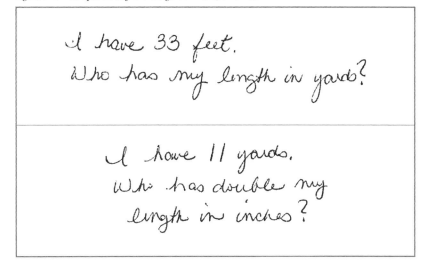

Another group is exploring how to more accurately measure lengths. The teacher has realized that Jennie, Robert, and Tom have shown some recent difficulty with measuring using an inch ruler.

Robert is trying to measure the length of a pencil to the nearest $\frac{1}{8}$ inch when he shares with the teacher, "I don't really know where the eights are on this ruler."

Jennie declares, "I know that there are halves and quarters, so I usually just round it to one of those. I don't think that you should really have to go any further than that." The teacher asks the group to consider reasons why they might need to measure to the nearest $\frac{1}{8}$ or $\frac{1}{16}$ inch, emphasizing, for Robert's benefit, the term *eighths* instead of *eights*.

Madigan and Liza are measuring across and around a variety of circular lids. They are inputting these points into a graphing calculator. After directing the calculator to create a scatterplot, Madigan notes, "Wow, these points are almost in a line. If we moved this one a bit higher, this one a bit to the left, and this one a little to the right, they'd be just right."

Liza replies, "Maybe they are in a line, but we just can't measure perfectly." The teacher decides this is just the right time to ask them to think about the ratios of the points.

Some of these students, such as those playing the board game, are at a similar level of learning, but some others, such as the students measuring weight, are not. The teacher likes to see students working in both configurations. She has learned that for game playing, teams need to have an even chance of winning and thus be at a similar level. However, in other activities, variety in abilities can lead to new possibilities. What's most important is that the students feel as if they are making progress and are enjoying gaining factual knowledge.

## Engaging Multiple Senses

Teachers often consider both Multiple Intelligences and multiple senses, when they think about different ways that students learn. When we look at learning through the lens of Multiple Intelligences, we focus on different types of intelligence and how they might be tapped in the classroom. When we think about multiple senses, we focus on how the learners' senses are involved in the learning process. Many, but not all, of us have a strong preference for one modality over others. For example, if you were about to learn a word that you have never seen or heard before, would you rather first see it or hear it? For some people it doesn't matter, others have a slight preference, and for some people, it matters greatly. As we learn from the following teacher reflection, when we are trying to remember something, it is helpful to have several senses engaged.

## Teacher Reflection

Last summer I read *Differentiation Through Learning Styles and Memory*, by Marilee Sprenger (2003), for a course I was taking. It really made me think about memory. One part of the book that struck me addressed the common worry, "How can we be sure we have turned off everything when leaving the house?" I can't remember if the example referred to an iron or a stove, but I remember the suggestion was to engage as many senses as possible—seeing, hearing, smelling, tasting, touching—when turning things off. For example, if I want to remember that I turned off the iron, I should focus on seeing the dial move and my fingers touching it—and say the action out loud (thus committing the task to my auditory memory). Just saying something like, "I am turning the iron off now," can really make a difference! I began to think more about how I could improve my ability to remember things. I started looking at the keypad when I wanted to memorize a telephone number. Making a visual pattern of the numbers was much easier for me than just remembering what I heard the information operator say or what I saw in a phone book.

*The students have more of a choice in how they practice and I try to make sure that over time, visual, auditory, and sensory memories are involved.*

Next I began to think about my students and how challenging it is for some of them to learn the factual equivalencies among measures. I wondered if I was including enough alternative ways for them to practice their memory skills. This year I have made practice time more varied. The students have more of a choice in how they practice and I try to make sure that over time, visual, auditory, and sensory memories are involved.

It seems to be helping. Just yesterday Billy asked me if we could add another practice time to our week!

When we are strategic and mindful of the purpose of the activities with which we ask our students to engage, we can make powerful instructional choices. When we think about both Multiple Intelligences and multiple senses in our planning, we greatly increase the likelihood of reaching more learners. When students have some control over their own learning, students are often more powerful learners. Let's think about these ideas and how they might relate to the learning of basic facts.

As many teachers know, not all students master their basic facts by the end of elementary school, and in middle school, there is even more of a stigma attached to not knowing these facts. Such a deficit is a barrier to many aspects of the middle school curriculum, such as multiplication and division of decimals, finding least common denominators and greatest common factors, computing surface area and volume, identifying prime numbers, and factoring quadratic equations. At this level students no longer use drawings or counters as freely as younger children do, and thus may not be taking advantage of their spatial intelligence or their preference for visual and kinesthetic learning. Some teachers worry about how to attend to these students' academic needs without causing them to get further behind in other areas or without embarrassing them.

Most difficult are students who have labeled themselves as those who just can't learn the basic facts. While we believe that there is a very small number of students for whom this may be true, we think this number is much fewer than those that claim the affliction. We also think that middle school may provide an opportunity to address this concern successfully. At this age students may be more able to follow sequential fact strategies, and thus take advantage of a logical-mathematical intelligence, than they were able to when such strategies were first introduced.

One classroom tutor finds it helpful to have students go through the facts and discover exactly which ones are not known. Students are often surprised by how many facts they actually are able to remember. When students realize there may be only twenty facts to learn, they often develop a more hopeful attitude. Then they can play hands-on or online games that address these specific facts and can chart their progress. Under these circumstances, students are often more open to relying on multiple senses to help them without worrying whether their approach is one that younger students might use.

## Reducing Anxiety

Anxiety can also be a barrier both to learning and to demonstrating what has been learned. Mathematics anxiety has received much attention in recent years. Though early studies focused on adults, it is now recognized that mathematics anxiety may begin early and is difficult to change once it is established. Earlier anxiety may intensify at the middle level as the mathematics becomes more complex and concern for peer acceptance increases. This anxiety is a major contributor to people's decisions to limit the number of mathematics courses they take later in life. Many people choose to take only required mathematics courses, which can greatly limit career options. Therefore, it's essential that we begin to address this learning anxiety in the elementary years.

While mathematics anxiety is not completely understood, experts recognize it as a specific anxiety, one that generalized anxiety alone cannot explain. Those afflicted with mathematics anxiety experience a severe dread of the subject and tension that interferes greatly with their ability to work with numbers or to perform mathematical tasks in front of others. Such anxiety can interfere with working memory to the point where new information cannot be stored or cannot be retrieved during a test.

One eighth-grade student explained, "I can't sleep well before a math test. I often wake up hot and sweaty from nightmares several times during the night. I always study hard, but as soon as I see the exam, my mind just seems to go blank."

**Take Action!**

Involve family members.

Family attitudes, social factors, teacher judgments, and negative classroom experiences can all contribute to mathematics anxiety. Ideally, parents, teachers, and other school personnel work together to prevent its occurrence in the first place. For example, family math nights help many parents recognize that learning and doing mathematics can be enjoyable. The evenings can also be structured so that those parents who have their own mathematics anxiety are comfortable identifying themselves. Follow-up conversations can help parents understand the importance of not modeling or perpetuating negative attitudes for their children.

Schools should be sure to project a positive attitude about mathematics. Most schools have ample displays of students' writing and artwork. To the extent that fire laws allow it, halls are often lined with posters related to books. Less often, we are greeted with a colorful and dynamic display related to mathematics upon entering a school building. Even a colorful bulletin board showcasing graphs in the news can help connect mathematics to the real world and make it more meaningful.

So what about our classrooms? It is clear that difficulty learning mathematics and low achievement in mathematics contribute to anxiety. Teaching mathematics in a rote, context-free manner makes it more difficult to learn and may result in more students suffering from anxiety. Providing rich contexts allows more students to relate to the subject and often suggests entry points to the problems being explored. Small-group work may be less threatening than whole-class discussions, and building concepts, rather than learning rote rules that can be forgotten easily, empowers students' faith in their ability to do mathematics.

There are some caveats, however, to the approach of providing rich contexts. Overemphasizing oral explanations and justifications can increase anxiety. Some students develop a great fear of doing mathematics in front of others, just as having the teacher walk by may cause some students to freeze.

One sixth-grade student said, "I have to ask my teachers not to call on me unless I raise my hand. I don't do so very often, but once in a while I feel brave or sure enough to talk in front of others about math. If I'm just called on, I immediately feel nauseous, which makes me even more anxious! If a teacher doesn't make this deal with me, I can't do a thing in class except worry about whether I'm going to be called up to the board."

Students who feel this way may benefit from writing and rehearsing explanations first and then reading them to the class. Also, some students may perform better when creating explanations with a peer who will report to the group. (Please see the following page for some other ways to prevent or reduce mathematics anxiety.)

It is easier to prevent mathematics anxiety than it is to reduce it. If students suffer from this affliction or appear to be developing attitudes and behaviors rooted in being anxious while learning mathematics, talk with their parents and the school's guidance counselor. The Mathematics Anxiety Scale (Chiu and Henry 1990) can be administered to children in grades 4 through 8. In most cases classroom interventions are not sufficient. Anxiety management training usually also involves breathing exercises, visualization techniques, "I can do it" mantras, and desensitization. In collaboration with parents and other professionals, teachers can help prevent or lessen any future concern in this area.

## Overcoming Learning Challenges

The need for outside help is not limited to anxiety. Barriers, both visible and invisible, are very real for many students. The list of diagnosable learning disabilities seems to be growing by leaps and bounds as we discover more about how our brains function and what happens if an area is underdeveloped or functioning in a unique way. The level of engagement, pace of learning, and expectations for individual student responsibility in our middle school classrooms are overwhelming. At this level, parents and teachers become less likely to believe that a student's problem is just devel-

**Take Action!**

Recognize student fears.

## Ways to Reduce Mathematics Anxiety

- Promote self-talk in which students verbalize what they are doing with statements such as "First I am going to . . ." in order to focus their attention and help them believe that they do know what to do. This is sometimes called *anchoring*.

- Build confidence by helping students recognize what they *can* do. Use questions such as "What do you know about this?" Keep samples of their work so that they can see their improvement over time.

- Keep number lines and calculators available so that students can use these devices to ensure accuracy.

- Use multiple sources of assessment and de-emphasize high-stakes testing. Understandably, teachers are under much pressure from all of the attention given to mandated tests. It is important not to share this pressure with the students. Test anxiety correlates highly to mathematics anxiety and vice versa.

- Have students keep a journal where they can record their feelings about mathematics, responding to prompts such as *When we start a new topic in math I feel . . .* , *When I am asked to explain my thinking in math I feel . . .* , and *When I am asked to come to the board in math class I feel. . . .* Teachers and students must be aware of these feelings to help students reduce them.

- Limit activities that are timed. Time is one more pressure that can greatly add to anxiety.

- Choose partners carefully. Some students may be most comfortable in a group that works at a slower pace. Others may need to work with the same partner throughout a unit.

- Let students set personal goals. When students set their own objectives, it gives them a greater sense of control, which in turn lessens anxiety.

- Integrate mathematics with other subject areas. Some students feel more comfortable performing mathematical tasks when the tasks are related to an area of strength or interest. A student interested in ancient Mediterranean civilizations may enjoy constructing a time line of that period, while a student whose favorite subject is science may be interested in collecting and analyzing data related to an experiment. Students also tend to develop more positive attitudes toward mathematics when they perceive it as connected to their world.

opmental and will improve over time. There is also significant pressure to "fix" it now so that the student can experience success in a college-preparatory curriculum.

While this is not a book about specific learning disabilities, we would be remiss not to take to heart the physical, emotional, and intellectual challenges of many students as they try to navigate the precarious terrain of mathematics. As we strive to get to know all of our students, we can also recognize that no one mathematics teacher can fully differentiate the curriculum for each and every student, every day. We need to be able to use all of the resources available to craft programs and meaningful experiences for each student. Strategizing with colleagues and working collaboratively with assistants, tutors, remedial staff, and special educators are essential. In many ways, each educator can have a critical piece of the puzzle and together, they can see the whole child more clearly. (See Chapter 8 for more on working with colleagues to manage differentiated instruction.)

Another challenge in the middle school mathematics classroom is that those trained to specialize in mathematics often lack study in special education. A website that posts several resources for middle school educators is www2.edc.org/accessmath/. The site is the result of a project of the Education Development Center in Newton, Massachusetts, Addressing Accessibility in Mathematics, that was funded by the National Science Foundation. We encourage you to take advantage of what the researchers have made available. We also recommend the book *Teaching Mathematics to Middle School Students with Learning Difficulties (What Works for Special Needs Learners)*, edited by Marjorie Montague and Asha Jitendra (2006). This book discusses a variety of issues and suggestions for working with struggling learners.

As students advance in the grades, parents who are able to do so sometimes seek tutors for their children. Tutors get to know students in a different way and see them work in a different environment. Ideally, tutors are in communication with classroom teachers;

*Tutor Reflection*

For twenty-two years, I have been working privately with math students in grades 5–12. Over the years I have learned a lot about how children learn and what prevents them from learning. Most of my relationships with my students begin with a phone call from panicked parents requesting help for their children. Typically, parents just received a report card or went to a conference and realized that the child is struggling in mathematics. Usually, middle school students recognize that they need the help and don't mind spending the time to get their questions answered. But, it is very important that they feel comfortable with me. So my work begins with building trust and helping the student to believe that I can help. The goals for tutoring are to build confidence, to help the student to learn the necessary math at grade level, and to sustain the learning beyond the tutoring session.

One student I tutored was in the seventh grade when her mother called me. She described her daughter, Cecilia, as a child who was very good at other subjects but not doing well in math. The mother and father tried to help her but every time they sat down with Cecilia, she complained that they weren't doing the math the way they did it in class. Both parents and student were getting frustrated. Cecilia and I spent our first sessions working through her homework questions, making sure that she could explain the answers in class in case the teacher called on her. In this way, Cecilia felt as though the tutoring sessions were worthwhile— she got done what she needed to accomplish. I learned a lot about how Cecilia learned and what she understood about the material that she was learning in class. In doing so, I gained insight into what might be causing her difficulty.

*At first Cecilia tried to keep it a secret that she really didn't know all of her math facts. Though she was too embarrassed to tell me this, every time she had to find 7 × 9 or 6 × 8 to continue a problem, I saw her counting with her fingers beneath the table.*

It turned out that there were several issues that contributed to Cecilia's frustrations. Working one-on-one with her, it became clear that she understood the problem much better if we worked on making a diagram or used some other sort of graphic organizer to better understand the problem. Once Cecilia learned how to make her own visual representations of problems, she felt much more confident and her task commitment increased.

At first Cecilia tried to keep it a secret that she really didn't know all of her math facts. Though she was too embarrassed to tell me this, every time she had to find 7 × 9 or 6 × 8 to continue a problem, I saw her counting with her fingers beneath the table. When we talked openly about this behavior, she seemed relieved. Eventually we talked with her parents about allowing her to spend time on the computer playing facts games. We also talked with her teacher about how successful she was when she made visual representations of problems so that her teacher would support this experience in the classroom.

Not all students recognize their weaknesses the way Cecilia did. When I met Mark, an eighth grader, he was in an honors algebra class

(*Continued*)

and really struggling after the third chapter of the textbook. He thought that he understood the material in class, did OK on his homework, and was confused as to why he kept "bombing the tests." His parents asked me to work with him on test-taking strategies. Mark told me that he seemed to do fine with the homework problems but thought that the problems on the test were a lot more difficult. We spent the first few sessions looking over his past homework assignments. When I examined these assignments, I noticed that Mark was skipping some of the harder problems or was getting them incorrect and not correcting his work. He was pretty good at hiding it because he would often write *IDK* for "I don't know," and the teacher's quick glances at his homework didn't always reveal empty spaces. We discussed that because he was in an honors algebra class, he was responsible for his own homework and for making sure he made the corrections. We also discussed that these were likely the types of problems that were on the tests, and that correcting mistakes on homework would help him to do better on his tests. Mark was willing to take responsibility for talking with his teacher. He asked his teacher for more practice problems on the challenging concepts that they were studying. Doing these additional problems before he took the tests made him feel more confident; it wasn't too long before his test grades improved. I also talked with his teacher, who agreed to examine Mark's assignments more closely until he was back on track.

insights gained from the tutors' sessions can inform classroom practice. Consider the following experienced tutor's reflection.

In both examples, the tutor was able to isolate difficulties and solutions and then gain the agreement of the students' teachers to give support accordingly. It doesn't always go so smoothly. Some students present more complex learning profiles and, of course, many students don't have access to private tutoring. We need to be sure we are utilizing all school resources available to us.

In many schools child study teams (CSTs) are formed as a venue for teachers to voice concerns about the lack of progress a student is making. Teachers are encouraged to share trepidations, raise questions, review student work, and tell anecdotes about what is happening in class. In preparation, teachers often complete a form about the student's strengths or weaknesses and answer a few guiding questions. Teachers may also wish to supply copies of current student work. Most teachers report a sense of relief following such meetings.

One teacher expressed, "I was worried that I was inadequate. My colleagues helped me to realize that I was making some good decisions. Just knowing that they were there to support me made me feel less isolated. I know I will bring more energy to my class now and feel more confident in the choices I make about this student."

This teacher also disclosed how much it meant to her that following the meeting, many of her colleagues checked with her to see how things were working. Their interest added to the teacher's belief that she could be successful. A special education teacher came to observe the class along with a math coach. Together, these three professionals developed an action plan and agreed to meet three weeks later.

More schools are looking at ways to increase instructional support in mathematics. System specialists now work closely with teachers and students on assessment, curriculum design, implementation, and direct teaching. Some school systems are hiring assistants and tutors who focus on mathematics, and special education staff, who often have stronger backgrounds in literacy learning, are beginning to augment their skills. Many schools, however, still find that budget limitations keep staff members from participating in professional development opportunities in mathematics or from receiving curriculum materials.

To remove barriers as successfully as possible, schools *must* provide these opportunities and materials to *all* professional staff and be committed to success in mathematics for all. Teachers must nurture open channels of communication with parents, specialists, assistants, tutors, and their students. They need to be willing to take risks, ask questions, examine their beliefs and behaviors, and make accommodations so that everyone achieves success.

## Connecting the Chapter to Your Practice

1. What classical mathematical puzzles or games do you integrate into your instruction?

2. How have language barriers affected your teaching?

3. How would you describe your own learning in terms of Multiple Intelligences and preferred senses?

# Chapter 6

# Scaffolding Learning

*Scaffolds*, a term related to architecture and construction, are temporary structures that remain in place as long as they are needed. Scaffolds are not permanent. Workers use scaffolds to get to parts of buildings that would otherwise be inaccessible. Another example of a temporary structure is training wheels. Training wheels are used when a child is first learning how to ride a two-wheel bike. These extra wheels allow children to ride successfully—something that would be impossible without the added support for balance. These wheels are removed when children establish their own sense of balance and are ready to ride without them. Similarly, we use scaffolds—temporary structures—to support students' learning.

Too often in the past our mathematics instruction has focused exclusively on students working independently, without support. Students spent most of the time working silently at desks. Teachers gave little or no assistance. At the end of a week or unit, each child took a test to determine what she learned. Fortunately, learning mathematics is no longer viewed as something that is done in isolation. Whole-class discussions and small-group work provide opportunities to share ideas and talk about what students have learned. These groups in and of themselves are a form of scaffolding. Many learners can do more when the classroom environment is communal. Help from a peer and collaboration with others are integral parts of the learning process.

With isolation no longer the norm, we can ask ourselves, "What can students do with support that they are not currently able to do on their own?" Another way to ask this question is, "What scaffolds can we put in place to allow students to be successful learners of mathematics?" Teaching with an emphasis on scaffolding presents a more integrated vision of teaching and learning. Teaching and learning are no longer separate, static activities, but interwoven events. The teacher develops a coaching style aimed at helping all students reach their potential. Scaffolding allows students to accomplish tasks that they would be unable to complete alone. Teaching, the act of supporting learning, is then viewed in a way more synonymous with how Vygotsky (1978) described the zone of proximal development. Effective scaffolds include asking questions, focusing on strategies, having students collaborate, making connections, teaching students to self-regulate, and having students use graphic organizers.

## Asking Questions

One of the ways that teachers support learning in the classroom is by asking questions. It is important that our questions require students to go beyond their current comfort level of understanding. Frequently, teachers pose simple questions at a level of thinking that requires only recall of information, for example, "What do we call a figure that has eight sides?" By analyzing the questions we ask, we can make sure that we are inviting students to engage in more complex and deeper levels of thinking.

The work of Benjamin Bloom is closely associated with cognition. He first published his taxonomies in the 1950s. His cognitive taxonomy describes six levels of cognition in ascending order of complexity: knowledge, comprehension, application, analysis, synthesis, and evaluation (Bloom 1984). A group led by one of Bloom's students, Lorin Anderson, updated Bloom's work (Anderson and Krathwohl 2001). The authors made four changes to the original taxonomy. They:

- changed the names of the categories from nouns to verbs;
- renamed three of the categories;
- reversed the order of two categories; and
- made the taxonomy two-dimensional.

The authors used verbs as they believed that this form of speech more accurately reflects the active nature of learning. They renamed Bloom's first category, knowledge, to *remember* because they thought the term better describes a form of thinking. Comprehension is now identified as *understand* and synthesis as *create*. They reversed the order of two of the categories because they believed that creative thinking is a more complex form of thinking than evaluating. The six categories of the revised taxonomy are listed along with associated tasks in the following chart:

| Revised Bloom's Taxonomy and Sample Activities | |
|---|---|
| **Cognitive Level** | **Sample Activities** |
| Remember | identifying, telling, listing, naming, and reciting |
| Understand | explaining, summarizing, paraphrasing, retelling, and showing |
| Apply | demonstrating, illustrating, solving, dramatizing, adapting, and incorporating |
| Analyze | comparing, categorizing, and deducing |
| Evaluate | judging, predicting, assessing, and estimating |
| Create | generalizing, inventing, formulating, transforming, and producing |

Perhaps the greatest change in Bloom's taxonomy is the addition of the knowledge dimension, making it two-dimensional. The knowledge dimension identifies four types of knowledge: factual, conceptual, procedural, and metacognitive. The six levels of cognition intersect with the four types of knowledge as summarized in the following table:

**Revised Bloom's Taxonomy**

**Cognitive Dimension**

| Knowledge Dimension | | Remember | Understand | Apply | Analyze | Evaluate | Create |
|---|---|---|---|---|---|---|---|
| | Factual | | | | | | |
| | Conceptual | | | | | | |
| | Procedural | | | | | | |
| | Metacognitive | | | | | | |

Since its inception, some people have viewed Bloom's taxonomy as linear and assumed that one can move to the next level only after mastering the current level. Other educators saw this view as problematic and believed students were being held back from potential learning opportunities because of it. No doubt everyone can think of students who naturally engaged in analytical thinking even though they found it difficult to recall basic factual knowledge. These students, though they could master advanced work, likely did not perform well on certain types of tests. Seeing Bloom's taxonomy as more fluid can help us better challenge and serve such students.

One way to use a cognitive taxonomy is to categorize the questions we ask or tasks we provide to make sure that students are exposed to all levels. For practice, try categorizing the level of each of the following questions or tasks. The generally agreed-on levels are identified at the end of this chapter. Note that more than six examples are listed and thus some will be labeled with the same levels. This repetition ensures that you have to think about the items carefully, not just label them using a simple process of elimination.

---

### Question Categorization Task for Teachers

Categorize each question below in one of the six cognitive dimensions (remember, understand, apply, analyze, evaluate, create).

1. How else could you explain what Chad was saying?

2. Which estimation of the dog's weight do you think is best? Why?

3. Invent a new way to multiply these expressions.

4. What is the name of this part of the fraction?

5. Which strategy do you think is best? Why?

6. How does Sally's method compare with Janet's?

7. How many of these numbers have a six in the tenths place?

8. What number do you think will be next in the pattern?

9. What is a story you could dramatize for seven and two-tenths divided by six-tenths?

10. Tell how prisms and cylinders are the same.

Although Bloom's taxonomy encompasses six levels of cognition, the levels are not necessarily discrete. For example, *evaluating* a pattern to predict what comes next requires that you first *analyze* the elements in the pattern that have been provided. Similarly, to model 7.8 × 3.4 (*apply*), one must first *remember* factual knowledge and *comprehend* multiplication of decimals, both conceptually and procedurally. Because of this overlap, it is sometimes difficult to distinguish one level from another. It is important to remember that the goal of the model is to help us ensure that all students are engaged in complex levels of thinking; we shouldn't get bogged down in matching tasks to each of the twenty-four cells on page 152.

Scaffolding is one way to help students reach more sophisticated levels of cognition. It does *not* require us to start with a simple query and build up to more complex questions, as illustrated in the following sequence of questions:

- What is the name of this shape? (cylinder)
- How would you describe a cylinder?
- What is the name of this collection of shapes? (prism)
- How would you describe a prism?
- How is the cylinder similar to the prisms?
- How is the cylinder different from the prisms?

A more challenging approach would be to simply ask, "How are cylinders and prisms alike or different?" Beginning with this question requires the students to do more of the work. They may want to draw the figures or think about how they look. Sometimes we ask more demanding questions and then backpedal when students do not seem ready for the challenge. But be careful—too often teachers backpedal after only two or three seconds, without giving time for students to collect their thoughts. Waiting longer can yield surprising results. To scaffold this task, instead of lowering its level, have geometric materials available in the classroom or ask students to first discuss their ideas with a partner.

Scaffolds are appropriate for our more ready students as well. If a task is really a challenge for them, they, too, need some form of support. As we see in the following reflection, until we push our more advanced students, we may not recognize their need for assistance.

I used to think my top students could just work independently no matter the task at hand. When I started to differentiate more and give them more difficult assignments, I found that they also needed my attention. It made me wonder whether I had ever been truly pushing their thinking or asking them to be in the domain of uncertainty that is often part of learning. I know that the students in my class who struggle may feel vulnerable as learners but I never challenged my top students until they too reached such points of vulnerability. I now think I have viewed feeling vulnerable as weak or bad as opposed to a temporary place of discomfort that can truly help learners move on to new ideas, information, and understanding.

*I now think I have viewed feeling vulnerable as weak or bad as opposed to a temporary place of discomfort.*

## Focusing on Strategies

Today's instruction in analyzing literature places an emphasis on strategies. This instructional focus asks students to preview, visualize, infer, make connections, predict, summarize, and draw conclusions as they read. They learn to identify character traits and think about character motivation; to describe the author's persona and use of figurative language; and to map cause and effect within the plot of the story. These good reader strategies are explicit. Teachers talk about the strategies during instruction and model them. Reminding readers of these strategies is a way to scaffold instruction. We need a similar cadre of explicit strategies for use when working with new mathematical content and tasks.

George Polya, in his seminal work *How to Solve It* (1945), suggests a four-step model of problem solving:

George Polya's Four-step Model of Problem Solving

1. Understand the problem.
2. Devise a plan.
3. Carry out the plan.
4. Look back.

These four steps are posted in many middle school classrooms and included in curricular materials. Unfortunately, it is less common to see significant time devoted to instruction related to each of these steps. As a result, the full power of the model is not developed. For example, *look back* is often translated to *check your work*, yet this is only one aspect of the fourth step in the problem-solving process. A series of questions can help students identify other actions that can occur as part of the looking back stage:

Questions for the Looking Back Stage of the Problem-Solving Process

- Is there another way you could solve this problem?
- How would you describe your thinking so that a peer could follow your problem-solving process?
- Is there another problem you can now solve because you have completed this task?
- How is this problem the same or different from other problems you have solved?
- What new problem can you create that could be solved in this same manner?

## Teacher Reflection

I remember that when I first started teaching we used to spend a lot more time teaching problem-solving strategies to our students. I had posters around the room outlining different strategies. I think there used to be ten that we thought were important for our students to learn. We would teach problem solving once a week by having students do Problems of the Day or a Problem of the Week. These problems were either required or allowed students to get extra credit (if they solved a particularly challenging problem). My students enjoyed learning the strategies and trying them out.

I can't imagine how I could spend a day per week in this way now. The curriculum is so full and we are expected to follow it carefully. My department head doesn't encourage us to bring other materials and problems to our classrooms; in fact, she seems much more concerned that such behavior might derail our students from their program of study. I like the program my school uses. There is much more real-world problem solving in it than in the program I first used, so I guess I don't have to supplement too much. But, I'm not sure my current students could name or use as many solution strategies as my earlier students. The other day we were solving a problem; the use of a diagram would have been helpful, but most of my students were trying to solve the problem in their heads. Maybe, if I had been teaching the problem-solving strategies the way that I used to, they would have come up on their own with the idea of drawing a picture of the problem. In this class I had to suggest that they consider making a picture.

One of my favorite teaching strategies used to be making an organized list. We used to do problems where we would play a game or do an experiment and help students determine how to make a list of the data that they found. It was a challenge for some of my students to figure out how to make a list, to figure out what was important to include and how to organize it. Today we are teaching more algebra concepts than we ever have before; my students would definitely benefit from being taught when it is important to make a list as well as how to make one.

As a result, I have made one change this year that I especially like. Once a month we have a challenge day. Each group of students submits a problem and we place them in a hat. I start the day by drawing one problem randomly from the hat and try to solve it. I think it's important for my students to watch what I do when I don't know a solution immediately. They see me try different approaches and hear me describe my thinking as I do so. Hopefully, this direct modeling of the problem-solving process makes it more explicit. It's great when I get stuck and one of them suggests something that I should try. I would have been much too frightened to do this when I first started teaching, but I've learned a lot about mathematics and about teaching since those early days. It is my hope that, when we are working on problems that my students encounter in their math curriculum, they will be able to recognize when it is important to use different strategies. "Let's use the working backward strategy" would be music to my ears!

> *I think it's important for my students to watch what I do when I don't know a solution immediately . . . It's great when I get stuck and one of them suggests something that I should try.*

## Student Collaboration

When we view every member of the classroom as a learner *and* a teacher, there are many more people in the room who can help others learn. Many teachers recognize the powerful possibilities that can arise when peers take on the teacher role. To help students engage in such behavior, teachers strategically structure situations that support peer teaching and learning.

When we engage in think-pair-share debriefings, we are using peer partnerships to scaffold learning. The thinking time may just be a few moments of silence or we might encourage students to make a drawing, build a model, or jot down some notes before talking with their partners. Talking in pairs can help students clarify their thinking or gain additional ideas. Sharing can then happen between two sets of pairs or among the whole group.

**Take Action!**

Use think-pair-share strategies.

Sometimes simply saying, "Turn to your neighbor and whisper your prediction," is enough to form partnerships. Direct modeling of how to work in pairs helps more efficacious peer partnerships develop. Ideally, partners develop a sense of trust, a sense of responsibility to help one another, and a commitment to doing their best individual work. Partners also need practice in learning to strike a balance—that is, to be as helpful as possible without becoming overzealous and doing all the work.

Sometimes, when more independent work is preferred, teachers suggest that math partners sit across from one another rather than in the adjacent position usually preferred for reading partners. Materials can be placed between the students. The amount of shared text is much less than when reading a story, and placing written directions between the partners is adequate. Depending on seating flexibility, you may want students to read tasks side by side first and then assume their working positions across from each other.

Teachers use a variety of strategies to foster peer collaboration. In some cases, when students are solving more than one problem, teachers give them one pencil to share so that they take turns being the recorder. Pairs can also alternate recording the work (list, drawing, or computation) and the explanation. Some teachers prefer students to do the work and write their explanations separately but then exchange their products for feedback, the same way as they trade essays they have written. Early in the year, teachers can help students practice how to be helpful to their partners by asking such questions as "If your partner couldn't remember how to find the slope of the line, what hint could you give to help?" Over time you can post a list of partner behaviors on a chart, as in this example:

## How to Be a Successful Partner

- Ask questions.
- Don't tell answers.
- Give hints.
- Respect each other.
- Listen attentively.
- Take individual responsibility.

**Computer Idea!**

**Strand:** Geometry

**Focus:** Classify angles.

**Context:** Using the computer applet Angles

Consider the following partner work story. A school is integrating the computer applet from the Shodor Interactivate website (www.shodor.org) titled Angles into a seventh-grade geometry unit. The students are exploring the relationships of the angles formed when two parallel lines are intersected by a third line, called a transversal. They have previously had a hands-on learning experience in which they explored various angles using rulers and protractors.

Madison and Ava are sitting together at the computer in the school's computer lab. They are equipped with one pencil and an activity sheet. Although it was initially challenging for both students to share the computer for these types of activities, they have now learned to do so with the help of assigned roles. Madison will record the work on the activity sheet and Ava will be in charge of the computer. The students have a choice as to how many transversals will be drawn by the applet. Madison would like to draw two right away. Ava suggests that, since they haven't used the program before, they should try just one first. (See Figure 6–1.)

Madison reads the activity sheet and says, "We're supposed to figure out what all of the angles are, whether they are acute, obtuse, or right angles. I know what those all are, so let's try it."

Ava notices that the first question asks the pair to determine what type of angles *b* and *h* are. They both agree that angle *b* is an

Figure 6–1  *Madison and Ava's transversal drawing in Angles applet.*

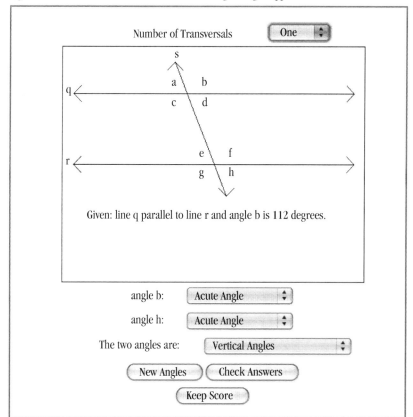

obtuse angle and angle *b* is an acute angle. They input their answers as such and move on to the next question. The computer program then asks them to determine the relationship between the two angles and requires them to use appropriate vocabulary for their answer. Ava immediately wants to input that the answer is corresponding angles and let the program tell them whether that's right or not.

Madison wants to think more carefully about their answer first and says, "Let's be sure before we put that answer in." She remembers that, when they worked on angle relationships in their classroom yesterday, they recorded this information in their notes. "I think we wrote this down in our notes. Let's look it up." As Madison looks in her notebook, Ava is working hard to be patient and not guess an answer right away.

Having found what she was looking for, Madison reports, "See, Ava, when the angles both make a straight angle like this example in our notes, then the angles are supplementary. So, I think that the ones in this question are supplementary, too."

Ava responds, "Oh, yeah, you're right. They do look like the same type as in the example and now that I see the picture I remember."

Their teacher has observed these exchanges and is pleased with the interactions. Each of the students contributed to their understanding of the task. They listened to each other's ideas and built naturally on previous knowledge. The teacher knows that partnerships don't always work out this well, but he works hard at helping his students learn how to work together.

Ava later explained, "My teacher used to just direct us to work in pairs without helping us learn how to do so. Now he knows better."

## Making Connections

**Take Action!**

Make connections with KWHL charts.

Making connections is another way to scaffold learning. Students learn more easily when they connect what they are about to learn to something they already know. This is one of the reasons that KWHL charts are popular. By completing the K, or *know*, section of the chart, students are establishing their own understanding of the topic. They are also providing their teacher with pre-assessment data. By declaring what they *want to learn* (W), they are providing input into their curriculum. The H, or *how*, section encourages students to identify how they want to learn. The final section (L) allows them to summarize what they *have learned* and reconnect to their original knowledge base by comparing the columns. An initial chart that seventh graders have generated for learning about integers follows. The Learned column is shaded because the class will not consider it until students have explored the content.

| KWHL Chart | | | |
|---|---|---|---|
| **Know** | **Want to Know** | **How** | **Learned** |
| There are positive and negative numbers. | Why don't we write the positive sign? | With thermometers | |
| Negatives are less than zero. | How to multiply a positive and negative number | With a number line | |
| Temperatures use negative numbers. | Dividing two negative numbers | Real stories of how we use positive and negative numbers | |
| Money shows positive as black and red as negative. | What is absolute value? | With chips like my older brother | |

Making a connection or an analogy to something that is already known or is within a familiar real-world context helps students make sense of new ideas and gain access to curriculum that would otherwise be too difficult.

One seventh-grade teacher, concerned that her students did not recognize the usefulness of learning to compute with integers, said, "They are just learning the rules and don't think this has anything to do with the real world. I think they would be more motivated and understand the material more deeply if they could see connections between their math class and their lives."

Although their curriculum did have some real-life contexts for integer arithmetic, this teacher believed that her students needed to produce some examples on their own, rather than just read about them in a mathematics book. She hoped that researching practical uses of integers would allow her students to truly take ownership of the math that they were learning.

She decided to ask her students to contribute to the section of her website that she calls "What's All This Math for, Anyway?" in which she often gives her own examples and provides links to interesting, related websites for her students to explore. She

*Activity Idea!*

**Strand:** Number

**Focus:** Develop meaning for integers.

**Context:** Compiling real-world connections on a class website had told her students that she is always interested in including their ideas for this section of her website, but this time she required them to add their own examples. Through this process, she believed, students would see how authentic the material can be. Here are some of the items that the students posted:

- I'm really interested in geography and I found out that elevations are sometimes written as negative numbers for places like Death Valley and the Dead Sea. I found out that Death Valley in California has an elevation of $-282$ feet and the highest place in California is Mt Whitney at 14,494 feet. I think that I'm going to have to figure out how many miles that is!

- When I visited my grandparents in Sweden last year their thermometer said that it was $-5$ degrees outside and I almost flipped out because I thought that I'd get frostbite. It turns out that it was Celsius degrees and I had to convert with negative numbers to Fahrenheit. I guess that it's always good to know how the temperature is measured.

- My brother keeps "borrowing" money from me and then seems to forget that he has to pay it all back so I made up a way to remind him. I made slips of paper that showed how much he borrowed and made it a negative number. When he pays me some of the money I make those slips show positive numbers. My parents called the negative ones IOU slips. I think that's really funny, but I also really hope that my brother will get it that he has to pay me back now!

The website of real-life examples continued to grow throughout the year as the students found more relevant uses for integers. Although the teacher monitored this section of her website for accuracy, she was pleased that the students were the initiators. They were cautious about posting material and conferred often with each other and with her before adding to the website. The students asked if they could post more real-life examples for the other mathematics topics. The teacher was happy to have them directly involved in their own learning.

## Self-Regulation and Self-Reflection

Metacognitive knowledge, or the ability to think about one's own thinking, is critical to learning. It allows learners to make plans, select strategies, and reflect on the effectiveness of choices made. Students who are encouraged to think about how they learn best are more able to inform the learning process and monitor their success. Ross,

Hogaboam-Gray, and Rolheiser (2002) suggest that we make students aware of our explicit criteria for evaluation in order to improve the work students produce. When we support metacognitive awareness in our classrooms, we are helping students become more confident, independent learners who can self-regulate their thinking.

Research suggests that students with learning difficulties are more successful when they self-regulate their thinking. It is important that teachers facilitate such students' metacognitive awareness (Montague 2006). Evaluating their experiences at the end of a class period, at the conclusion of a unit, or when test results become available involves students in the authentic measurement of their own success.

One sixth-grade teacher, interested in learning more about her students' self-evaluation, gives opportunities for students to sort themselves. She asks her students to place themselves on a learning continuum through dot charts or bull's-eyes. (See Figure 6–2.) Today, Abbie knows that she will be asked to place a dot on the chart posted in the back of the classroom to indicate where she sees herself at the conclusion of the lesson. She begins to consider where she should place her dot. Her choices today are to place it under the statement "I do not know how to find the volume of a cylinder," "I think that I know how to find the volume of a cylinder," or "I can explain how to find the volume of a cylinder to others." Abbie must consider her classroom experiences and self-determine in which group she belongs. When teachers allow students to post

Take Action!

Incorporate self-assessment.

Figure 6–2   *Examples of self-sorting prompts.*

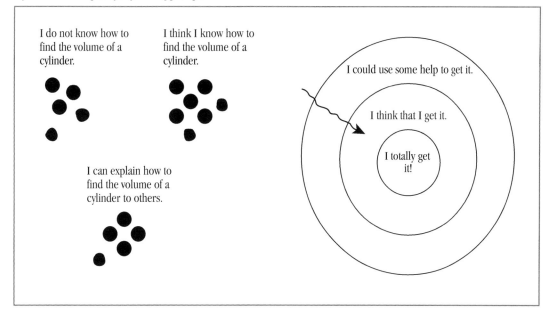

their dots anonymously, responses are more likely to be accurate. Such distinctions will also help the teacher determine how to structure the next day's lesson to better meet student needs.

Kalen's teacher often prepares exit cards for his class. Known in his class as tickets to leave, these slips ask students to complete prompts as in the following:

---

**Tickets to Leave**

Today I learned that . . .

----------------------------------------

I was surprised when I figured out that . . .

----------------------------------------

A question that I still have is . . .

----------------------------------------

The representation that made the most sense to me . . .

----------------------------------------

I am still struggling with . . .

----------------------------------------

One thing that I didn't understand today is . . .

----------------------------------------

The best thing about this math lesson today was . . .

----------------------------------------

I took the best notes when . . .

---

When you are about to give a unit quiz or test or have just administered one, you might include these prompts:

---

**Tickets to Leave (Test Related)**

Before the test on Thursday, I'd like to review . . .

----------------------------------------

I need to study these vocabulary words before we take the test . . .

----------------------------------------

I studied for today's test by . . .

----------------------------------------

My test results that surprised me . . .

---

It is still common practice in some schools for teachers to briefly return corrected tests and then collect them again for future use. While it is often helpful for teachers to review results later or to reuse test items, this approach does not allow students to consider their tests beyond the class period or to reexamine their work before the teacher supplies correct answers. In contrast, some teachers ask students to reflect upon their errors prior to giving the correct answers or to evaluate their work based on a rubric that provides specific criteria. Connor's teacher makes a regular practice of asking his students to complete a self-reflection handout after he hands a test back. (See Figure 6–3 on the following page.) Connor must consider how he responded to each individual question on the test and then reflect on his thinking on the test overall.

Writing responses to these types of questions provides students with the opportunity to practice reflective thinking. Reading the responses provides teachers with valuable feedback about the day's lesson that can allow them to better differentiate instruction the following day.

## Graphic Organizers

Graphic organizers—visual representations that provide a prompt or an organizing framework for retrieving, storing, acquiring, or applying knowledge—are also a way to scaffold learning. The more we use both linguistic and nonlinguistic representations in our classrooms, the more we can help our students learn and remember. Graphic organizers often contain both linguistic and nonlinguistic features.

Concept maps or webs are a way to graphically represent relationships among ideas. The maps help students develop a framework for what they already know and provide a model that they can elaborate on as their learning increases. Maps or webs also provide important assessment data and can be developed at the beginning, in the middle, or at the end of units. The main concept can be written at the top or in the middle of the map. Rays or arrows then span out from that main idea. As the rays fan out, the ideas move from more general to more specific.

One eighth-grade teacher knows that his students have had experience using concept webs in several of their other subjects. For the most part, though, they have only used webs shown in their textbooks or constructed by their teachers to help review for tests in history or science. This teacher wants to engage his students in preparing their own concept webs about probability. He believes that he can learn a good deal about their understanding of this topic by having them brainstorm their ideas and then learn to organize the ideas within a web. As students develop their

Lesson Idea!

Strand: Data

Focus: Probability

Context: Creating concept webs

**Variables Unit Test ~ Self-Reflection**

**Problem 1**

**a.**

☐ I made a table with two variables labeled at the top of the two columns.

☐ I used these two variables in my table: _____ and _____.

☐ I correctly labeled my *x*-axis and *y*-axis.

☐ I used an appropriate scale for my *x*-axis and *y*-axis.

☐ I used a descriptive title.

**b.**

☐ I gave the correct answer.

☐ I clearly explained the reasoning for my answer.

**c.**

☐ I used a variable for *total cost* and a variable for *number of shirts*, and I wrote an equation to find the total cost, given the number of shirts.

**Problem 2**

☐ I told a story about a money amount changing as time increased.

☐ In my story the money amount increased rapidly to a certain point and then decreased at a slower pace.

**Problem 3**

☐ I explained that the daylight hours increased from 10 to 15 and then decreased back to 10.

☐ I explained that the change is related to the month number because of the changing season.

☐ I pointed out that the greatest increase occurred from February to March, and the greatest decrease from September to October.

**Problem 4**

**a.**

☐ I made a table with three columns. They were labeled *# of CDs*, *Taylor's Cost*, *Buyer's Cost*.

**b.**

☐ I wrote an equation using two variables for the total cost of buying CDs at Taylor's.

☐ I wrote an equation using two variables for the total cost of buying CDs at Buyer's.

**c.**

☐ I correctly answered the question.

☐ I showed my work by indicating the price changes in the table.

**d.**

☐ I correctly answered the question.

☐ I showed my work by indicating the price changes in the table.

**Underline one:**

I am satisfied with my test score.

I would like to do better on my next test.

Figure 6–3 *Post-test self-reflection.*

**Now that I have reflected on my responses, I realize I should have:**

a.

b.

**What will I do differently on the next unit test?**

a.

b.

**My teacher can help me by:**

a.

b.

Figure 6–3  (*Continued*)

webs, the teacher hopes that they will make connections among the various aspects of probability. He knows that their thinking may be somewhat sparse now, as they are just beginning to study the topic, but as they progress, they can either add to their webs or re-create them to match the complexity of their thinking.

The teacher believes that if the students work in small groups, more of them will participate in the initial brainstorming session. Consequently he has students sitting in groups of four with a small stack of index cards in the center of each table. The teacher is interested in learning what the students remember from previous experiences with probability. He has placed a larger index card at each table with the printed title "What We Know About Probability." He tells the class, "I know that you have studied probability before and I'm curious to know what you remember."

Several students raise their hands to make suggestions; the teacher tells them that he would like them to have this discussion in their small groups. As they brainstorm an idea, they need to decide what to name it and write the name on an index card from the pile at their table. As he walks around the room, the teacher hears his students make comments such as:

- "I remember using spinners to see how many times we landed on red."
- "We wrote our results to look like fractions."

- "I think that we tried to decide how likely something was to happen or not."
- "We used a computer program to make a lot of flips of a coin happen really fast and then we had to analyze the results."

The teacher sits with one group for a short time, encouraging the students to think about how they could name what they remember.

Ashlyn says, "I know that when we used materials like spinners and coins that we were doing experiments. Then we would compare our experiment results to what should happen."

Tomas confirms that this activity occurred in his class as well. The teacher asks, "If you had to give a name to all of the ways that you collected data, what might you say?"

Juddy responds, "How about if we called it conducting experiments?" The group agrees and Juddy writes this phrase on an index card.

Moving on to another group, the teacher observes the students writing the following on their index cards:

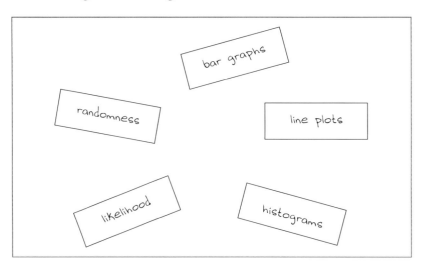

The teacher asks these students to consider how the information they have included on their first three index cards is related.

Grant responds, "They are all of the ways that we used to show our results when we did experiments. Do you want us to make an index card to tell what they all are?" The teacher takes a moment to talk with the class about making labels to help organize the ideas on their cards.

Once the teacher is satisfied that all of the groups have had ample opportunity to brainstorm a list of their past experiences with probability, he places a small bundle of coffee stirrers at each table. He asks the groups to cluster their idea cards around the label cards that they made. He uses the example of the students who made a label titled "Data Results" and asks the students to show some of the index cards that they will cluster with this label.

Next the teacher places index cards and coffee stirrers backed with magnetic tape on the board to demonstrate how students can use the stirrers to connect the cards at their own tables. He places the "Data Results" card in the middle and several related cards around it. When he places a stirrer from each example card to the label card, he seems to spark his students' thinking about how they, too, might connect their cards. The students begin quickly to unpack their bundles of stirrers and move their cards around to make connections. As the teacher overhears one group discussing whether to put their idea card "Likely or Not?" with the card labeled "Randomness" or with another card labeled "Events," he makes a mental note to be sure to address this aspect of probability within his unit.

As each group completes its initial web, the teacher brings the class back together as a whole. He explains that he would like the students to be able to keep the webs they have made so far and to add ideas or make changes as they learn more about probability. The teacher introduces students to a graphic software tool that allows them to create webs. He demonstrates how to make the labels (replacing their index cards) and how to draw arrows (replacing their coffee stirrers).

Each group of four students gets a laptop computer from the cart and begins to transfer work from the physical model to the computerized version. (See Figure 6–4 on the following page.) As they learn to use the software and re-create their webs, students make even more connections among the ideas in their webs. The teacher is hopeful that the students recognize how much they have learned already about probability and that they can draw upon this knowledge as they continue to investigate.

Venn diagrams are another example of a graphic organizer. Although the use of Venn diagrams was traditionally limited to mathematics and science, they are now often utilized in literacy and social studies, for example, to compare two or three stories, characters, heroes, or events. Introducing these graphic organizers during math time can help students view mathematics as a useful tool.

In the middle grades, students can use Venn diagrams to organize the prime factors of numbers to find their greatest common

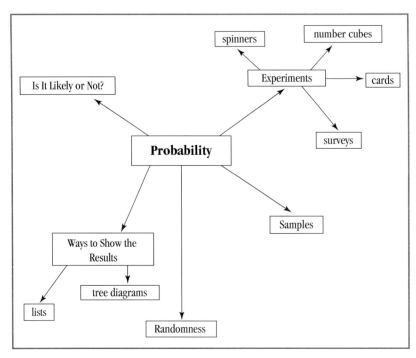

Figure 6–4  *Student-created probability web.*

factor (GCF) and least common multiple (LCM). Given a two-circle diagram and the numbers seventy-five and forty-five, for example, students can place the prime factors of each number in the appropriate circle, making sure to position factors of both numbers in the intersection. (See Figure 6–5.) To find the GCF, students find the product of the factors, in the intersection, in this case, $3 \times 5 = 15$. The LCM is found by determining the product of all of the factors, or $5 \times 5 \times 3 \times 3$, or 225.

Euler circles are also used to show the relations among sets. The difference is that Euler diagrams make subset and discrete relations more visible. Instead of just having some empty regions, Euler circles change position. Teachers can provide a visual arrangement of the circles and ask students to identify possible labels. Figure 6–6 shows examples of subset and discrete relationships between sets. Euler diagrams are also used to show the nested relationship within natural numbers, whole numbers, integers, rational numbers, real numbers, and imaginary numbers.

Another graphic organizer that focuses on mathematical vocabulary is a word bank. When designing a task, a teacher may choose to scaffold the students' ability to explain their thinking by providing a bank of words at the bottom of the assignment sheet. (See Figure 6–7 on page 172.)

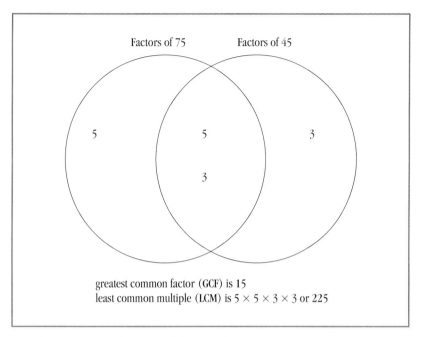

greatest common factor (GCF) is 15
least common multiple (LCM) is $5 \times 5 \times 3 \times 3$ or 225

Figure 6–5    *Using Venn diagrams to find GCM and LCM.*

Some teachers prefer to include this organizer but leave the bank empty. (See Figure 6–8 on the following page.) Students first brainstorm and record words in the bank before they begin the task. Note that this form also provides further scaffolding for questions that require students to make comparisons.

Figure 6–6    *Euler circles showing subset and discrete relationships between sets.*

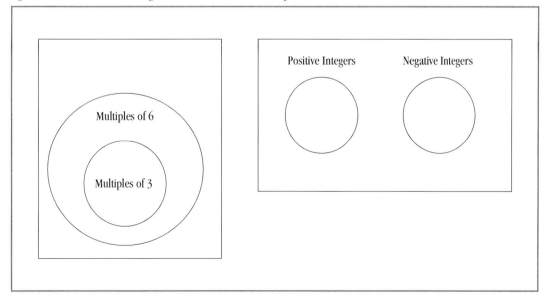

How are a pyramid and a cone different?
How are they the same?


Word Bank:

| | | |
|---|---|---|
| curve | polygon | solids |
| lateral face | prism | three-dimensional |
| perpendicular | rotation | vertical point |
| polyhedra | simple closed curve | vertices |

Figure 6–7 *Task with accompanying word bank.*

More teachers are considering such formats in the struggle to help their students respond to open-ended questions in mathematics. When examining student responses, teachers find that too often, students lack the vocabulary to be able to adequately address the questions.

Another graphic organizer is a vocabulary sheet. One eighth-grade teacher in a bilingual classroom has students complete a sheet whenever she introduces a new term. The sheet begins with

Figure 6–8 *A blank word bank template.*

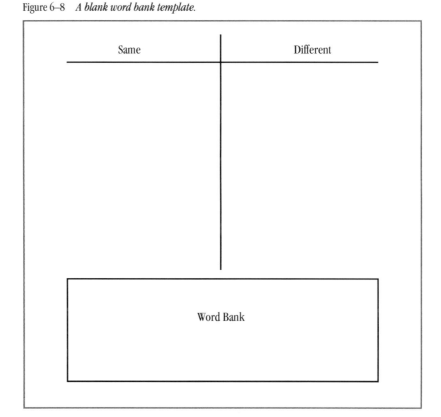

asking students to provide the definition found in a dictionary or glossary. Next students write the definition in their own words. This teacher purposely has students provide both types of definitions with hopes that students will begin to make connections between the two versions. She believes strongly that students need to make their own connections with a term in order to internalize its meaning. Providing blank space rather than lines in the "Examples" and "Nonexamples" portions of the form allows students to choose to draw diagrams or write words. (See Figure 6–9.) Students place these sheets, in alphabetical order, in the back of their mathematics journals so they can refer to them easily whenever they need be reminded of the meaning of one of the terms. They are also encouraged to add to their pages as they deepen their understanding of the terms.

Figure 6–9   *Vocabulary template.*

New term: _____

Definition in glossary or dictionary: _____

_____

_____

_____

Definition in my words: _____

_____

_____

_____

Examples:


Nonexamples:

You can also encourage students to create their own graphic organizers to help them remember vocabulary associated with specific mathematical terms. One sixth-grade teacher encourages students to think about vocabulary or concepts associated with particular terms that they have trouble remembering. As the group brainstorms examples, it is common for another student to comment, "Oh, I have trouble with that one, too." The teacher then suggests that they create a graphic that will help them remember. She tells them, "Create something so memorable and meaningful that you could never forget again."

Gus, who always seems to forget the relationships among the U.S. standard units for liquid measures, makes a picture to depict them. As shown in Figure 6–10, his drawing includes two containers that look like cups in each of two containers labeled with *P*s (for pints), which are within an outline labeled with a *Q* (for quart). At the very top he has written $4Q = G$ so that he can generalize to gallons.

Denise, Carolyn, and Shanna always get confused about the terms *multiple* and *factor*.

Carolyn says, "Oh, the multiple is the big one and the factor is the little one, like four times five equals twenty." Shanna agrees and suggests that they close their eyes and think of a small thing that begins with F on top of a large thing that begins with M. Carolyn closes her eyes and then reports with excitement that she saw a small frog on top of a big mountain.

Denise is less certain about this idea and wonders about $4 \times -5 = -20$. She asks, "Doesn't this mean that the multiple can be less than a factor?"

Figure 6–10  *Gus's graphic to remember the relationships among the U.S. standard units for liquid measures.*

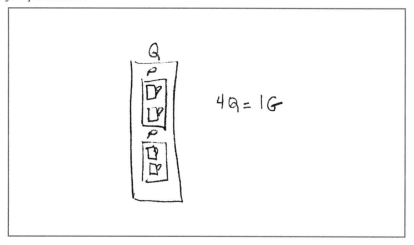

Figure 6–11 *Shanna's graphic to remember* factor *and* multiple.

Shanna, ever the peacemaker, says, "Wait, let's focus on something else. There are always two factors and one multiple. We can make a picture with two frogs sitting on one mushroom." This image causes some giggling and the girls each begin to make a drawing, one of which is shown in Figure 6–11.

Dean and Janice decide that they have trouble remembering that one is not a prime number. Janice writes *1* and the word *prime*, and then crosses out *prime*. Dean looks at her drawing for a bit and then starts talking about the television show *Numb3rs* and how the name is written with a 3 instead of an E. They decide to write *prime* with a 1 instead of an I and then cross out the 1. Their graphic is shown in Figure 6–12.

Some teachers present problems in a way that graphically organizes a student's work. One example is a structured form

Figure 6–12 *Dean and Janice's graphic to remember that one is not prime.*

There are 4 blue marbles and 6 red marbles in a jar.
You reach in and pull out 2 of them randomly.
What is the probability that they are the same color?
Explain your thinking.

| Facts: | Drawings: |
|---|---|
| | |
| **Computation:** | **Answer:** |
| | |

Figure 6–13    *Graphic organizer: problem-solving scaffold.*

that requires students to complete different components. (See Figure 6–13.) Sometimes students just need a less structured form with the problem presented at the top and a clearly designated place to record the answer. (See Figure 6–14.) Such graphics can scaffold students through the problem-solving process, but they should not be used with all problems or be implemented for any length of time. It's important that scaffolds, even simple ones, be removed or modified as the student progresses. Remember, the goal is for the student to organize the problem-solving process and to take responsibility for deciding if making a drawing would be helpful and for remembering to identify the answer within the work.

Forms with spaces for multiple answers also scaffold student work. For example, if you ask students to name all possible combinations, you might provide a table that indicates how students should organize the data and provides space for the types of answers you want students to identify. (See Figure 6–15.) Again, such multiple-response scaffolds should be used only with students

Brianna and Madelyn were counting their stickers.
    Brianna said, "If you give me two of your stickers,
I'll have twice as many stickers as you."
    Madelyn replied, "Yes, but if you give me eight of your stickers,
then I will have twice as many as you."
    How many stickers does each child have?

Show your work:

Answer: _____

Figure 6–14    *Graphic organizer: less detailed problem-solving scaffold.*

who would be unable to work with a more open-ended presentation. Some students can use this problem (without the scaffold) as an opportunity to create their own methods for deciding if they have identified all the correct responses. But for some students this task is too overwhelming at first. The scaffold, or response template,

Figure 6–15    *Graphic organizer: scaffold for problem with multiple responses.*

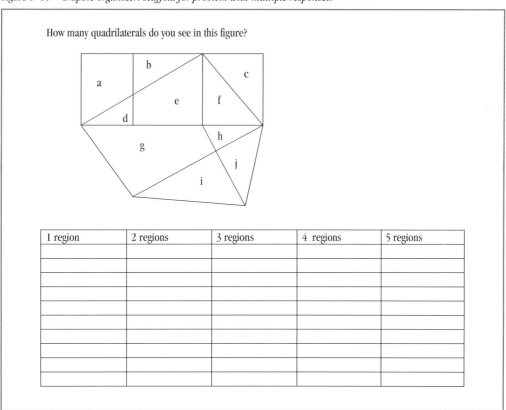

How many quadrilaterals do you see in this figure?

| 1 region | 2 regions | 3 regions | 4 regions | 5 regions |
|---|---|---|---|---|
|  |  |  |  |  |
|  |  |  |  |  |
|  |  |  |  |  |
|  |  |  |  |  |
|  |  |  |  |  |
|  |  |  |  |  |
|  |  |  |  |  |
|  |  |  |  |  |
|  |  |  |  |  |

provides a systematic way for them to give the problem a try, and the structure can help students who find the empty page, or the requirement to find multiple answers, too intimidating.

We cannot overemphasize the importance of providing only those scaffolds that are needed and lessening or removing them as soon as possible. It is also important to use scaffolds that support robust concepts. Too often students who reach the middle grades and still experience difficulty with mathematical concepts are provided with rote approaches only, keeping them from gaining the conceptual frameworks necessary for success with algebraic tasks.

We also have graphic organizers of our number system. Number lines and pictures of decimal squares graphically represent relationships among numbers. Students are known to have difficulty placing fractions and decimals on number lines, which indicates a less than complete understanding of these numbers. It is similarly important to provide continuous and discrete models for students of arithmetic with integers. While use of chips of twocolors emphasizes the importance of the identity element for addition and subtraction, a few learners find the number line model easier to understand. For them, the kinesthetic memory of walking along the line in different directions, forward and backward, is easier to retain.

A graphic that is helpful for solving percent problems is a 10-by-10 grid, known as a *unit square*. Students can begin by determining the value of the unit square given the value of one small square, or the value of one small square given the value of the whole grid. Then you can ask more complex questions.

This visual model allows students to gain a conceptual understanding of percent problems. Students can avoid the need to memorize specific algorithms for different types of percent problems, as well as the common misuse of cross multiplication.

A group of seventh-grade students has just been introduced to the use of grids to represent proportional relationships. They are working on the tasks shown in Figure 6–16. Bella and Kieji are discussing their responses to the last question in Task 3: *If 20 squares represent $15, how much money would be represented by 70 small squares?* Bella finds the value of one small square, which is $\frac{15}{20}$ or $0.75, and then multiplies by 70 to find $52.50. Kieji thinks of 70 as $3\frac{1}{2}$ groups of $15 or $45 + $7.50 = $52.50. The visual model of the grid helps these students construct their own solution strategies as well as follow each other's thinking. The teacher is confident that over time, as their conceptual understanding deepens, these students will be able to visualize the grid without

**There are 500 students at the Meadowbrook Middle School.**

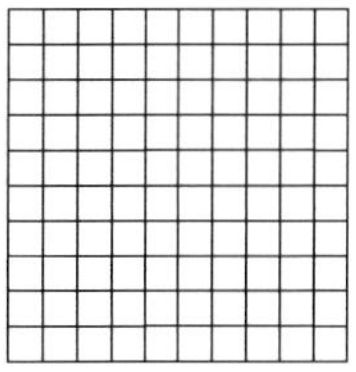

1.  If the unit square to the right represents the
    students, how many students are represented by
    one small square?

2.  If one small square of the grid represents 7 students,
    how many students would there be in the whole school?

3.  If a unit square represents 200 iPods, how many iPods would be represented by
    *   50 small squares?
    *   20% of the small squares?
    *   $\frac{1}{2}$ of a small square?

4.  What percent of the unit square would represent 150 iPods?

5.  If 20 squares represent $15, how much money would be represented by
    *   the unit square?
    *   1 small square?
    *   150% of the unit square?
    *   70 small squares?

Figure 6–16   *Tasks that encourage students to use grids to represent proportional relationship.*

needing to actually construct it. Furthermore, the mental images of the grid will allow them to proceed arithmetically.

Graphic organizers that help students develop their conceptual understanding of computational procedures are particularly helpful when teachers use the organizers across grade spans. One middle school teacher explained, "I used to really get upset with the way some of my sixth-grade students multiplied. They used these boxes and it all looked so juvenile. I just told them that they were in middle school now and didn't need that technique anymore. Then I went to a workshop and learned that the same technique could be used with algebraic expressions. I had really made a mistake!" (See Figure 6–17 on the following page.)

As you can see from the numerous examples of graphic organizers in this chapter, these visual tools are powerful models for conceptual development, as well as simple ways to illustrate a particular task or process. In the same spirit, asking questions, focusing on strategies, having students collaborate, and making connections are valuable ways to support learning. Such ways make the work more accessible for all students as they pursue tasks, make choices, and solve problems.

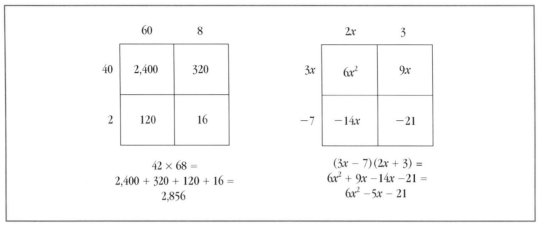

Figure 6–17 *Graphic organizer for finding partial products in arithmetic and algebra.*

| **Answers to Question Categorization Task, page 153** |
| --- |

*1. understand 2. evaluate 3. create 4. rememember 5. evaluate 6. analyze 7. remember 8. evaluate 9. apply 10. analyze*

## Connecting the Chapter to Your Practice

1. How would you help a colleague better understand the difference between *analyze* and *evaluate* in the new version of Bloom's taxonomy?

2. From your experience, what are your two favorite stories of student collaboration?

3. What graphic organizers do you find most helpful for students?

# Chapter 7
# Supporting Choice

*O*ur society places value on making choices. Making choices helps us feel autonomous, confident, and competent. Choice is highly motivating and is one way that students can take responsibility for their own learning. Making a choice involves self-expression, which is a form of creativity. We honor our students as learners when we allow them to make choices. We are also able to differentiate instruction by providing choice. Though having more choices is frequently associated with growing older and being able to handle responsibilities, students often view school as a place where choice diminishes as they advance through the grades. How do we make room for choice and how do we structure choices for students to make in the middle grades?

Though there is rarely time in a typical middle school class period for the kind of choices that are permitted in the early years, we believe teachers can integrate choice into current instructional strategies as they expand their pedagogical repertoire. The major goal is to realize that including choice does not mean veering from learning expectations. As we learn from the teacher reflection shown on the following page, providing students with choices does not mean that everyone can do anything they want. Rather, students can choose among tasks, with each option designed to support the instructional goals in the classroom.

This teacher offers us several key ideas to think about in terms of providing choice in our classrooms. Making smart decisions, managing time, holding students accountable, and building choice into the classroom practice provide us with a framework for thinking about how to design and implement choice in our

I began my career as a kindergarten teacher. I used to marvel at the way my students focused during choice time and how activities during that time led to exciting new areas of study. These young students were used to making decisions about what materials to use, much as they did at home with toys. Choice time allowed them to do something they really cared about, to have some control of their learning environment. When I became a sixth-grade teacher I quickly realized that choice time was not something that was built into the schedule at this level. I missed the comfortable way I was able to interact with students during this time and worried that I was giving my older students the subtle message that I didn't have confidence in the decisions they would make.

In response, I decided to offer project time during the last Friday of the month. It worked well for a couple of months and then slowly things began to deteriorate. Too many students were getting off task and, as a result, behavior problems started to increase. After some reflection I realized that the projects weren't really connected to what we were studying. No wonder the students began to think of this opportunity as free time. I decided to decrease the time to twenty minutes and to make this a time for math games that allowed students more practice with math topics that we had previously studied. Both changes helped and over time, I developed different levels of each game to be sure that student readiness was addressed.

Now that I have been teaching at this level for quite a few years, I have found a number of ways to provide choices for my students to make. I look for times when they can choose their own partners, find their own work space, or decide which task to do first. At the beginning of the school year we spend some time establishing routines and expectations for making decisions. We discuss what it means to make a good choice and they know they will be held accountable for their selections. I now incorporate choice into my curriculum on a frequent basis. In this way students recognize choice as part of our classroom practice, rather than as a sign that it is time to fool around, and that, within that choice, they will still be expected to demonstrate what they have learned.

> *I look for times when they can choose their own partners, find their own work space, or decide which task to do first.*

classrooms. There are managerial implications around time, work habits, disposition for learning, behavior, and ways to monitor student progress that require our attention as well.

Being offered a choice implies the need for reflection and self-direction. Many adolescents are adept at this; many are not. Adolescence is a journey toward independence and self-discovery. Parents and teachers alike recognize that adolescents need predictable structure, clear expectations, and innumerable opportunities to explore, practice, make mistakes, and learn. Teachers and parents also recognize that adolescents need the time and opportunity to practice decision making as well as learn how to compromise. In many ways, offering choices requires more preparation than merely directing students to complete a task, but the gains are worth it. Choice provides powerful opportunities for additional practice and differentiating instruction and also leads to natural extensions for learning. For students who struggle with learning mathematics, choice can provide the motivation needed for success.

Acknowledge the benefits of providing choices for students.

There are a variety of choices we can offer our students. Some of them are listed in the following chart:

| Choices to Offer Students |
| --- |
| • which tasks to complete |
| • what materials to use |
| • with whom to partner |
| • where to work |
| • how long to work on a particular task |
| • which topics to study |
| • the order in which to complete assignments |
| • how to represent and present ideas |
| • how to demonstrate what is understood |

Letting our students make such choices can have a positive impact on their learning and their self-esteem. The extent to which this potential impact is realized often depends on the ways in which teachers structure and organize choice in the classroom. Math workshops, projects, menus, think-tac-toes, RAFTs, and learning stations are effective ways to organize and manage classroom choice as we strive to meet individual needs.

## Math Workshops

Some teachers use *math workshops* as a term to describe the kind of activity that occurs when students are given choice in the mathematical ideas they investigate. Such workshops are also a time to work on specific skills such as computing with decimals, fractions, and percents; solving and graphing equations; and finding surface area and volume. Ideally, math workshops are designed to support authentic mathematical investigation, provide opportunities for skill development, and set expectations for high-quality work.

Consider this seventh-grade classroom, where students are investigating measures of central tendency: Snap Cubes, color tiles, rulers, balances, sticky notes, and graph paper are available to construct models. To provide choice within this workshop, the teacher encourages students to choose the data set with which they want to work (data sets are entertainment, environment, music, politics, or sports) and to choose which materials they want to use as they determine how (if at all) the mean, mode, and median change when data in a set are amended. The teacher has assigned a few students to use specific materials based on their readiness for this content. For example, a couple of pairs will use the Snap Cubes to represent their chosen data because those manipulatives will allow them to create sturdy models. Conversely, a couple of other pairs are assigned to use sticky notes or the balances, as these materials will provide students with a wider variety of options and a greater challenge. For example, they can cut the sticky notes to represent fractional or decimal parts. Although they have to work with the assigned materials, these students can still choose a partner with whom to work, the data to use, and the ways in which they will represent the work.

Task questions are also tiered. Some students are expected to determine the changeability of just the mode or the median and to study how the mean changes only after they have fully explored these two measures of central tendency. Some students are expected to explore how all three measures change, and their data include more complex numbers than other groups. For example, some of these students are answering such questions as *If another student decides to run the race and finishes with a time of 5 minutes and 35 seconds, how will the mean change?* and *By how much do you think that the mean will increase or decrease if Susan's next test grade is 87.5?* Some students are asked to create their own data sets from information available on websites the teacher has identified and to generate questions for their classmates to explore.

During this time, the teacher is working with a small group of students who require more instruction with how to model the three measures. At the end of that focused work, they will investigate how changing the data affects the median. All students must

**Workshop Idea!**

**Strand:** Data

**Focus:** Measures of central tendency

**Context:** Making choices in a math workshop

provide exit information regarding their activities, responding to these two prompts:

- What have you learned about how the median changes when the data change?
- Provide an example of a situation in which the median does not change despite a change in the data.

In this workshop most students choose or collect their own materials. Providing easy access to materials is one of many managerial strategies that supports learning. As students learn to use mathematical manipulatives and come to expect them to be available for use, the students are also developing the good work habits and positive behaviors that are indicative of successful, independent learners. Ironically, we find primary and elementary school students often have more choice in material use than middle school students. Materials in primary and elementary classrooms are often housed in open bins or plastic tubs at a level that makes them easily accessible to young students. In middle and high school classrooms, however, materials may be stored in out-of-the-way shelves, file cabinets, or closets. We must all find places in our classrooms to store manipulatives that suggest students are free to use them as needed. Everything should be reachable, labeled, and easy to maintain. (See Chapter 8 for a fuller discussion of organizing classroom space.)

Provide access to materials.

## Projects

One way to allow our students to pursue their own interests is to involve them in projects. Projects provide students opportunities to apply concepts and skills as they wrestle with important ideas and in-depth study. Projects usually require significant research and organizational skills and therefore might be better pursued during the second half of the year. Some teachers find it helpful to provide a specific time line for a project. For example, a seventh-grade class working on an end-of-unit project involving positive and negative integers has specific tasks and deadlines that have to be met along the way. (See Figure 7–1 on the following page.) The articulation of these tasks helps the students break down their project into daily goals and allows the teacher to easily identify students who are falling behind the intended schedule.

Support project work.

Other teachers allow for more open-ended projects and thus require students to complete a contract committing them to their topic and plans. (See Figure 7–2; see also Reproducibles.)

Check off each task as you complete it.

**Complete by Wednesday, January 5**

☐ Choose a topic for your integer logic puzzle.

**Complete by Friday, January 7**

☐ Prepare a draft of the clues for your puzzle.

☐ Choose artwork to go along with your puzzle (either hand drawn or computer generated).

**Complete by Tuesday, January 12**

☐ Complete a computerized version of your logic puzzle.

☐ Be prepared to exchange logic puzzles with a peer reviewer in class today.

**Complete by Thursday, January 14**

☐ Make corrections to your puzzle based on feedback from your peer reviewer.

**Complete by Friday, January 15**

☐ Submit your final draft to your teacher.

☐ Complete your reflection sheet.

Figure 7–1    *Checklist for project deadlines.*

Figure 7–2    *Project contract.*

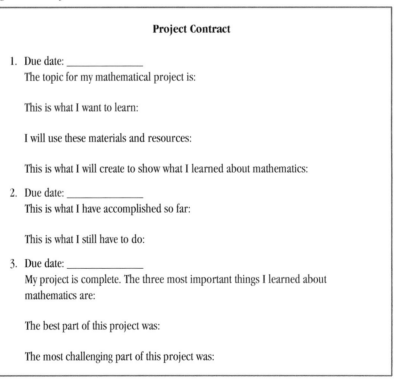

**Project Contract**

1.  Due date: _____
    The topic for my mathematical project is:

    This is what I want to learn:

    I will use these materials and resources:

    This is what I will create to show what I learned about mathematics:

2.  Due date: _____
    This is what I have accomplished so far:

    This is what I still have to do:

3.  Due date: _____
    My project is complete. The three most important things I learned about mathematics are:

    The best part of this project was:

    The most challenging part of this project was:

Some teachers provide specific projects for students to complete. Consider the following example from an eighth-grade algebra class. The teacher decides that she wants to engage students in project activities that will require them to collect data and then analyze that information to determine whether it represents a linear, quadratic, or exponential situation. She tells the students that Wednesday will be project day and that they are to bring in various types of small balls that bounce such as table tennis balls, bouncy balls, lacrosse balls, tennis balls, and softballs. Engaging the students in gathering the materials gets them excited about the project day; as they leave the room, they are chatting among their peers about what they might be doing.

When the project day arrives, the teacher has gathered metersticks and stopwatches and prepared project sheets for students. The sheets explain the tasks and provide space for students to record their data. Each self-selected group needs to choose a ball and gather other necessary materials. They will use the class period to collect their data and then they will use the upcoming week to interpret their results and determine appropriate functions. Students will conduct three experiments. (See Figure 7–3; see also Reproducibles.)

Each group of students finds that collecting the data for these experiments is challenging. They don't always agree on where the ball bounces and they have to brainstorm different ways to best determine

Figure 7–3   *Project sheet.*

---

**Project Sheet**

You are about to become an expert on bouncing balls. Pick the ball of your choice and then conduct the following three experiments. Remember that when we measure, it is best to measure three times and average the results.

**Experiment 1**

Drop your ball from an agreed-upon height on the meterstick and determine its height after one bounce. Do this three times from the same height and then take an average. Then, drop your ball from various other heights. Relate the initial height and the bounce height.

**Experiment 2**

Drop your ball from an agreed-upon height and record its height after the first bounce. Then, drop the ball from the height that it reached after the first bounce. Relate the bounce number and the height it reached after this bounce.

**Experiment 3**

Drop your ball from an agreed-upon height and measure the elapsed time until the third bounce. Be patient because measuring the time of the bounce takes practice! Relate the initial height and the time after the third bounce.

---

**Strand:** Algebra and Data

**Focus:** Linear, quadratic, and exponential functions

**Context:** Conducting experiments with bouncing balls

its height on the meterstick. Some students put their stick on a desk to get a better viewing angle. Another group sees this approach and decides to use it as well. Unfortunately, they take several measures before realizing that they have placed their stick upside down.

Once all groups have collected their data, the work to interpret the results begins. The teacher explains that the students have only one week outside of class time to produce a project document. During the last two minutes of the period, students plan times to meet and complete their projects. As the teacher explains in the following reflection, projects often require work in uncharted territory but usually lead to worthwhile results.

## Teacher Reflection

I began teaching algebra about five years ago and found that I often didn't have time for the chapter that required students to identify the various types of functions that we had explored during the year. I felt as though my students were adept at recognizing linear functions and I assumed they understood the difference between an exponential function and a quadratic function because they had, overall, done well on those chapter tests. However, after school last week, I was helping one of my students study for a high school placement test and realized that he was unable to recognize the difference between a graph of an exponential function and that of a parabola. The next day, I decided to give the problem to the entire class and was surprised to find that they, too, were uncertain about the identity of the functions.

I didn't want to just review what we had done, so I decided to have the students complete a project with different types of balls. As my students worked, I realized that few were adept at collecting experimental data. I was exhausted by the end of that period. But the students did demonstrate that they had learned a lot this year about how to represent data in tables and graphs and how to interpret their results. Even so, as these data were real, not contrived, students spent a good deal of time trying to determine the appropriate functions.

*Making these experiments into a weeklong project rather than a day's activities allowed students to delve more deeply into this content.*

Some students went home and tried the experiments again. Others were interested in exploring how their graphing calculators could help them to display their data. Two groups decided that they wanted to try using another kind of ball so they could compare their results. Still another group needed to find extra time to conduct their experiments again, as they had misread the directions the first time.

I wasn't certain at first how long this project would take. I knew that collecting the data would take time on that first day, but I didn't know how quickly students were going to be able to interpret the results. Making these experiments into a weeklong project rather than a day's activities allowed students to delve more deeply into this content. I'm going to plan to do these experiments next year, too.

There are many project ideas that are appropriate for students in grades 6 through 8; some examples are included in the list below. You can also have students brainstorm their own ideas and add them to the list. If your students are not familiar with mathematical projects, give them a few examples to prompt their thinking.

## Project Ideas: Grades 6–8

Create a poster titled "Everything You Wanted to Know About a Trillion."

Design an outdoor track and field day where you collect and analyze data from field day events.

Find out about number systems without a zero.

Make a kaleidoscope and explain how symmetry is involved with how a kaleidoscope works.

Interview three adults about how they use mathematics at work.

Investigate cell phone calling plans to determine the best deal.

Investigate how mathematics helps engineers.

Learn about card tricks that depend on mathematics.

Make a model of an inanimate object that is increased or decreased by a chosen scale factor.

Make a pendulum and collect and analyze data about it.

Lead a group in making a mathematics mural for the school's front lobby.

Pick and follow a stock portfolio.

Plan and plant a school garden.

Start a school store.

Summarize the life of a famous mathematician.

Tutor a younger student in mathematics.

Write a chapter to extend the story *The Number Devil: A Mathematical Adventure* (Enzensberger 1998).

Projects can also be shared across grade levels. For example, some related websites allow students of different grade levels to visualize a million objects and observe representation of one million in various number forms. The website A Million Dots on One Page (www.vendian.org/envelope/dir2/lots_of_dots/million_dots.html) gives students the opportunity to visualize a million dots in various forms, including grouping them as $10^2 \times 10^4 = 10^6$ or $10^3 \times 10^3 = 10^6$. The MegaPenny Project, found at www.kokogiak.com/megapenny/default.asp, demonstrates various representations of one million pennies as compared with other objects such as trucks, football fields, and skyscrapers.

One middle school engaged in a schoolwide mathematics project related to collecting various objects to represent one million. Each homeroom in the school, grades 6 through 8, chose a different object to collect. Some homerooms worked together to collect the same object, hoping to actually get to a million. Bottle caps, soda can tabs, toothpicks, buttons, and beads were among the objects collected. A number of homerooms were content, by the close of the school year, to collect lesser amounts and still benefited from collecting a great number of objects and grouping the objects by tens, hundreds, and thousands as they counted.

One eighth-grade homeroom wanted to collect as many pennies as possible, hoping to someday get to one million pennies. These students, determined to collect enough pennies to reach a million, wanted to continue collecting past the school year in order to reach their goal. They convinced their teachers to involve all students in the school and created a schoolwide penny project. The original goal of the project was to donate the money collected to a local charity, but student interest steered them toward erecting a memorial in which each penny collected would represent the life of a child who died in the Holocaust. So, the goal of collecting 1 million pennies grew to collecting 1.5 million pennies. This led to several questions such as *How much will 1.5 million pennies weigh?* and *How much space will 1.5 pennies take up?*

Each homeroom housed a large container for collecting pennies, which were brought to a central location every few weeks. Once there was a large collection of pennies, students across the grades were recruited to become part of the counting process. The community became involved when various businesses throughout the school district put out collection jars and the news media assisted the school with promoting the project. The news spread and Holocaust survivors became involved as well as other interested people across the state and from other parts of the country.

**Project Idea!**

**Strand:** Number

**Focus:** Understand large numbers.

**Context:** Collecting a million pennies

All students were involved with significant counting and grouping, but the number of pennies increased rapidly, and teachers decided the counting was taking too much time away from other work. Fortunately, they discovered that pennies could be sent to an off-site location to be rolled and then made into $25 bricks. This led to questions about how many bricks would be needed in all and how much they would weigh. When the pennies returned as bricks, they were distributed to each homeroom, as evenly as possible. The homerooms were then responsible for unrolling the bricks when the time came to add the individual pennies to the memorial. Most students estimated that the bricks would weigh 5 to 6 pounds. One group of students brought a brick to the scale in the nurse's office and was quite surprised to find that it actually weighed about 14.5 pounds.

Local families assisted the students in determining the appropriate dimensions for a clear, plastic memorial with the capability of holding such a great number of pennies. They decided that the type of material used to make the shark tanks at aquariums would be sturdy enough to house the pennies. Students were also engaged with identifying an appropriate place in the school where the flooring would be able to sustain that weight. The final step was for students in each of the homerooms to unroll the pennies so that they could be added to the memorial.

There was a myriad of opportunities for each homeroom teacher to engage students in estimation, data collection, and the study of large numbers as this project progressed. Having students of all grade levels involved allowed the entire school to share excitement about mathematics and led to a permanent memorial at their school. The project also created connections to other disciplines such as history and engineering. It is important to relate mathematics to other disciplines. Projects often support such links across content areas while simultaneously providing students with a variety of avenues through which they can make personal connections to mathematical study.

## Menus

Marilyn Burns and Cathy Humphreys suggested the use of menus to organize student choice (Burns and Humphreys 1991). This type of menu features approximately five activities. Just as one chooses an entree from a restaurant menu, students choose an activity from the math menu. During the span of a week, students may try two or three items on the menu. For example, an eighth-grade class that

Menu Idea!

Strand: Algebra

Focus: Systems of linear equations

Context: Choices on a menu board

is working with systems of linear equations may have a menu like the following:

| Menu: Systems of Linear Equations |
|---|
| Use a Gizmo applet to explore the cat-and-mouse activity involving *modeling linear systems* (see www.explorelearning.com), which focuses on graphing equations to determine whether or not the cat catches the mouse. |
| Solve systems problems using a graphing calculator. |
| Write a note to a friend explaining which method of solving a systems of linear equations problem is easiest based on the type of situation. |
| Create problems to include in a problem deck: a collection of word problems that include mixture, work, and rate problems. |
| Order the steps to reveal a hidden picture by doing the activity at www.quia.com/pp/11581.html; you'll be given a series of steps to solve a pair of simultaneous equations using substitution. |

You can create a special menu board to list the options and make a recording sheet to keep track of students' choices. (See Figure 7–4.) Some activities on a menu board might remain for a significant amount of time. Through repetition, students are able to explore a certain activity over the course of days or weeks, thereby developing comfort and confidence. Over time, you can also modify a menu task by changing the numbers, the complexity of the problem, or the specific rules for play. You might want to make a particular choice available for a long time to give more students an opportunity to try it while you change other activities frequently based on need. Rotating out some activities leaves room for new and expanded ideas to be developed while still keeping some of the familiar choices available.

Teachers organize choices according to their style and classroom management preferences as well as students' needs. Many teachers add a "required" element to the choices. Carol Tomlinson (2003) provides menus with required features. Students must complete the main course listings and choose one or two side dishes; desserts are optional tasks that students particularly interested in the topic may wish to complete.

*Record your menu choices each day. Write a sentence to tell something you learned or practiced.*

|  | Monday | Tuesday | Wednesday | Thursday | Friday |
|---|---|---|---|---|---|
| Using a Gizmo Applet |  |  |  |  |  |
| Using a Graphing Calculator |  |  |  |  |  |
| Writing a Note to a Friend |  |  |  |  |  |
| Creating Problems for the Problem Deck |  |  |  |  |  |
| Ordering the Steps |  |  |  |  |  |

Figure 7–4  *Recording sheet: students' menu choices.*

A sixth-grade teacher wants to create such a menu. To begin, the teacher thinks about her key question for the menu and identifies it as *How is symmetry related to art?* She then notes the key objectives that she has for students:

- Identify types of symmetry.
- Describe symmetry observed in art.
- Create a visual representation of one type of symmetry.

She decides she will introduce the topic by reading to her students *The Optical Artist: Exploring Patterns and Symmetry,* by Greg Roza (2005). This popular book provides a variety of interesting examples of symmetry from the works of M. C. Escher and other artists.

The teacher then thinks about how to create a menu as a follow-up to the story. She identifies three activities that focus on her

Strand: Geometry

Focus: Symmetry

Context: Exploring symmetry in art through menu activities

objectives and includes them within the main course section. She thinks of side dishes as ways to reinforce these ideas, so she includes six options that focus on specific applications of symmetry. Finally, she creates two desserts—activities that she thinks her students might enjoy doing, but that she doesn't think are essential. (See Figure 7–5; see also Reproducibles.)

As needed, the teacher can easily tier the menu for less or more ready students. For example, creating one page of an original version of *The Optical Artist* (Roza 2005) could be required, or a specific type of symmetry, such as rotational, could be identified to help students focus. For more challenge, students could work

Figure 7–5   *Menu: Symmetry in Art.*

---

**Menu: Symmetry in Art**

**Main Course (You must do each one.)**

- Make a list of items for a class scavenger hunt that requires your classmates to find different types of symmetry in your school. Be sure to indicate specific types of symmetry for each item on the list.

- Create a symmetrical spinning top that you can share with a younger child. The design should include three line symmetries and a rotational symmetry of 60°.

- Choose one object in nature that has symmetry and study that object in depth. For example, you may choose to study the symmetry in butterflies. Be sure to include discussion of centers of symmetry in your report.

**Side Orders (Complete two.)**

- Make a kaleidoscope that makes symmetrical patterns when turned.

- Interview an artist about how he or she uses symmetry in his or her artwork.

- Reread *The Optical Artist*, by Greg Roza (2005), and write your own description of one of the symmetrical pictures in the book.

- Make a slide show of symmetry in nature.

- Choose one of the symmetry websites that have been saved as favorites to explore.

- Find three representations of optical illusions that are interesting examples of different types of symmetry.

**Desserts (Do one or more if you are interested.)**

- Read three other books about symmetry and write a review of one of them for your classmates.

- Write a poem about symmetry and visually display this poem in a symmetrical format.

as a team to make a quilt that includes a combination of symmetries similar to those found in the book.

## Think-Tac-Toe

Think-tac-toe is another format that you can use to structure opportunities for students to make choices. A think-tac-toe board is usually a 3-by-3 matrix with nine cells, resembling the familiar tic-tac-toe game board, though you could create a grid with more cells. (See Figure 7–6; see also Reproducibles.) One option is for students to complete a task in each row. The tasks in the first row of this example focus on communication about ways to perform operations with fractions. The tasks in the second row provide computation practice with fractions and use of the guess-and-check problem-solving strategy. The tasks in the third row make connections such as inclusion of fractions in a newspaper, a classmate's way of thinking about fractions, and word problems. Another

*Organizing Choice Idea!*

**Strand:** Number

**Focus:** Computation with fractions

**Context:** Think-tac-toe format

*Photocopy It!*
See Reproducible 7D

Figure 7–6 *Think-tac-toe: fractions.*

**Think-Tac-Toe: Fractions**

*Choose and complete one activity in each row.*

| | | |
|---|---|---|
| Draw a picture that shows a model of $2\frac{1}{4} \times 1\frac{1}{2}$. Make connections between your drawing and how you use paper and pencil to find the product. Dictate your ideas to a friend. | Your brother divided $6\frac{1}{3}$ by $\frac{1}{2}$ and got the answer $3\frac{1}{6}$. What could you show and tell your brother to help him understand why his answer is wrong? | Write directions for two different ways to find $4\frac{3}{8} - 2\frac{5}{16}$ when you use paper and pencil. |
| Place the numbers $\frac{1}{16}$, $\frac{3}{16}$, $\frac{5}{16}$, $\frac{1}{8}$, $\frac{3}{8}$, and $\frac{1}{4}$ so that the sum of each side is $\frac{5}{8}$. ○ ○ ○ ○ ○ ○ | Place $+$, $\times$, or $\div$ to make a number sentence that is true. Add parentheses if needed. $\frac{1}{4} \square \frac{1}{8} \square \frac{3}{4} \square \frac{1}{2} = 1$ Write two more problems like this one and trade them with a classmate. | Which two numbers should you exchange so that the sum of the numbers on each card is the same? $\frac{1}{2}$ $\frac{2}{3}$ 1 \| $\frac{3}{4}$ $\frac{2}{3}$ $\frac{7}{12}$ $\frac{5}{12}$ $\frac{1}{4}$ $\frac{1}{2}$ \| $\frac{1}{12}$ $\frac{3}{4}$ $\frac{5}{6}$ Write two more problems like this one and trade them with a classmate. |
| Make a collage from newspaper ads or articles that include fractions. | Interview a classmate about what he or she knows about fractions. Find out as much as you can in three minutes. Write the teacher a report with suggestions for teaching. | Your friend solved a word problem by multiplying $2\frac{1}{2}$ times $\frac{1}{3}$ and then subtracting the product from 3. Write two interesting word problems that your friend could have solved this way. |

option in using a think-tac-toe board is to direct students to complete three tasks in a row. It is also possible to tier the choices, so that each row contains more challenging tasks than the previous row or each offers tasks more conducive to a different learning style and preference.

### RAFT

A RAFT activity is a strategy for differentiating learning that can also provide choice for students. The acronym stands for *role*, *audience*, *format*, and *topic*. To complete a RAFT activity, students create a product according to these four categories. For example, as a historian (role) speaking to children (audience), a student might create a presentation (format) to explain how our number system evolved (topic). As there is a specific purpose for each suggestion within a RAFT, this instructional strategy emphasizes the usefulness of mathematics and offers students an opportunity to think about how we use mathematics beyond the classroom.

A seventh-grade teacher decides to create a RAFT task about probability. He is concerned that his curriculum does not apply this topic enough to real-world applications. He is also aware that most students and adults tend to have many misconceptions about probability and wants students to explore the topic further. He tries to think about a variety of roles that might appeal to his students and different products they could create and comes up with the options in Figure 7–7 (see also Reproducibles).

## Learning Stations

You can use learning stations to augment a current unit, to highlight an important concept, or to maintain previously learned skills. They can provide opportunities for students to investigate topics further or to be introduced to new ways of thinking about mathematics. Stations are particularly helpful when there are not enough materials for the whole class to engage with at the same time. For example, a learning station focused on measurement might include a trundle wheel and a weight scale, items that would not be available in classroom sets. There might be one station that students rotate through as appropriate, or there could be several stations arranged about the room, with some students working at each one. These stations are temporary structures in the classroom that may be made available for a day, a week, or a couple of weeks. Learning stations add variety to our instructional patterns while providing choices for students.

| RAFT: Probability | | | |
|---|---|---|---|
| **Role** | **Audience** | **Format** | **Topic** |
| Meteorologist | Middle school students | PowerPoint presentation | How I use probability on my job |
| Financial advisor | People trying to save money | Song | Why you shouldn't buy lottery tickets |
| Game maker | Game company boss | Game | Game with just the right combination of skill and luck |
| Stockbroker | Clients | Report | Probability of making money in the stock market |
| Sports analyst | Team manager | Convincing argument | Creation of a dream team |
| Fill in your | choice here | Check with the | teacher for approval. |

Figure 7–7  *RAFT: probability.*

Photocopy It! See Reproducible 7E

A seventh-grade teacher is thinking about ways to help students make connections among content they have studied throughout the year. Because of the emphasis on standardized tests, her school has initiated a planned review session once or twice a month, but she would like her students to make connections and retain the mathematical ideas learned throughout the year. She knows that proportional reasoning permeates the middle school curriculum and is critical to success in all branches of mathematics. She believes students require time and repeated opportunities to deepen and apply proportional thinking and decides that learning stations would address this need. This month she will extend the review session to two days and expect students to deepen their thinking as well as review content.

Identifying the learning goals that will be supported or extended through station activities is her first step in the planning process. She wants to emphasize skills that benefit most from extended exploration with hands-on activities. She also wants the stations to help students connect proportional reasoning to the real world as well as to several branches of mathematics. After

Organizing Choice Idea!

Strand: Number

Focus: Proportional reasoning

Context: Working at learning stations

identifying these broad instructional goals, she decides the stations will focus on the following content:

- comparing or determining equivalence of ratios
- representing proportional relationships in multiple ways
- determining and using scale factors
- using proportions in a variety of contexts

Her next step is to choose or design appropriate activities that will meet the learning goals and appeal to a variety of interests and learning styles. She wants the tasks to be somewhat open-ended, but also self-sustaining, because she cannot be at several stations at once. She also wants the activities to feel linked, not random, to the class, so that students can make connections as they further explore proportional reasoning.

She brainstorms a number of options and decides on four stations that will involve several content strands and focus on proportional reasoning. She will cluster desks to delineate the stations. To allow for multiple groupings, she will make three laminated copies of the task card for each station.

At the first station she places three closed boxes, each containing all blue, all yellow, or all red cubes; a cloth to drape over each box; adhesive dots; and copies of an article about three techniques used to estimate wildlife populations. The task card tells students that it is their job to estimate the entire population of the trout in each pond, represented by the cubes in the boxes. They may place the cloth over a box, remove the cover, capture a maximum of twenty-five trout without looking inside the box, mark them with a dot, return them to the pond, and mix them into the population. They can take up to ten samples of twenty-five fish. The task card tells students what they must do to complete the activity:

1. First make a plan for your experiment that includes how many trout you will capture and mark, how many samples you will take, and how you will use your data.
2. Explain your conclusions about the populations.
3. Read the article and compare your experiments with the work of the wildlife experts.

At the next station, which focuses on relationships among a country's population and its consumption of food or energy, the teacher has gathered two maps of the world, two computers, a digital camera, and two containers of raisins. The task card for this activity reads:

1. You will focus on North America and two other continents (excluding Antarctica) of your choice. Use the websites in the Continent folder (saved in the Favorites section) to find information about the population and consumption of each of the three continents. Make notes about the data as you read.

2. Assume that 100 raisins represent the population of the world. Place the appropriate number of raisins on the map to represent the populations of North America and the two continents you chose. Explain your thinking in your portfolio, and then label your map (population) and take a picture of it.

3. Clear the map and now place raisins to indicate the continents' consumption of the world's food or energy. Again, explain your thinking in your portfolio, label your map, and take a picture of it.

4. Write about your findings in your portfolio.

At the third station, students will focus on scale factors with Cuisenaire rods, metersticks, masking tape, and flashlights. The station is placed near a bulletin board with a large piece of plain white paper on it. The task card for this site states:

1. With your partner(s), choose a rod, hold it upright, and turn the flashlight on directly behind it so that its shadow is formed on the white paper. Mark your position on the floor (with tape) and measure your distance from the wall as well as the length of the rod's shadow. (Use centimeters.)

2. Using the same color rod, repeat this process standing at different distances from the wall.

3. Make a table and a line graph to show your data.

4. Write conclusions in your portfolio about how the length of the shadow changes in relationship to the distance from the wall.

5. Repeat this process, standing at the same marked positions with a different-color rod.

6. Choose a third rod and make predictions about the data you will collect. Explain your thinking in your portfolio. Check your predictions.

The fourth station focuses on scale factors. It has rulers, compasses, protractors, string, construction paper, three new pencils (sharpened), masking tape, and staplers. The task card informs students that they are to make a model of a pencil for a 40-foot-tall giant. The card states:

1. Make a plan for determining the dimensions of the pencil. Record your thinking in your portfolio.
2. Record the measures you take and describe how you will use the data to determine measures for the giant's pencil.
3. Construct your model.
4. Reflect on your work. Include sources of measurement errors.

Finally, the teacher places a hanging file organizer with a folder for each student next to her desk. Each folder has a recording sheet along with several blank pieces of paper stapled together. These folders will serve as the students' portfolios. It is important that students record their work and document their station activities. This system will allow students to be independent and help the learning stations run smoothly.

During math time the next day, the teacher spends a few minutes introducing the tasks and related materials at each station. She wants her students to be aware of the purpose of the stations and the goals for learning. She does not model how to complete the activities, but rather briefly describes each one, showing the materials, articulating her expectations for working with a partner, and demonstrating how to complete the recording sheet. She emphasizes that the students are expected to work at one station today and at a different one tomorrow. She then allows the students to choose a station, telling them that no more than six students may be at a station at one time. There's a bit of shuffling about at first, but within a couple of minutes the students have found a place to work and begin to engage with the tasks.

Some teachers prefer to have only one station in a classroom that students explore over time. An eighth-grade teacher provides a station for exploring Fibonacci numbers during a week focused on geometry, art, and nature. The class is divided into three groups for the duration of this topic and each group is given a weekly schedule that involves group work, independent tasks, skill workshops with the teacher, and time at the learning station. Each student will spend two half periods at the station during the week. The station is designed to allow a small group of students to work independently or collaboratively while additional learning opportunities are taking place in other areas of the classroom.

To designate space for the station, the teacher moves a rectangular table alongside the bulletin board and places four chairs at the table. He hopes this arrangement will separate the station from other activities and provide a more private space to work. He usually puts a station near a bulletin board, as the board provides space for sharing ideas and serves as a visual reminder of the work being done. This teacher's board works particularly well because it is near the classroom's two computers. The station offers several tasks that students may choose to complete. Though time does not allow students to explore all of them, students become aware of the tasks through other students' explorations and notes left on the bulletin board. The activities include:

- Solve the problem: A robot can take a step that is 1 ft. long or 2 ft. long. How many different ways can it travel the distance of 10 ft.? (White and red Cuisenaire rods are available to represent the steps.)
- Choose the rectangles you find most pleasing and measure them to compare their length-to-width ratios. Do the same with pictures of famous buildings such as the Parthenon.
- Complete the activity sheet *Are We Golden?* which requires measuring various parts of your body and computing identified ratios (Reeder 2007).
- Investigate the spirals on real objects such as celery stalks, pinecones, pineapples, and nautilus shells.
- Make a list of the numbers in the Fibonacci sequence and draw conclusions about the positions in the list of multiples and greatest common factors.
- Examine patterns in baskets and woven placemats to find examples of numbers in the Fibonacci sequence and then create your own patterns with yarn and cardboard looms.

Stations such as these take time to develop and organize. In the interest of being resourceful, the teacher might consider making stations only for those topics that will be explored yearly. Ideally, station materials are stored in a plastic tub or folder (without the related manipulatives and tools) so that they are ready to be used in subsequent years. Some teachers need to store stations in such ways all the time, because they need the stations to be portable. Portable stations can be used in different parts of the room or even be put away for a few days, if necessary. Ample space is a rare commodity in many classrooms. As the following teacher reflection makes clear, making strategic decisions based on availability of space, time, and amount of materials is an ongoing process.

I value the need for setting up, maintaining, and rotating learning stations in my classroom. Learning stations have helped me be able to offer more choices to my students. In my mind this equates to more opportunities to practice and to learn. Once a station is up and running, my goal is for it to be self-sustaining. I want to be able to engage with other students at their point of need or to have a chance to sit back as an observer. I try to design stations that do not require any teacher direction after the initial introduction.

Since I have been teaching for a few years, I have been able to reuse learning stations as a unit comes up for study in later years. Over time I have been able to test out how self-sustaining an activity may be for the majority of my students. I know I always have to be open to different learning styles and preferences. I have to give particular consideration to my English language learning students and think about what they can read or write to fulfill learning expectations at any given point in the year.

I also need to consider what I use to define the space for the station. Have I given ample room? Have I separated stations from other work areas so that students are not unnecessarily distracted? Have I provided all the necessary materials for success? Do these materials need to be placed at the station or do my students know where to find them when they want them? Students know where to find resources in our classroom. I have set an expectation that students are the ones who know what they need at any point in time and are encouraged to act responsibly on that need.

*Students know where to find resources in our classroom. I have set an expectation that students are the ones who know what they need at any point in time and are encouraged to act responsibly on that need.*

Maintaining stations can take a lot of time. In some cases I can store all of the materials for a given activity in one box and when students have completed the work, I can store it away for another time. More typically the manipulatives used at one station are used repeatedly. I cannot store these away. When I have more than one station running at the same time, I may have to borrow materials from another teacher. I have to think about the best ways to juggle all of these things, but I always find the extra effort worth it.

This teacher uses a word in her reflection that sounds familiar to all teachers: *juggle.* Juggling is part of the art and craft of teaching and learning. Determining what will happen at each station and feeling confident that the activities are aligned to the curriculum must always be in the forefront of our thoughts. The following questions can help guide the implementation of learning stations:

| Key Questions for Planning Learning Stations |
|---|
| 1. Who decides what materials or activities are available and when? |
| 2. Who decides if a student will engage in this work? |
| 3. How will time be managed? How long will students be given to complete a task? |
| 4. Who initiates what goes on at a station? |
| 5. How will activities at a station be assessed? |
| 6. How will I support discussion and closure of stations? |

These questions are among a host of decisions that teachers must make to create and implement learning stations. Consider as well the other instructional strategies for structuring choice that have been presented in this chapter. Taking all of these into account, here are our answers to the previous questions.

## 1. Who decides what materials or activities are available and when?

Once teachers determine curriculum objectives, they identify which materials might be needed to help students meet those established goals. If the materials are new to students, the students need to learn how to use them and where to store them. Once the materials are familiar, however, most can be made available to students at all times, to be used whenever needed. In the spirit of choice, we recommend that students choose materials whenever that choice does not hinder safety or greatly reduce the likelihood that learning will be successful.

## 2. Who decides if a student will engage in this work?

Often teachers operate from a mind-set that all students should complete every activity. This mind-set may stem from our desire to support inclusive and equitable classrooms. We need to balance this desire with the realization that for a class to be equitable, each student must get what he needs based on readiness, interest, and learning style; this does not mean that we should feed the student every activity. All students do not need to complete every activity in order to support a classroom community. Also, we need to open our minds to the possibility that students themselves can participate in making these decisions. In fact, they can often be quite helpful. For example, one sixth grader explained to her teacher, "I need to know fractions better before I do problems like this." Conversely, sometimes a student might select a more difficult task than the teacher would have assigned. When students are motivated and supported, they often can achieve and understand more than we expected.

## 3. How will time be managed? How long will students be given to complete a task?

Every teacher has an ongoing battle with the classroom clock. We can all agree there is never enough time. Part of this dilemma stems from the fact that no two students work at the same pace or learn at the same rate. Some teachers plan for an average amount of time that it will take most students to complete a task and then have to be flexible for those students who finish early and those who require more time. Students who finish early can be encouraged to move on to another activity or station instead of waiting for everyone to be done. We can also make stations available for an indefinite amount of time, especially if they take up little classroom space. If the station remains intact for a few days, students who need more time to complete a station activity can have that opportunity during another class period. What is of utmost value is the recognition that students need different amounts of time at different points of learning.

## 4. Who initiates what goes on at a station?

This question brings up the notion of the teachable moment. Certainly teachers make initial plans for learning stations, but we always want to be open for ideas that students offer us as a direction for learning. There is an art to finessing these ideas, offering students permission to share their thoughts, and giving them time, space, and materials to follow their interests. Unfortunately this conflicts with some of the current trends in our educational practices. Coverage of material included in curriculum guides and standardized tests seems to be of major concern; student questions that do not immediately map onto an easily recognizable curriculum objective are sometimes viewed as unnecessary tangents. This concern has increased as school systems have adopted pacing guides as well as expectations that textbook programs be followed exclusively. It is important to remember that activities that include choice are not intended as detours. Teachers can create stations that allow students to meet required curriculum objectives through alternative approaches.

We do not want our students to think of school as a place where we disregard what they want to learn. Often, when we stop and think about how we can relate the topic of study to a current interest, we can find a path. For example, an interest in iPods could lead to an investigation on how size, capacity, weight, and cost may or may not be related.

### 5. How will activities at a station be assessed?

When an activity results in a product of some kind, teachers often feel that assessment is more manageable and they become more confident in their decision making. The review of and reflection on student work samples is an important step in evaluating students' learning. Also, take time to observe students in action and to engage students in conversations as they work. A natural strategy for capturing these moments is to keep anecdotal records. Digital or video cameras can also be wonderful ways to document learning. Assessments of activities at learning stations come full circle, as do all assessments, back to the learning goals that led to the development of the stations in the first place. Being mindful of our goals—and letting students know them—helps us focus assessment in any learning environment, whether there is a tangible product or a set of scenarios that tell the story of learning.

### 6. How will I support discussion and closure of stations?

One of the ways we let students know that something is important is to take time to discuss it—to exchange strategies, consider alternative conclusions, and highlight connections and extensions. Such discussions also allow us to firmly link the activities to the original learning goals. Observing our students at work and reviewing their portfolios can help us determine the order in which students report, so that the complexity of ideas builds and allows students to extend their thinking as they follow the discussion. When more than one station has been explored, this is an opportunity to help students make connections among the various activities. Finally, this is a time to return to pre-assessment responses or to a KWHL chart (see page 161 in Chapter 6) and reflect on what has been learned.

Answering the questions posed here can be difficult. These questions require that we make decisions that can be demanding of our time and our efforts. The best decision is always rooted in

*Take Action!*

Support debriefing.

the context of our own school settings and our students' needs. We must also remember that these decisions are not set in stone. Flexibility is key; as we gather new information or learn new instructional strategies, we can revise our practice to better meet the growing needs of all of our students.

## Keeping the Interest Alive

Along with empowering our students, providing choice in our classrooms helps us tap into their interests. But just having choices available does not guarantee interest. Any parent who has heard the lament "There's nothing to do!" understands this well. Part of the attraction of making a choice is that it can lead to something new and exhilarating. Changing the available materials on a regular basis adds a fresh look. Having a familiar material or activity disappear can pique curiosity or even be a relief. Having it come back again in a few weeks or months may also be a welcome change.

Engaging new senses, such as smell, can provide unexpected attention. Multimedia presentations can also create new interest. Introducing topics in novel ways piques interest. Gigantic footprints across the ceiling to introduce a unit on proportional reasoning or a set of clues to help students make guesses about a new topic adds intrigue to learning. Adding a little surprise to our classrooms can be fun and helps students view mathematics in new ways, even when routines or objects are highly familiar.

Earlier in this chapter a teacher helped us consider making good choices. Helping students self-monitor this criterion is not easy. Yet it is our role as teachers to support our students in their individual decision-making processes. Holding class meetings or individual conversations is a strategy frequently used to support students' growth in this area. It is the establishment of expectations, trust, accountability, and security that can support our students as they make choices in our classrooms. As we get to know them as individuals and they get to know themselves as adolescent learners, we can encourage, direct, redirect, and applaud their efforts. All of this must happen within a full and lively classroom that changes in atmosphere and mood throughout the week and over the course of a year. Creating and maintaining learning laboratories like these presents unending questions as to how to balance the needs of the class as a whole with those of individual students. Discovering ways to orchestrate this complex process is a daily challenge.

## Connecting the Chapter to Your Practice

1. How do you think teachers of mathematics compare with teachers of other subjects, in terms of providing choices to students? Why do you think this is the case?

2. Of the various strategies for organizing choice presented, which ones are you most likely to incorporate in your teaching? Why?

3. What materials in your classroom are easily accessible to students?

# Chapter 8
# Managing Differentiated Instruction

*T*he role of a teacher has been compared to that of a coach or a conductor. Both lead a group of individuals with different talents and do not assume that those talents should be nurtured in the same manner. Coaches and conductors know how to motivate each member of their group and aim to develop all of the participants' strengths and work on weaknesses. They hold practices with the whole group, identified subgroups, and individuals. Each athlete or musician has slightly different tasks to perfect, and yet in the end, the goal is for everyone to work together to produce a unified and masterful performance on the field or in the concert hall.

Teachers also need to develop a sense of a unified classroom while addressing individual students' strengths and weaknesses. In a differentiated classroom where students are more likely to be engaged in multiple tasks that support their different levels of learning readiness, learning styles, and interests, it can be challenging to also develop a mathematical learning community that comes together to build, discuss, and verify ideas. Yet this is a challenge we must address. Differentiated instruction is not the same thing as individualized instruction. We do not believe that students should learn mathematics in isolation or that they should be deprived of the joy of being an active member of a well-functioning community group.

Teachers must also figure out how to manage different tasks going on at the same time. They need to distribute and collect materials in ways that do not require a lot of time and effort. They are challenged to find ways to have other students engaged in meaningful activities while they work uninterrupted with a small group. There is a necessity to create classroom spaces for noisy activities and quiet ones. Teachers need to think about the limitations of space, materials, and time as they make their plans. They may also need to think about how to share their classroom with a coteacher or instructional aide. They must take the intricate components of classroom life and the complex needs of adolescent learners and create a masterful learning environment.

While we do not want to promote the idea that a teacher must create a masterpiece each day in the classroom, we do believe that a well-managed classroom that supports students' learning while maintaining a sense of community is a masterpiece—one that begins its composition the moment students walk in the door on the first day of school. In a differentiated classroom, right from the beginning, values, routines, expectations, and cooperative relationships need to be established to develop an environment conducive to learning. Teachers must manage differentiated instruction through classroom space, respect for differences, routines, student groups, time with individual students, ragged time, whole-class work, and teaching partnerships.

## Classroom Space

Ample space is a rare commodity in many classrooms. We need to make careful decisions about how to use limited space to support a variety of groupings and activities. The following guidelines help teachers think about ways to arrange a classroom to support diffe rentiated instruction; we recognize that most teachers need to find their own creative solutions to provide enough space for both groups and individuals to work.

---

**Managing Classroom Space for Differentiated Instruction**

**Choose tables**

If you have room only for desks or tables, and you have a choice, choose tables. In general, tables are more useful because they can accommodate individual or small-group learning and provide additional space for shared materials. Round tables are more conducive to small-group work because they allow everyone seated there to easily see one another's face. If tables are not available, consider arranging desks in clusters to form a similar work space that supports collaboration and conversation. If at all possible, avoid chairs and desktops or writing spaces that are attached, as these offer the least flexibility.

---

*(Continued)*

## Managing Classroom Space for Differentiated Instruction (Continued)

### Consider removing your desk

If you are asking your students to function without desks, think about doing the same yourself. While you need personal storage areas, removing the teacher's desk may allow you to add an extra learning station or private space in the classroom. This may seem out of the question or unrealistic to you at first. Allowing yourself the chance to consider this option may lead to new possibilities for use of space in your classroom. It may also lead to reflecting on how space and arrangement may influence teaching and learning.

### Maximize storage space

Ample storage space is essential to organized and efficient classrooms. Materials should be easily accessible and labeled to ensure proper return. Just as with our drawers and closets at home, having too many materials in too little space results in disorganization. Store materials used occasionally or during specific units in a supply closet or in higher cabinets in the room.

### Consider traffic patterns

Make sure that students can travel easily from one table to another, to and from the classroom door, and to the various mathematical supplies and manipulatives in the room. Make these pathways wide enough so that you and the students can move back and forth without asking other students to move or interrupting their work.

### Designate space for the essentials

Designate space for essential materials such as recording sheets or packets for student work, finished-work baskets, portfolios, or other assessment-related data. Some teachers use hanging file folders as a way to organize incoming and outgoing work. Teachers sometimes place all of the activity sheets related to a new unit in an open file box that is labeled so that students can easily get a new sheet without asking. Many teachers place a hanging file or an open file box for incoming work beside the place where they do their planning. In this way, teachers can easily access student work as they plan for the next day, prepare for student or parent conferences, or write report cards. Teachers can also easily file students' work in portfolios or other data-type collections.

### Consider work spaces beyond your classroom

Hallways, computer rooms, and media centers may provide additional working space for small-group or independent work. Some teachers take advantage of having strong, positive relationships with colleagues in adjacent classrooms, occasionally identifying one room for small groups and one for quieter, individual work.

The following reflection shows how a teacher's idea of how to best set up a classroom can change over time.

## Teacher Reflection

When I first started teaching eighth grade, I used to spend hours and hours making attractive bulletin boards that displayed all kinds of interesting information for my students to absorb. I had charts that showed measurement conversions and posters that showed the ways in which numbers were used in the real world. I always made fancy borders for the bulletin boards so that they would look attractive. It took me days to put up these boards. By the time I got finished decorating, I realized that I had precious time left to think about how to arrange my classroom's furniture. I just put the desks into tightly knit groups, hoping that the arrangement would allow everyone to see the board when necessary.

It took me a year or so to realize that a number of my students had significant growth spurts over the summer between their seventh- and eighth-grade years and that I needed to provide enough room for them to sit comfortably and to move around the classroom easily. And, although my students did seem to appreciate the attractiveness of my classroom, they didn't spend a whole lot of time using the resources that I had provided. So, as I prepared for my third year of teaching, I spent a lot more time thinking about how to arrange my room and much less time on bulletin boards.

*So, as I prepared for my third year of teaching, I spent a lot more time thinking about how to arrange my room and much less time on bulletin boards.*

I traded in my desks for round conference tables and chairs that had a shelf underneath for students to put their extra books. I have the students sit in a way that leaves a seat for me at each of the tables. That way, I can join my students when they are working in small groups and not just stand over them. They have gotten used to me sitting down, listening in, and only sometimes participating. Using these round tables in place of desks gives my students more room to move around and also allows me to bring in other furniture. I now have a storage unit to keep all of my materials and a special place for my students to get their own handouts when appropriate.

Each table of students has a "distribution manager," who is in charge, for the week, of getting necessary materials and handouts for activities. This has worked much better than me handing out everything. I also now have space to put my display computer and don't have to set it up every time I want to use it. My lessons seem to flow a lot better now that I have put the time into making sure that everything is accessible to my students. Even though I still have bulletin boards, my students now contribute to them more and the efficient classroom setup better supports learning.

# Respect for Differences

In order for differentiated classrooms to function well, all participants must know that you require respectful behavior. During the adolescent stage of development, formation of identity is critical and peer acceptance takes on a dominant role. Thus it is essential that everyone respects others' learning needs and styles and realizes that all class members have the right to have their needs met. Activities that identify and celebrate differences help students better understand why their classrooms are organized the way that they are. These activities help students get to know themselves and each other better. This knowledge allows students to better support each other individually and to feel more connected as a community of learners.

One teacher has students complete a survey form sometime during the first week of school. The form is called *What Matches You?* and provides twenty-five different statements about learning for students to consider. (See Figure 8–1; see also Reproducibles.)

Figure 8–1    *Survey: What Matches You?*

---

**What Matches You?**

*Try to find two classmates who match each description. Have them sign their names in the boxes they match. No one may sign more than three boxes on one sheet.*

| | | | | |
|---|---|---|---|---|
| I learn best through hands-on experiences. | I like to solve problems. | I prefer to work alone in mathematics. | I find it helpful to write about my mathematical ideas. | I sometimes get confused when others explain their thinking. |
| I understand fractions better than percents. | I like to measure things. | I use drawings to understand a problem. | I learn best when the teacher writes on the board. | I find a number line helpful when working with integers. |
| I am better at division than multiplication. | I like rotating shapes in my mind. | I need it to be quiet when I work. | I prefer fraction strips to fraction circles. | I prefer to work with others. |
| I know my basic facts well. | I like digital clocks better than face clocks. | I am better at solving equations than graphing them. | I like reading and making maps. | I like learning different ways to solve problems. |
| I like to brainstorm ideas with a group and then follow up alone. | I like logic games and puzzles. | I want rules for solving problems. | I would like to use a calculator all of the time. | I read tables and graphs in the newspaper. |

Some of the items are general statements about learning, such as "I need it to be quiet when I work." Other statements focus on mathematics, such as "I am better at fractions than percents."

As we learn from the following teacher's reflection, this form can spark conversations about learning and about mathematics.

## Teacher Reflection

For a couple of years I used a form like *What Matches You?* during the first day or two of school. It got students walking around and talking to each other and learning something about their classmates. Four elementary schools feed into my middle school and so the students can be a bit overwhelmed by the sea of new faces during the first week. I used to put in items such as "I like to play baseball" or "I like chocolate ice cream." This year I decided to focus more on learning.

> I recognized that students would eventually find out about each other's recreational and food preferences, but that they might never talk about how they each learn.

I recognized that students would eventually find out about each other's recreational and food preferences, but that they might never talk about how they each learn. Also, I was hoping this activity might help them to gain an intuitive sense of why I strive to provide differentiated learning opportunities in our classroom.

Their responses took somewhat longer to be formulated. They used to know right away whether they liked chocolate, but deciding if they wanted rules for solving problems required some reflection. Some students were amazed to find that everybody didn't think a digital clock was better than a face clock and others were pleased to find someone else who preferred to work alone.

After we did this activity, we talked about the differences in our classroom and how it was important to respect these different ways of learning. We made a list of what we learned. Marcus said, "I have to be quiet sometimes so that Billy can think."

Jamie said, "I might want to try using the fraction strips."

Ellie said, "It's good that we are different. Otherwise, it would be boring." It felt wonderful to hear the students articulate these ideas.

Immediately following this conversation we began our first differentiated learning activity. I introduced it by saying, "Many times in our classroom we will be doing different activities from each other. Why do you think that is so?"

Several hands popped up and I called on Ricardo, who said, "Because we are different." What a great way to begin!

**Take Action!**

Establish schoolwide expectations for respect.

Some teachers are able to take advantage of middle school teams, establishing expectations for respect for differences across the subject areas. When rules for respectful behavior are team- or schoolwide, it increases the likelihood that students will follow them. One middle school started a schoolwide campaign about respect in and out of the classroom. The principal arranged to have guest speakers come in to talk about what bullying means, to have students talk in their homerooms about what it means to respect each other's differences, and to involve parents in his campaign. The classroom teachers worked with their students to determine how to best respect learning differences in their specific subjects.

One seventh-grade teacher involves students in brainstorming respectful alternatives to statements such as these:

- You're wrong.
- My way is better.
- Why are you doing it that way?

She also engages students in open discussions about how they feel when disrespectful behavior occurs. She finds that these discussions lead to stronger empathy for one another and commit students to behaving differently. She knows that her seventh graders need to broaden their understanding of what it means to be respectful in the classroom; many of her students believe that it just means to not make rude comments. But, as she and her students learned during their assembly on bullying, there are many ways to disrespect each other's way of learning.

**Take Action!**

Support classroom discourse.

In tandem with these discussions, she begins to model ways for students to work side by side with others in a classroom with a wide range of learners. In the beginning of the year she reminds them, "Please raise your hand when you are ready to share your solution." She is consistent about students needing to raise their hands, as she wants all students to have time to think about their answers before some students call out a response or let everyone know they're done by exclaiming, "I got it!" She also asks questions such as "Do you have a different idea?" and "Did anyone approach this problem differently?" to encourage alternative responses. She encourages other students to restate what they hear and to begin their comments by building on what the last student has said. She asks questions such as "Why do you think that Margaret solved the problem the way that she did?" and "Nathan, would you be willing to add more to what Leah said about this problem?"

Through her own actions and the manner in which she encourages her students to respond to each other, both in small groups as well as in whole-class discussions, this teacher sets the tone for a classroom in which all students respect each other's ways of thinking. This level of respect often results in students learning a good deal more from each other and exploring pathways to learning that would not have been there otherwise.

## Routines

Routines serve several purposes in a classroom. Once students recognize ways to walk into class, get into groups, distribute assignment papers, put away materials, and turn in homework, these activities occur quickly and efficiently. Though considerable time and effort are needed to establish classroom norms, once they are established, students adhere to them with minimal energy and teacher supervision. This is particularly important in a differentiated classroom where students are expected to manage themselves, more frequently and often for longer durations, while the teacher is working with other students.

Routines also instill feelings of safety and security. When the same procedures are followed on a daily or weekly basis, students understand what is expected of them and can predict what will happen next. Such regularity helps students feel emotionally safe and thus more able to participate in the learning process. Established routines also create community. As students identify and describe the ways in which their classroom runs, they are forming their understanding of the unique culture of that classroom.

Transitions can often be challenging. Moving from the whole class to small groups, especially if moving furniture is involved, can be quite time-consuming. In many schools math periods are already much too short and we cannot afford to waste any of those precious minutes. Some teachers have students practice getting into groups while they race against the clock. You might use stopwatches to encourage students to beat previous times; with practice, more efficient transitions become routine.

Upon entering the classroom, there are always students who want to talk with their teacher about the previous night's baseball game or ask a question about an ongoing project. One middle school teacher manages this entry time by having a "do now" task on the board or at her students' desks. She also has a list of what the students will need for the day's lesson on the board. Students

Take Action!

Start class periods.

learn to follow the routine of gathering necessary materials, either from their own personal supplies or from the classroom materials, and engaging with their tablemates in the "do now" task. The teacher varies whether or not she has a classroom discussion about the problem. If her lesson allows time to go over it that day, then she will. Other times, she provides the students with a correct response and then asks them to put their work in their pocket folder. Students are expected to submit a corrected version at the next class meeting.

Many middle school teachers also establish routines for how they review homework with students. There is a myriad of ways in which homework may be checked, both for completion and for accuracy. One middle school teacher lists the problem numbers on the board, and at the beginning of each class, students individually, or as a group, put a check mark next to the problem number that they would like the teacher to go over with the entire class. Some students begin their class period with discussions of their homework in small groups, sometimes with an answer key. As they do so they learn to assist one another with determining how to approach difficult problems and to engage in alternative ways of thinking. In this approach, the teacher is often able to minimize the time needed to review homework and allow more time for the day's activities.

As an exit routine, one sixth-grade teacher often finalizes his lesson about five minutes before the end of the class period to give students time to return materials and complete a ticket to leave. The questions on these tickets vary. There might be a mathematical question related to the day's lesson, such as *Does a square have rotational symmetry?* Or questions may focus on students' general understanding of the day's work, by asking, *On a scale of 1–10, how well do you think that you understand the formula for surface area of a cone?* or *What else do you think that you need to review at home before the test on Friday?* For more ticket examples, see page 164 in Chapter 6.

## Flexible Grouping

Another way to maximize learning is to think critically about group work. Though whole-group teaching can be very powerful and some teachers believe it promotes equality by ensuring that all students are taught the same lessons, it is not always the most effective way to learn. As we have explored throughout this book, differentiation is focused on finding the most effective ways of meeting our students' various needs and interests. Organizing students into groups can simultaneously promote individual learning.

Grouping for differentiated instruction is different than working in groups. Group work has been long recognized as a way to break up the whole-class instructional pattern, to engage students more actively in their learning, and to provide greater opportunities for communication and social interactions. Traditionally, each group completes the same task. The teacher rotates among the groups, supporting their work and informing their thinking. While that is a useful instructional strategy, grouping for differentiated instruction is even more intentional.

Within differentiated instruction, grouping is flexible; that is, groups are formed with a specific focus and then reconfigured when a new purpose is identified. The formation of groups may be based on readiness, learning styles, or interests and can be heterogeneous or homogenous. Groups may be formed for a day, a week, or a few weeks. This flexible grouping keeps students from being labeled and allows them to work with a variety of their peers.

Take Action!

Form flexible groups.

It takes time and thought to group students. Thinking about why you are grouping and whether groups will be designed around a specific learning goal, learning style, interest, product, or behavior is all part of the process. You have to identify the appropriate size of the group, the amount of time the group should work together, and the composition of the group. You also need to think about how groups and their materials will be identified and organized.

Sometimes groups are formed at random. Some teachers keep a deck of cards with stickers on them. If six groups are needed and there are twenty-four students in the class, teachers use four different kinds of stickers. Teachers shuffle the deck and students randomly select a card. All students with the same sticker form a new group. Sometimes these cards correspond to tables or areas of the room and as students pick a card, they know right away where to go to meet their new group.

Sometimes students choose their own groups or partnerships. Allowing students to make this choice is one of the ways we can share our classroom authority. Many teachers find that they are most comfortable with this option only when dyads are being formed, when groups will be intact for a short period of time, or when partners or groups will work together on the basis of interest.

More often, differentiated instruction requires teachers to form groups intentionally; that is, teachers match students specifically in ways to best meet learning needs. One teacher frequently changes student groups in her classroom. She keeps a large magnetic board and a set of name tags backed with magnetic tape to help her organize this process. When she plans an activity that requires new groups, she moves the names on the board according to her criteria. She explained, "I used to do this on paper. When the grouping was obvious, this worked fine. Sometimes, though, I find it challenging to make groups and change my mind several times. With the board, I can try out several formations easily. Then when I am done, the list is already there for my students to see."

Many teachers keep a log of the groups that are formed during the first few weeks of school. The log can serve as a place to keep notes about groups that function particularly well together or partnerships that seem to require more supervision. A teacher can also make sure that everyone has the opportunity to work with all the other classmates during these first weeks of community building. It can also be worthwhile to note how the groups were formed so that over time, students work according to readiness, learning styles, and interests.

It is essential to keep students' social-emotional development in mind. Note that though a middle school student might feel isolated at any time, forming partners and groups can actually heighten such feelings. Some students may wonder why they are in one group versus another. Others may worry about being chosen or welcomed. Still others may have fears about how they will be able to contribute to a particular group. Concern for isolation, safety, comfort, friendships, and working relationships must always be part of the grouping process.

We must also recognize that middle school is often the first time that students are tracked. If your school insists on this organization, we encourage you to lobby for broader bands of ability levels or to delay the structure until eighth grade. You may want to organize a study group of colleagues to read and discuss *Detracking for Excellence and Equity* (Burris and Garrity 2008). We also recommend that you examine data about students in honors algebra and basic review courses. School officials are often surprised when they consider the percentage of students who receive free or reduced-price lunches who are enrolled in these classes. Such data can stimulate our thinking about hidden inequities and illuminate the need for earlier interventions. Finally, we must remember that even when classes are supposedly organized by ability levels, they still include a diverse group of learners.

## Individual Time

There are times when teachers and students need and want to work one-on-one. While some may consider this a luxury in a busy classroom, many teachers find such work to be one of the most enlightening aspects of their day. Working with an individual student provides time for getting to know the student better, for assessing a specific skill or competence, or simply for getting to the depths of a problem. Individual time can be rewarding and informative to both the student and the teacher and nourishes a necessary supportive, trusting relationship.

Differentiated instruction supports opportunities to work with individual students by building expectations for different learning activities to occur simultaneously. Other students do not expect the teacher to always be available to them and thus develop their ability to work independently. Teacher-student partnerships become just one of the various configurations within the classroom. Such acceptance also supports longer individual interactions such as interviews, tutoring, or follow-up to a lesson.

Many teachers can relate to the image of keeping several plates spinning in the air. We work tirelessly to keep every student engaged and learning. Sometimes, even in our best attempts, plates fall. In these moments it is important to have ways to work with individual students. Sometimes we can anticipate a falter and a quick spin or adjustment will help the student get back on track. Sometimes the student needs more intensive work. For example, in one seventh-grade class, students are asked to solve for $p$ in the following equation:

Take Action!

Discover misconceptions.

$$3p - 6 = 12$$

Brin has experienced success with solving similar problems, such as $3p + 6 = 12$, by subtracting six from both sides. Unfortunately, she continues this approach, again subtracting six from each side. As this does not isolate the variable, she subtracts again. She tries this approach mentally one more time before frustration takes over. She sighs heavily and eventually regresses to a guess-and-check method. (See Figure 8–2.)

Upon questioning her, Brin's teacher realizes what type of error she is making, but it takes a few more questions to determine why she is consistently subtracting. Brin is insistent that she needs

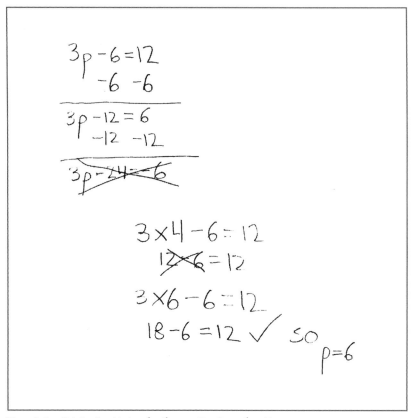

Figure 8–2 *Brin's attempts to solve the equation* $3p - 6 = 12$.

to subtract six from both sides because "It needs to go away." Although Brin has experience with negative numbers, she fails to understand that the subtraction sign is essentially modifying the six and needs to be considered as a part of what she is trying to remove from that side.

Brin's teacher reengages her in several problems where she utilizes the visual model of coins and pouches as outlined in the curriculum and then helps Brin to retransition to solving the equations without the visual model. Interestingly, another student in Brin's group notices what they are doing and comments that he is having the same difficulty. This student, too, becomes interested in visualizing the problem, and the idea that you always subtract from both sides is quickly dispelled. If Brin's teacher had not sat with her, the teacher may never have uncovered the source of Brin's misconception.

Other times, a one-on-one conversation with the teacher is necessary to better understand how students' attitudes influence their learning. Collin has been coming after school to work with his teacher for several sessions prior to a test. He has been frustrated by his test grades. He believes that he understands the content, yet his grades suggest otherwise. His teacher also thinks Collin understands more than the tests demonstrate; he is always an active member of whole- and small-group discussions and is able to contribute in many positive ways. As his teacher works with Collin after school, she again concludes that he seems to understand the content. So, she decides to move away from the conversation about the mathematics and asks about taking tests in general. Collin reveals that he gets anxious and does not finish tests on time. He shares that this happens to him only when he takes math tests and he thinks this is because he feels a lot of pressure to do well. He also tells his teacher:

> *My older brother is a math genius and I want to be just like him. I get frustrated when math seems to take me so much longer than my brother. I start to feel anxious whenever other students in class walk around the room to get supplies. How do they have time to get up at all? I also get really distracted when other students bring their tests to your desk. It makes me even more aware of how slow I am.*

A look at Collin's previous tests reveals an interesting pattern. He always gets the problems correct on the first two pages, but then as the test continues, he starts making computation errors and his work on the last two or three problems looks rushed. Collin's teacher had thought that this was just because the problems were becoming more difficult, but by talking with Collin she now learns that he becomes increasingly anxious as the test continues. A few changes for Collin make a big difference for him. The teacher gives him the opportunity to take the test in an adjoining room, where he is not concerned about what the other students are doing. Further conversations with him about how to be more efficient when solving problems lead to greater speed. Over time, Collin becomes less anxious and his test grades improve.

## Ragged Time

When students are involved in different tasks and work at different rates, this creates what some educators refer to as *ragged time*. Helping every student transition to another appropriate activity when the assigned task is completed would occupy an unrealistic amount of a teacher's time, so it is important to have activities that

*Take Action!*

Discover important attitudes.

students can go to naturally. Such activities are sometimes known as *sponges*, as they soak up the extra time between early and late finishers.

A number of options are possible and different choices may be available on different days or within different units. For example, during a geometry unit one sixth-grade teacher always sets up two sponge activities: origami and a jigsaw puzzle. She places these activities at a table in a corner of the room. Over three or four weeks, her class completes a thousand-crane project (folding a thousand origami cranes) and finishes the puzzle. Sometimes the teacher picks out a few puzzle pieces and places them strategically so that each student can contribute. The class feels a great sense of accomplishment when these activities are completed.

One teacher launches her discussion of proof by using Sudoku puzzles. She finds examples online that are appropriate for her students. At first, many of her students respond, "I just think it should go there," when they explain the placement of a particular digit. During the course of the week, she uses these puzzles to help students understand what it means to prove that an identified digit, and only that digit, must be placed in a particular cell. Later, the teacher refers to this experience whenever she thinks her students need to be reminded about what it means to prove something. She also collects a group of puzzles that students can pursue when their work is finished. The puzzles are purposely color-coded by difficulty and students are comfortable saying, "I'm taking a red one, because these puzzles are new to me."

Most classes support the choice to practice computation skills during ragged time. Students might play a game together that emphasizes mental computation or take advantage of computer software. Some teachers set out a collection of unit-related literature and nonfiction books when beginning a new topic. These books can be placed in a special location and explored when the day's specific math task is completed. Students may also work with problem decks, technology, menu choices, and stations. Some teachers provide each student with a problem pack at the beginning of each unit, with the expectation that she will complete it during these ragged times. All sponge activities don't have to be related to the current topics; in fact, bringing back some favorite choices can be a way to maintain skills.

What's important is that students know what to do when they finish their work and that they continue to be involved in mathematical explorations throughout the time designated for mathematics. Too often middle school students are merely

**Take Action!**

Manage ragged time.

directed to start their homework. While an efficient solution, it limits the time students spend on mathematics each day. We want them to spend their entire math period engaged in activities that will increase their learning of mathematics in addition to the time they will spend on completing homework assignments.

## Whole-Class Work

Whole-class lessons remain important. Often the notion of all of the students working on the same thing at the same time seems contradictory to the notion of differentiated instruction. As we have seen throughout the stories shared from various classrooms, however, whole-class lessons are vital. They provide common experiences and expose students to a greater array of thinking. They help develop common vocabulary and a sense of community. They offer an efficient means for introducing new content that can then be continued later as students work in small groups, in pairs, or individually. There is a time and a place for each form of instruction; knowing your intent and figuring out the best way to meet your goals is what is critical.

Even during a whole-class lesson, teachers have ways to support individual needs and strengths. Often a quick think-pair-share time can lead to a more successful whole-class endeavor. Many students prefer being able to stop and reflect or having the support of a partner in a large-group setting. Waiting before letting students respond, encouraging several students to respond, and teaching students how to connect their comments to those of the previous speakers are all ways to support differentiated instruction in whole-class discussions.

Some teachers find it helpful to get a general sense of students' understanding during these discussions. Students can hold up quick response cards or raise their thumbs (up for solid understanding, down for lack of understanding, and sideways for unsure) to give teachers immediate feedback. One teacher developed the habit of asking students who had their thumbs directed sideways to explain their thinking. Other students can then ask questions or elaborate on the thinking of these students. Through this process, students have the opportunity to learn from and with each other.

Though differentiated instruction emphasizes meeting individual needs, we must not lose sight of the importance of the collective experience in this process. Participation in a learning community is powerful. What we learn together can far exceed what any one individual can learn alone or any single teacher can teach. Finding ways to bring a class of students together to share their experiences is essential.

Even when students are working on separate tasks, you need to have designated times for students to gather and share their new knowledge, ideas, and strategies. Whether in class meetings or debriefing sessions, students should have time together to report findings, review ideas, and raise new questions. Within these discussions, students can see how others take on new challenges and make sense of new material. Yet when students have not worked on exactly the same task, sometimes sharing becomes less important to them—even irrelevant or confusing. Teachers need to orchestrate these conversations in ways that build commonalities while respecting and celebrating differences.

Looking for common ground is a place to start. That's why we always identify the curriculum goal or standard before we design tasks, form groups, and make other decisions about customizing instruction. Refocusing students on the common threads of their individual learning experiences helps them see that it makes sense to share. Sometimes simply asking students to describe one new thing they learned today, this week, or during this unit can both honor and link individual experiences. Recording personal responses in a concept web may unearth more similarity and common ground than first perceived.

Class discussions can focus on process as well as content. Sometimes, talking about how we organize our data, visualize a relationship, or represent our thinking is more informative than sharing an answer or a solution. Further, as students learn more about each other's thinking, they are able to more authentically validate frustrations, make note of growth, and celebrate success.

## Teaching Partnerships

In today's classrooms, volunteers, student teachers, paraprofessionals, coteachers, or math coaches may be working together to support student learning. Having more than one adult in the room can often better support multiple activities and meet the needs of a diverse student population, but clear and shared expectations are necessary to maximize joint efforts.

When working with volunteers, student teachers, and paraprofessionals, it must be clear that the classroom teacher is in charge. This hierarchical structure may help you avoid potential pitfalls. The teacher chooses how the volunteer can best support learning

**Take Action!**

Look for common ground among different activities.

goals, and often the volunteer works with students individually. Some teachers find themselves benefiting from particularly talented individuals or from long-term partnerships. Such team members can be true collaborators who effortlessly balance one another as they move about the classroom.

Coteaching, involving the pairing of a general education and a special education teacher, is becoming more common in our inclusive classrooms. The general education teacher tends to bring the most knowledge about the content area and the curriculum as well as experience with whole-class instruction, while the special education teacher brings expertise related to making instructional adaptations and managing individual behavior. Together, they share ownership of the students. With careful planning, this collaborative relationship can greatly benefit students. When you are used to working alone, sharing all of the decision making involved in classroom teaching can also lead to a disaster; careful management of these partnerships is essential.

A variety of educators including Cahill and Mitra (2008) and Boudah, Schumaker, and Deshler (1997) have identified different ways in which general education and special education teachers can share the responsibility for teaching the same students. Some of these ways are listed here:

---

### How General Education and Special Education Teachers Can Work Together

**Lead-and-assistant model**

In lead-and-assistant models, the general education teacher usually leads the lesson, while the special education teacher pays particular attention to students with IEPs. Roles are particularly clear in this model, but all students do not benefit from the special educator's expertise; a sense of "your students" and "my students" might prevail, which would not support collaborative planning.

**Parallel teaching model**

Teams who follow a parallel teaching model ideally plan lessons together, but they deliver them separately. They may each provide instruction to half of the class, or they may teach in separate spaces, with the general education teacher in the regular classroom and the special educator in the resource room. One drawback to this approach is that such teams don't always have time to plan together. As a result the special education teacher's lessons might overlap with lessons that the general education teacher is planning or has already done with the whole class.

---

(*Continued*)

## How General Education and Special Education Teachers Can Work Together (Continued)

**Taking turns**

Taking turns allows both teachers to serve as the lead and the assistant teacher. Teachers may decide which role to assume based on preference, content knowledge, or an established every-other-day schedule. In this model, both teachers have the opportunity to provide whole-class instruction and individual or small-group support.

**Complete coteaching**

True coteaching is possible only when teachers are equally involved in the planning, delivery, and assessment of instruction. Often seen as ideal, this approach takes considerable openness, time for joint planning, and administrative support for success.

Consider the following reflection of an eighth-grade teacher who has cotaught for the past three years. Through her reflection, we gain many insights into what can go wrong and what is needed for coteaching relationships to thrive.

This teacher identifies many aspects of a positive coteaching situation: one partnership per teacher; input into the formation of

## Teacher Reflection

I had just completed my third year as an eighth-grade math teacher when the district decided that my school would become an inclusive school and that all classes would be cotaught. We were told that we would receive professional development in August and know our partners at that time. I was floored. How was I supposed to share *my* classroom? I thought about looking for another position, but the pay was good in my system and I only had a ten-minute commute. I decided it was too late to find something comparable and that I would have to give it a try. Boy did I regret that decision! In August, I learned that I would have one coteacher for three of my eighth-grade classes and a different one for my other two. One of the coteachers was new to the district and the other, new to my school. I was now going to share my students with complete strangers!

It was a difficult year and to be honest, I have forgotten some of the many things that went wrong, probably because

> *It was a difficult year and to be honest, I have forgotten some of the many things that went wrong, probably because they are too painful to remember.*

they are too painful to remember. One of my coteachers expected me to do all of the planning and grading, even though our salaries were the same. She didn't have time to plan after school, and special education meetings were held at the same time as when the math department met. She did not hesitate, however, to criticize my style of teaching. She wanted everything to be structured, with step-by-step instructions given to the students. That's just not how I taught. Students pick up on things so easily; it was clear to them that our teaching styles were in conflict. Parents of the students with IEPs began to talk only to her and at a Back-to-School Night one of them asked, "Is it true that you won't teach my son exactly how to factor a quadratic equation?" The arrangement was a failure and the students suffered because of it. I now recognize that there were ways that I could have created a more positive relationship. I might have suggested that we do something out of school to get to know each other better or I could have been more open to her suggestions about ways to change my teaching, but at the time I was just too miserable and had a bad attitude about the whole thing.

I got along much better with my other coteacher, Tim, though it was still challenging. His teaching philosophy seemed to match mine and as he didn't have a young family, he was always willing to stay after school to plan together. That really mattered to me as it allowed me to plan just a day or two ahead instead of organizing a whole week or unit in advance. I like to make adjustments based on what's going on in the classroom. Also, as Tim didn't have much training in mathematics, it took time to go over the material with him. My social life took a definite dive that year.

Tim had a great sense of humor and the students really liked him. In fact, sometimes I felt jealous of his relationship with them. He was almost $6\frac{1}{2}$ feet tall and they seemed to automatically do anything he asked. We were willing to try different models of coteaching and once in a while, we began to really teach *together*. The problem was that he would often get called out of the classroom to help with an emergency with another special education student, to evaluate a student, or to attend an IEP meeting.

I wasn't the one having problems; changes were made the following year. We had more say about who our partners would be and Tim and I asked to work together. He took a mathematics course that summer, I took a special education course, and we spent a day every two weeks reviewing the curriculum, creating rubrics for assignments, and talking honestly about what we each needed to teach well that fall. After another year of working together, we really hit our stride. It still takes extra time to plan together, but Tim is now able to really share the planning and grading responsibilities. He's learned a lot more mathematics and I've learned a lot more about how to teach. We've become real friends and the students are getting a much better education!

the partnerships; time to work together; willingness of both teachers to expand their knowledge; lack of responsibilities outside of the classroom; and open and honest discussions about needs and preferences. Ideally, schools provide time for coteachers to work together within the school day and support both teachers' attendance at content and special education professional development opportunities. Coteaching requires considerable investment, but research suggests it can have a significant positive impact on student learning.

As teachers gain experience with differentiated instruction, they identify their own ways to organize classroom space, build student awareness and respect for differences, develop classroom routines, form groups, work with students individually, provide interesting activities for students who finish early, lead whole-group lessons and discussions, and share their classrooms with other professionals. They develop their own methods for supporting the important work of differentiation—for building the masterpiece of a well-functioning classroom that meets individual needs while maintaining classroom community.

## Connecting the Chapter to Your Practice

1. What's one change you could make in your classroom space to better support differentiated instruction?

2. How would you respond to a new teacher who asks, "What classroom routines should I establish during the first week of school?"

3. Would you like to coteach? Explain.

4. For you, what is the ideal percentage of instructional time students should spend working as a whole class, in a group, or individually? Why?

# Chapter 9

# Teaching with the Goal of Differentiation

$W$e hope that you too believe that it is essential to differentiate mathematical instruction and now have some additional ideas about what that means and how it might look in your classroom. Even with this recognition and vision, however, differentiated instruction is a long-term goal, and working toward and maintaining such a goal is often difficult. Just as you would require encouragement, reminders, and support to make other significant changes in behavior, you need to find ways to keep your differentiation lens in focus—to act on your belief that students' readiness, learning styles, and interests should inform the ways in which you teach. What can you do to keep your spirit for differentiation high? Here are ten suggestions.

| **Keep Your Spirit of Differentiation High** |
| --- |
| 1. Identify where you already provide differentiation. |
| 2. Recognize where you are along the journey. |
| 3. Start small and build up your differentiation muscles. |
| 4. Capitalize on anticipation. |
| 5. Expect surprises. |
| 6. Let students help. |
| 7. Work with parents. |
| 8. Find sources of professional development. |
| 9. Reflect on your journey. |
| 10. Keep the vision. |

# Ten Ways to Sustain Your Efforts

## 1. Identify where you already provide differentiation.

It's important to remember that differentiation in mathematics is not brand-new. You are most likely already grouping students, working with students individually, and making accommodations to meet students' needs. With differentiated instruction, you will make these decisions more deliberately and with more specific needs in mind. Instead of making changes after a lesson has been problematic, make adjustments in the planning process. Sometimes just tweaking a familiar activity allows the learning experience to be more on target, deeper, and richer for students.

Some teachers begin by thinking about the students who have had unsuccessful experiences with the curriculum. Perhaps there are three or four students in your class who need much more support or challenge. Putting the effort into making lessons work for these students may take more time in the beginning, but the end result will be worth it. For example, one teacher expressed, "Now I work more ahead of time, so I don't have to work so hard when I am teaching."

Don't lose sight of what you can do and, in fact, what you are doing already. Whether you make differentiated instruction in mathematics a priority, you still need to assess what students know and align your curriculum to national, state, and local standards. These assessment and alignment processes jump-start your goal of differentiation. It is valuable to do them; they give you a secure foundation on which to base instructional decisions and to build activities that better meet individual needs. Be clear about what new work is needed and what is required already. As we learn from the following teacher reflection, this clarity is not always present.

## Teacher Reflection

I spent all day Sunday getting ready for new mathematics activities I wanted to try. I had been to a workshop on differentiated instruction and decided to do some things differently in the measurement unit. I had given my students a pre-assessment on Friday and spent much of Sunday morning looking at their work and rereading my school's curriculum. It was a beautiful day, and my husband and children were headed out for a hike. I wanted to go with them and was feeling grouchy that my schoolwork kept me from joining them. I was beginning to wish that I had never started this work. I complained to my husband, who said, "But you always spend a Sunday working on stuff before you start a new unit. Isn't this comparable to cleaning the house?"

I had to laugh at myself then. Just yesterday I had been complaining about how much work it was to have his parents to dinner.

*I sometimes start out new projects with a bit of pessimism. It's important for me to remember why I am doing something and to be clear about what the actual costs are.*

In the morning we cleaned the house and shopped for food; by midday we hadn't even started to cook. My husband had been clear then, too. He reminded me that we always went food shopping and cleaned the house on Saturday mornings whether his parents were coming to dinner or not. How did I forget that? When I looked at it that way, the additional time wasn't that great and it turned out to be a lovely evening.

I sometimes start out new projects with a bit of pessimism. It's important for me to remember why I am doing something and to be clear about what the actual costs are.

## 2. Recognize where you are along the journey.

Many teachers provide a task in September that students complete again sometime in November or December. The comparison of these work samples provides students and parents with concrete examples of growth. Such evidence can boost morale, particularly for students who struggled initially or who may not realize how their abilities have changed. Just as initial benchmarks help students appreciate what they have gained, teachers also benefit from learning how their teaching abilities have adapted, sharpened, broadened, or transformed. So, before you begin your new commitment to differentiated mathematics instruction, you might want to self-assess your current level of differentiation in mathematics.

We encourage you to make a copy of the Self-Assessment of Differentiation Practices form. (See Figure 9–1; see also Reproducibles.) Complete it now and put it in a place where you can find it at a later date. If you keep a personal calendar, mark a date two to three months from now when you will complete this form for a second time. (You may also want to note where you are putting your original response!) Most teachers who do this find that there are significant differences between their responses. For some teachers, just knowing they are going to complete the form again encourages them to try new instructional strategies.

## 3. Start small and build up your differentiation muscles.

Once teachers recognize the need for differentiated instruction, they sometimes feel as if they have to differentiate every lesson for every

**For the Teacher**
**My Self-Assessment of Differentiation Practices**

Rate your agreement with each of the following statements.
1—disagree strongly  2—disagree somewhat  3—agree somewhat  4—agree strongly

| | | | | | |
|---|---|---|---|---|---|
| I feel confident in my ability to facilitate the learning of mathematics at my grade level. | 1 | 2 | 3 | 4 |
| I can challenge my most mathematically able students. | 1 | 2 | 3 | 4 |
| I know how to support my least mathematically able students. | 1 | 2 | 3 | 4 |
| I can meet the individual needs of my students in mathematics as well as or better than I can in literacy. | 1 | 2 | 3 | 4 |
| I have enough knowledge of mathematics to support a variety of models, representations, and procedures in my classroom. | 1 | 2 | 3 | 4 |

Rate the likelihood of the following activities occurring within a week of mathematical instruction. 1—very unlikely  2—somewhat unlikely  3—somewhat likely 4—very likely

| | | | | | |
|---|---|---|---|---|---|
| I work with students individually. | 1 | 2 | 3 | 4 |
| Students are grouped by readiness. | 1 | 2 | 3 | 4 |
| Students are grouped by interest. | 1 | 2 | 3 | 4 |
| Students are grouped by learning preferences. | 1 | 2 | 3 | 4 |
| Different students are working with different materials and tasks. | 1 | 2 | 3 | 4 |

Check off each instructional strategy that you have tried in your teaching of mathematics. Give yourself two points for each check mark.

☐ transformation of tasks to make them more open-ended
☐ RAFT
☐ learning station
☐ menu
☐ think-tac-toe
☐ compacting
☐ tiered task

Total score: _____

Scores range from 10 to 47.
Are you comfortable with where you are on this continuum of differentiation?
What next step(s) do you want to take?

Figure 9–1   *For the Teacher: My Self-Assessment of Differentiation Practices*

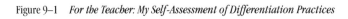

student. This would be an overwhelming task, especially if differentiated mathematics instruction is a new practice for you. Just as if you were beginning a new exercise program, it's best to start slowly and extend your goals as you build your skills and experience success. Exercising too much too soon can result in injuries, frustration, and a sense of failure. These repercussions cause many who make an initial commitment to fitness to conclude that exercise just isn't right for them. Keep this in mind when integrating differentiated instruction! Begin slowly and increase the differentiation in your teaching as your skills and confidence grow.

One way to start is to begin with the mathematics strand you believe you know the best or the one that would benefit the most from differentiation strategies. For middle school teachers, this may vary by grade level. For sixth-grade teachers, number and operations is the likely strand, while at the eighth grade, algebraic thinking is most likely. These topics get much attention at these grades, and if you have been teaching for a few years, you probably have the greatest number of supplementary resources for these areas. Once you have selected a strand, narrow your focus to a unit, a series of lessons, or a particular outcome. Students' abilities to compute or to make algebraic generalizations vary widely. These differences are often apparent quickly and can be challenging to address within the same activity. This difficulty is in contrast, for example, to the way student differences seem to be addressed more easily within the data analysis and probability strand.

Most middle school teachers find that they can easily engage all students with the same task of conducting a survey if they allow students to choose what data they will collect and how they will organize that data. Interest will influence the topics students choose. Readiness will affect how students state the question. For example, "Did you like the format of the geography bee or the spelling bee best?" is much easier to negotiate than "What do you like best about the geography bee?" Learning preferences may influence how students keep track of the collected data; make sure that everyone has the opportunity to respond. Readiness, learning styles, and interests may inform how students display the information and what conclusions they draw. Most important, these differences occur naturally and do not require much teacher intervention. This is less likely to be the case with number and operations or algebraic thinking. The following reflection shows how choosing a familiar strategy and topic can be a positive way to begin.

I teach in a self-contained sixth-grade classroom. I decided that I would try to incorporate some of the instructional strategies I use in reading in my mathematics program. I often select books with a similar theme that span a wide range of reading levels. In this way I feel like I can place the right book in the hands of every student—books that will challenge their levels of comprehension while being well within the instructional range of their skill levels for reading. At the same time, we can have a class discussion about themes that emerge in each story and students can be regrouped to share with those who may not have read the same book. There is usually enough commonality to sustain a dynamic conversation. If I have selected nonfiction material, students can compare details and share facts, thus allowing everyone to benefit by the different books they read.

> *I decided that I would try to incorporate some of the instructional strategies I use in reading in my mathematics program.*

Attempting to set up a similar dynamic for math has not been as straightforward, but I wanted to give it a try. Focusing on number and operations, I selected a word problem and then created three versions of it. The structure of each problem was the same. I created a story around a set of twins who each earned an allowance for doing chores. Within the three versions of the problem, I differentiated the amount of money each child earned, the number of times each chore was completed, and how the problem was worded. I predetermined which students would answer each problem. Students initially worked alone; then I paired them with other students who were working on the same problem. Once I felt as though everyone had solved and compared with at least one other classmate, I grouped children in triads with one student representing each version of the problem.

In this new configuration, students were asked to share their problems, answers, and solution strategies. My hope was that students would act as the experts for the problems they were presenting to the group. Once everyone had familiarized themselves with the three problems, I wanted them to discuss what was the same or different in each problem. This seemed to work well. Students made comments such as "In your problem, Julio and Rita each did the chores a lot more times," "Rita earned more money than Julio in my problem," and "We all used division to get the answers."

This was a small step for me, but it was one that really worked. I could see doing something like this once a week without too much trouble. The students were successful with their individual problems, but also were exposed to other levels of thinking and solution strategies. Maybe next time I could change problem settings as well, choosing contexts that I know would appeal to different students' interests.

## 4. Capitalize on anticipation.

Teachers are often thinking about what will happen next. Sometimes this anticipation can be to our benefit. Sometimes it can lead to trouble. We need to think about how to use anticipation to our best advantage.

On the positive side, being able to anticipate the time and resources a specific activity will require is very helpful. Haven't we all started a lesson, only to realize that we had not made enough copies of the activity packet, or that there really wasn't enough time to complete the new lesson (it took much longer to launch than expected and now the students have to be in their next class!)? Decisions that avoid situations like these come with experience, though even the most seasoned veteran makes similar errors in judgment from time to time. Not having the right resources can derail a potentially successful differentiated lesson, so it's important to make sure that required manipulatives, worksheets or packets, directions, calculators, and any other supplies or tools are readily available. We have to consider purpose and quantity, need for replacement during completion of the task, how students can assist with management, and the mathematical implications of the types of manipulatives or technology available.

Visualizing a future event is part of anticipation. It is important to think about how we envision a lesson unfolding. Keeping in mind our goal(s), where a given lesson falls in the learning progression, and the current levels of our students' understanding, what responses might we anticipate? What leaps in students' understanding might occur? What questions might students ask? What possible errors might they make and what misconceptions might they have? Drawing on our knowledge and past experiences can help us anticipate our responses to new insights, questions, errors, and incomplete understandings. We consider what distractions or diversions may present themselves and identify key questions that we want to ask. We determine ways to scaffold learning and plan groups that will work well together and support the students in their pursuits. Basically, by trying to do as much work up front as possible, teachers reduce potential roadblocks to learning. They also increase the likelihood of being available to work with a small group or support individual students.

Establishing blocks of uninterrupted time for students to focus on the task is also helpful. Check your schedule. Many teachers comment that any time they want to start a new unit or are planning a debriefing session, they want all students present. Many students receive support outside of class; it is important to be mindful of what is happening for each student as you prepare and schedule new lessons. Consider inviting special education teachers to observe and participate in a new lesson; they can then continue your ideas during their time with particular students. Also, build in extra time for students to explore new materials in the lesson. Don't forget that captivating models and tools such as pattern blocks, geoboards, and algebraic tiles are distracting when they are first introduced.

We need to be fresh and ready for new challenges and possibilities. One way that anticipation can lead us into trouble is the overanticipation of behavior. It is only natural for teachers to want to set up the most positive learning environment for students. Keeping everyone's behavior in check can be part of this mindset. Sadly, we can all describe a time in our classrooms when a student's behavior overshadowed or impeded learning. To avoid this from happening, many teachers overanticipate how a specific student might respond and then provide unnecessary scaffolding. Though a natural instinct, this form of anticipation can be short-sighted and limit student potential. As we strive for differentiation in our math classrooms, part of our goal is to support students in all areas of their development. Many teachers have found that when they create tailor-made assignments, negative behavior is diminished. So, for example, under new and more comfortable learning conditions, students may no longer need overly supportive prompts or a separate space to work. Also, even students who have had difficulty working together in the past can learn to appreciate others' strengths.

Many teachers lament about how impossible it is to differentiate mathematics instruction. This attitude and worry can defeat them before they even begin. Part of anticipation is looking forward. Try to visualize how you want your students to succeed, how you want them to develop a rich understanding of and appreciation for mathematics, and how you want them to gain self-confidence in their abilities. Get excited about the possibilities; visualize yourself as the key ingredient in making this happen. Change is scary, it's risky, and it can be problematic. It also can be exciting, rewarding, and fun.

### 5. Expect surprises.

Throughout this book we have presented classroom vignettes that contained surprises. Sometimes students didn't react to materials in the way the teacher expected; sometimes they experienced unexpected difficulty with a representation. This happened even though experienced teachers took time to plan lessons carefully and anticipate students' needs and reactions. But instead of halting the students' work or getting frustrated, these teachers appreciated the opportunities to learn more about their students' thinking.

Sometimes we are surprised to find out that a student knows more than we thought or exhibits a more positive attitude toward mathematics than we believed possible. When choice is involved or mathematics relates to students' interests, students are often able to make mathematical connections in new ways. For example, one student, Isabel, explained, "When I was learning about rotational symmetry in my math class, it took me a while but I finally understood how it worked with the rotations of the angles. But it wasn't until I went to my art class and we made quilt squares that we all put together in a rotational symmetry quilt that I really saw how it worked in real life. Now I see rotational symmetry lots of places, even on roadway signs and on logos on websites."

Parents can also be the source of surprises. Teachers have found that when parents understand how much differentiated instruction helps their children, many ask more questions about mathematics and offer more help. They no longer make statements such as "Well, I wasn't very good at mathematics, so I'm not expecting my child to be a whiz at it either," and they recognize that their children can succeed under the right circumstances.

Teachers tell us they have been surprised to learn that though making plans for differentiated instruction is time-consuming at first, it in fact saves time in the long run. Another surprise teachers have expressed is that when they differentiate instruction, they feel more creative and empowered as decision makers. Teachers are also surprised at the amount of mathematics they are learning. For example, when Thomas asked, "So why can't you divide by zero?" his teacher realized she, too, needed to find out and they researched the topic together.

Surprises are part of the joyful mystery of teaching. They keep us interested and help us learn. They are stimulating and sustain our commitment to differentiated instruction.

## 6. Let students help.

Classrooms require significant management of people, paper, and materials. Differentiated instruction often requires even more organization and record-keeping skills. You will be more successful if you let your students take some of the responsibility. Following are some tasks students can manage independently.

| Responsibilities Students Can Take on in the Classroom |
| --- |
| Organize and distribute materials. |
| Review one another's work. |
| Keep track of their own choices and work. |
| Make sure a partner understands an assigned task. |
| Lead a discussion or familiar game. |
| Answer peer questions when working with a group. |

**Practice Idea!**

**Strand:** Number

**Focus:** Computation

**Context:** Math games

When you encourage your students to take more responsibility for the operation of the classroom, you are fostering their confidence and helping them be more independent. Their involvement may also increase the likelihood that differentiated activities will succeed.

Sometimes the summer months provide teachers with time to tackle projects that never seem to get accomplished during the year. One summer, Christa decided to create a library of math games. Every year she recognized that most of her students would benefit from more practice with computation with decimals, fractions, percents, and mental arithmetic. She decided that offering math games as a portion of Thursday night's homework would give the students extra practice as well as involve their families in their learning.

Christa identified six basic games and then designed three levels of each by changing a few rules or the specific numbers involved. She wrote directions for each of these eighteen game versions and collected the materials—such as cards and dice—that were needed. She wanted four copies of each game so four students could take home the same activity on any given day. She decided to store the games in sealed plastic bags that would protect the games as they traveled back and forth to school. In each bag she put a direction sheet, a materials list, the needed supplies, and a reflection sheet that posed the questions *How did this game help you?* and *What did you learn while playing this game?*

In the fall she organized a storage area for the games and made additional copies of the directions, materials lists, and reflection forms for replacement. She also stored extra packs of cards and dice. She had a student teacher that fall who was given responsibility for distributing the games on Thursdays and checking them back in on Fridays. The process involved collecting the reflection slips, following up on any missing materials, inserting new reflection sheets, and putting the games away. Students were eager to get their Thursday-night homework and Christa noted a marked improvement in their skills. She also found that a number of her students gathered after school, at each other's houses, or in the town library to play the games. Some even engaged their siblings and friends from other classes.

Following the winter break, Christa's student teacher returned to his college campus and Christa took over support of this activity. She was surprised at how difficult it was to accomplish this process without losing precious instructional time. After the second Friday she was certain that this ritual would need to end; she just couldn't support it. She shared her disappointment with the school's math coach, who responded, "Could your students be taught to take care of this themselves?"

Christa had to admit that she hadn't thought of this and at first didn't believe that it would work. She ultimately decided it was worth a try. To her surprise, the students became quite adept at completing these tasks quickly. The six basic games were assigned to captains, who distributed the needed materials to identified peers at the end of Thursday's class and checked them in on Fridays while other students completed quick "do now" problems. The fact that the materials were clearly labeled facilitated the process. Every three weeks, the captains rotated. Christa explained, "I am so glad this was suggested to me. Instead of being frustrated with having to give this up, my students have taken over and it really works!"

It's worth thinking about some of the clerical and custodial tasks that you are performing. Could your students take more responsibility for them? Are there more important things you could accomplish with this time?

## 7. Work with parents.

As you know, parental support can make the difference between success and failure. It is important that your students' parents understand how your classroom works. You can begin by asking parents to help you know their children better, perhaps by completing surveys (see Reproducible 3E) or by talking with you informally before or after school. Most parents support efforts to make sure their children's individual needs are met, but often they need to believe that this is really going to happen. The first back-to-school meeting in the fall is also an opportunity to gain parents' understanding and support.

When one teacher was on an errand, she started to think about the ways she met her own children's needs. She was buying her three children socks; one child wanted high basketball socks, one wanted tennis socks so low you could hardly see them, and her youngest wanted tube socks because, as he explained, "the seams hurt [his] feet when [he had] shoes on." She chuckled as she thought about how not having the right socks could ruin a morning for the entire family. She decided to share these thoughts at back-to-school night and to ask the parents additional questions, such as "Do each of your children need the same amount of sleep? Enjoy the same activities? Want to eat the same food? In what ways do you adjust to meet these individual needs and interests?" She found parents enjoyed talking about these differences with others who were also trying to meet children's needs that didn't always match. It was simple to then help the parents understand that these same differences exist in the classroom and must be addressed.

Evidence of their children's growth is often the most persuasive argument. Before the first parent-teacher conference, collect early work so that it can be compared against later samples. Help parents see the specific concepts and skills their children have gained. Let them know how differentiated instructional strategies supported this improvement. Conferences can also be a time to address their particular concerns about the way you are teaching. Be prepared to help parents understand that

- all learning activities are directly tied to curriculum goals and standards;
- differentiated instruction is not a secret method for tracking the students—groups change often and for a variety of reasons; and
- they are always welcome to visit the classroom and participate in the learning activities during parent shadow day or some other designated time when parents share their children's classroom experiences.

Follow up initial meetings with newsletters and notes. Emails describing new units can help parents realize the common instructional threads in the classroom. This tends to lessen parents' fears that their children are missing out on something.

Sometimes talking about their child's particular learning strengths and weaknesses reminds parents of their own learning profiles. Parents may have struggled in their schooling because learning needs weren't met. Many teachers find that when they share observations with parents about their child's learning profiles, the parents ask questions that suggest they identify with what they have just heard, such as "I wonder what kind of learning disability they might find for me if I were just starting out in school today?" or "I loved math class because I didn't have to read as much. But I'm worried about how much more reading my son needs to do in math class today. Do you think my negative feelings about reading could be turning him off?"

Parents' feelings are strong and their insights about their child's learning are often profound. It is not always easy for parents to open up about their school experiences, but they often do so once a level of trust has been established. For example, at a teacher-parent conference held nearly two months after school has begun, an eighth-grade teacher tells a father that his son is struggling academically in algebra class. The teacher describes classroom situations in which the student often tries to interject a more complex idea than is necessary to solve a problem. The teacher explains, "Consequently, your son is often not successful at completing all of his homework problems and his grades on quizzes are lower than I would expect." The father and teacher have an informative initial discussion about why this student might be so interested in more complex mathematical concepts. The parent agrees to have a conversation with his son. The following week the father sends an email to his son's teacher, reproduced here in the form of a parent reflection.

## Parent Reflection

I had a conversation with my son a few nights ago about his interest in sharing ideas that might fit better in an Algebra II class than in his current class. My son has told me that he always thought he would be considered smarter in the eyes of his teacher and his classmates if he added complex math terms into conversations. He talked about how impressed the classmates at his table were that he had a handout that included all of the square numbers from one to ten thousand and how the principal was impressed that he knew that there were imaginary numbers. He also said that he enjoyed learning this information from me, as I am an engineer and have always enjoyed math myself. I think he thought that I would connect more with him if we talked about more complicated math concepts. When

> *My son has told me that he always thought he would be considered smarter in the eyes of his teacher and his classmates if he added complex math terms into conversations.*

*(Continued)*

we were going over his math homework last night, we talked a little further about how he sometimes gets too caught up in trying to sound smart and needs to try to slow down a little to understand what the teacher is doing in class.

I have to thank you for talking so openly with me about my son. I believe that together, we can help him to focus more on his current studies. Perhaps we can talk about how I can help him at home to understand the connections between what he is currently learning and some of these more complex ideas that he is interested in. I admit that I have to learn not to push my agenda on him so much and let him get what he needs as a foundation in math before I encourage him to think about higher-level math topics, even though he might be ready for them. I look forward to having continued conversations about how we can work together to help him become a better math student.

The teacher is honored to receive this email and knows that this parent's trust is a wonderful gift—one that will ensure that his son's needs will be better met.

## 8. Find sources of professional development.

Ideally, you are working with colleagues as you strive to further differentiate your mathematics instruction; your school system has provided you with coaches, consultants, time, and resources. Such circumstances are increasingly rare, however, and so it is more than likely that you will need to find ways to support your efforts. Sometimes it's sufficient to find one other teacher that will work with you. Here is a list of activities for teachers to engage in with one or more colleagues:

## 9. Reflect on your journey.

When we reflect on our teaching, we take the time to actively deliberate about what is working and what needs further attention. In the evening we might sift through what happened that day, maybe even replay conversations in our mind. Sometimes we uncover something that we didn't know was bothering us; sometimes we develop new insights and ideas. Over time, reflecting on what happens in our classroom helps us transform as well as reaffirm our teaching habits and beliefs. Though reflecting on our teaching is always important, it is particularly helpful when we are adjusting our practice.

Some teachers reflect with others about their teaching; others spend alone time—such as during their commute—to mull over the day. A few teachers keep a journal. When we write our reflections,

## Activities for Teachers to Support Each Other

- Use planning time or arrange coverage for your class so you can visit each other's classroom. It will help you understand how things are currently working and the challenges each of you faces.

- Connect more with the special educators at your school. Find out what teacher resource books they find most helpful and try to attend a conference with them. See what you can learn from each other about how best to meet the needs of your struggling learners.

- Attend mathematics conferences in the local area to gain new ideas and connect with a wider group of teachers.

- Contact a local college library to see if it has videos on the teaching of mathematics or the general practice of differentiated instruction. Watch these videos with other teachers.

- Work more closely with instructional specialists. Many specialists are eager to work with teachers who want to transform their practice.

- See if your school system has a membership in the National Council of Teachers of Mathematics (NCTM) and read its journal *Mathematics Teaching in the Middle School*. If the magazine isn't accessible, explore NCTM's website, www.nctm.org.

- Talk with your principal to find out what support is available and if any local grants might be used for attending conferences or purchasing resource materials.

- Engage in instructional debriefing with other teachers, focused on what is happening during math time.

we have a record that we can return to and reread; this record helps us identify patterns and track our changes over time. One teacher reserves Wednesday afternoon for journal writing. Her reflection tells us about this tradition.

Some teachers prefer to take notes rather than write in prose. One teacher has a daily note-writing practice. Each day she makes notes on a file card in answer to two questions, "How did I address individual needs today?" and "What did I learn about my students today that will inform what I do tomorrow?" When she comes in the next morning, she rereads the notes to help her focus on the

## Teacher Reflection

Early on in my career, I found that by Wednesday, I needed to spend time working after school. By then plans made over the weekend needed more attention and my desk was a bit unorganized. Also, like many, I think of Wednesday as hump day and so working a bit longer on that day made sense to me.

At first, it would take me a while to get started. I'd collapse in my chair and check my email. Sometimes it would take me an hour to get back up to speed. Then I learned about journaling and how that can give you energy and help you focus. I decided to try it on Wednesdays and it really worked for me. Now when my last class is over on Wednesdays, I immediately take out my journal and set the minute timer for fifteen minutes. It might take me a minute or two to start writing, but soon the words begin to flow and I'm often surprised by what I write. I get so focused that I'm usually startled when the timer goes off. Maybe it's the quiet, the focus, or the introspection, but after journal writing I have the energy to tackle the other things I need to do.

> *Maybe it's the quiet, the focus, or the introspection, but after journal writing I have the energy to tackle the other things I need to do.*

new day. Some teachers follow a similar process but record these notes in their plan books. Following is a list of questions to help us reflect on our practice of differentiation.

| Differentiated Learning: Reflection Questions for Teachers |
| --- |
| • Did the pace of today's mathematics instruction work? For whom? Why? Why not? |
| • Are all students being challenged mathematically? |
| • Have I touched base with each of my students over the past few days? |
| • How did I address students' interests this week? Did I learn anything new about an interest a student has? |
| • How were different types of learning styles addressed today? |
| • Are there students I want to meet with individually tomorrow? |
| • Is there a student I am worried about in terms of mathematics? |
| • Would some of my students be more successful using different mathematical manipulatives, representations, or recording systems? |

### 10. Keep the vision.

There will no doubt be times when you question the goal of differentiated mathematics instruction, or at least its viability or sustainability. Perhaps a principal will express reservations about your instructional style, a parent will complain about her child not doing the same work as the neighbor's child, or a colleague will suggest that you are making too much work for yourself. At these times it's important to remember the significance of the goal and the sense it makes. Focus on what is working well in your classes and what is best for your students. Remember that differentiated instruction is a long quest—a journey that never truly ends. It serves as a lens, however, to remind us to focus on how we can best support the individual differences among our students. It provides us with a vision for organizing our classrooms and implementing our curriculum. It takes courage and passion to sustain our differentiated instruction efforts; never lose sight of the vision of all of our students becoming successful learners of mathematics.

## Connecting the Chapter to Your Practice

1. In terms of differentiation, where would you place yourself along the continuum of novice to expert? Why?

2. What responsibilities do your students have in the classroom?

3. How do you help parents to understand the goals of the mathematics curriculum?

4. Who in your school system is most likely to help you identify worthwhile professional development opportunities?

# Reproducibles

# Parent or Guardian
# Questionnaire:
# Your Child and Math

Dear Families:

I am always so excited about the start of the school year and a roomful of eager students. I am eager to get to know each and every one of them, as well as their families. As no one knows your child as well as you do, I am hoping that you will have the time to answer these few questions. There are no right or wrong answers, just responses that will help me meet the needs of your child when learning math. I am very interested in helping students see that math is an important part of the world and thus exciting to learn. I believe by connecting the learning of math to other important aspects of your child's life, I can make it more relevant and exciting. Please feel free to call me if you have any questions. Thank you.

Student's Name _____

Completed By _____

1. What are your child's favorite hobbies, interests, pastimes, books?

2. In what ways is mathematics part of your child's life at home?

3. What, if any, concerns do you have about your child's knowledge of mathematics?

4. What is a mathematical strength that you see in your child?

5. Describe your child's experience with math homework.

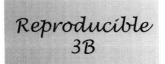

# Parent or Guardian Survey:
## Your Child and Math

Dear Parent or Guardian:

It's been a wonderful start to the school year. I am excited about getting to know each of my new students. I am hoping that you will help me by completing this questionnaire about mathematics. There are no right or wrong answers! Please feel free to call me if you have any questions. Thank you.

Student's Name _____     1 = agree
Completed By _____     2 = somewhat agree
                                                    3 = somewhat disagree
                                                    4 = disagree

| | | | | |
|---|---|---|---|---|
| My child will stick with a math problem, even when it is difficult. | 1 | 2 | 3 | 4 |
| My child lacks confidence in mathematics. | 1 | 2 | 3 | 4 |
| My child has strong computational skills. | 1 | 2 | 3 | 4 |
| My child's favorite subject is mathematics. | 1 | 2 | 3 | 4 |
| My child becomes frustrated when solving math problems. | 1 | 2 | 3 | 4 |
| My child does math homework independently. | 1 | 2 | 3 | 4 |
| As a parent, it is my job to help my child with math homework. | 1 | 2 | 3 | 4 |
| Math is talked about at home and is part of our everyday life. | 1 | 2 | 3 | 4 |
| I do not always understand the way my child thinks about math problems. | 1 | 2 | 3 | 4 |
| Math is taught better today than when I was in school. | 1 | 2 | 3 | 4 |

Comments:

# General Interest Survey
## for Students:
## What Interests You?

Name: _____     Date: _____

1.  What activities do you like to do after school?

2.  What are your favorite sports or games?

3.  What music do you like best?

4.  If you could plan a school field trip, where would the class go?

5.  Who is your favorite character from a book or a video?

6.  Which of these things do you like most? Put a 1 there. Which of these things do you like second best? Put a 2 there.

    ____ music                    ____ reading
    ____ sports                   ____ nature walks
    ____ acting                   ____ drawing or art projects
    ____ being with friends       ____ building things
    ____ science experiments      ____ field trips to historical places

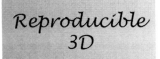

# Learner Survey:
# Who Are You as a Learner?

Name: _____     Date: _____

1.  If you could learn about anything at school, what would you choose?

2.  What do you know a lot about?

3.  How do you work best in school?
    __ alone   __ partner   __ small group   __ large group

4.  Where do you like to work in a classroom?
    __ desk   __ table   __ hallway   __ floor   __ library area   __ other

5.  You learn best when your classroom is
    __ quiet   __ somewhat quiet   __ somewhat noisy   __ noisy

6.  You like schoolwork to be
    __ easy   __ somewhat easy   __ somewhat hard   __ hard

7.  What else do you think helps you learn?

8.  What do you think makes it hard for you to learn?

# Math Interest Inventory

Name: _____     Date: _____

1.   Math is important to learn because . . .

2.   When I am learning math I feel . . .

3.   One thing I am good at in math is . . .

4.   One thing I am not good at yet in math is . . .

5.   This year in math I want to learn about . . .

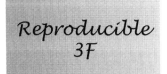

# Mathematics
# Autobiography

Name: _____     Date: _____

Directions: Write an autobiography that focuses on your experiences with mathematics. Use the following questions to guide your thinking. Be sure to explain your answers. You don't need to answer every question, but comment on at least five of them.

1.  How do you feel about yourself in math classes?

2.  What is your first memory of using mathematics?

3.  What do you remember about learning to count or using numbers?

4.  What kinds of things have your math teachers done to help you enjoy math?

5.  What is your favorite topic in mathematics (geometry, computation, logic, algebra, problem solving . . .)?

6.  What kind of math equipment, tools, or games do you like to use when learning mathematics and why?

7.  What are two examples of when you have used math outside of school?

8.  When solving problems, do you prefer working alone or in a group? Why?

9.  What math topic is a strength for you?

10. What math topic do you find most challenging?

# What's the Secret Code?
# Red Group

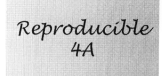
Name: _____     Date: _____

1.  Use the clues to find the code number.

    • The code number is between 3,600 and 3,800.
    • There are six places in the number.
    • All of the digits are odd numbers.
    • The number is 0.41 less than a whole number.
    • The digit in the tens place is one-third the digit in the hundredths place.
    • The digit in the tenths place is four more than the digit in the ones place.

2.  What's the code number?

3.  Pick two clues and explain how they helped you find the code.

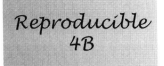

# What's the Secret Code?
## Blue Group

Name: _____     Date: _____

1. Use the clues to find the code number.

   - No digit is used more than once.
   - It is between 6,600 and 6,800.
   - When multiplied by 4, the result is a whole number.
   - The digit in the tenths place is one-fourth the digit in the ones place.
   - The sum of the digit in the hundredths place and the digit in the tens place is even.
   - There are six places in the number.

2. What code numbers fit these clues?

3. Pick two clues and explain how they helped you find these possibilities.

4. Write one more clue so that there is only one possible code number.

# What's the Secret Code?
## Green Group

Name: _____     Date: _____

1. Use the clues to find the code number.

   - It is between 8,500 and 8,800.
   - When multiplied by 8, the result is a whole number.
   - The digit in the hundredths place is $\frac{3}{4}$ the digit in the thousands place.
   - The sum of all the digits in the number is 26.
   - The digit in the hundredths place is 200% of the digit in the tenths place.
   - There are no zeros in the decimal places.

2. What code numbers fit these clues?

3. Explain how you used all of these clues to find these possibilities.

4. Write one more clue so that there is only one possible code number.

# Who Won What?
# Red Group

Name: _____    Date: _____

Without knowing what was inside, Abe, Belinda, Carlos, and Dani each chose one of these boxes as their prize.

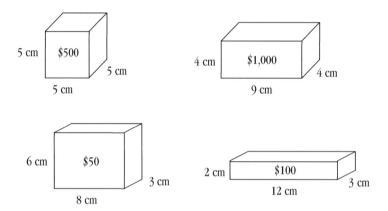

5 cm  $500  5 cm  5 cm

4 cm  $1,000  4 cm  9 cm

6 cm  $50  3 cm  8 cm

2 cm  $100  3 cm  12 cm

Use these clues to determine how much money each player won.

- The boys chose boxes with the same volumes.
- Belinda chose the box with a surface area of 132 cm².
- The box Carlos chose has a surface area greater than the surface area of the box Abe chose.

1. Abe won _____

2. Belinda won _____

3. Carlos won _____

4. Dani won _____

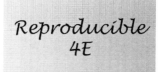
# Who Won What?
## Blue Group

Name: _____     Date: _____

Without knowing what was inside, Evan, Fredrika, Gwen, and Hank each chose one of these boxes as their prize.

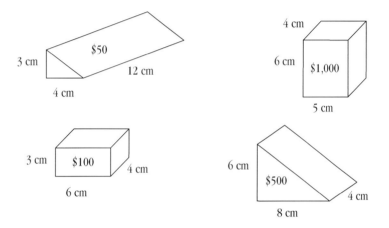

Use these clues to determine how much money each player won.

- Fredrika did not choose a box with a volume of 120 cm$^3$.
- The box that Hank chose does not have the same volume as the box Gwen chose.
- Hank chose a box with a surface area less than 148 cm$^2$.
- The box that Gwen chose has the greatest surface area.

1. Evan won _____

2. Fredrika won _____

3. Gwen won _____

4. Hank won _____

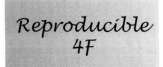

# Who Won What?
## Green Group

Name: _____     Date: _____

Without knowing what was inside, Isabella, Joseph, Kevin, and Ladonna each chose one of these boxes as their prize.

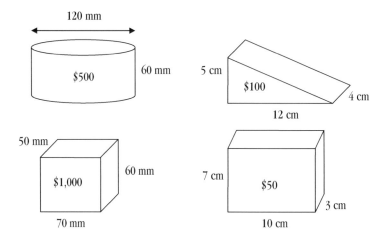

Use these clues to determine how much money each player won.

- Ladonna did not choose the box with the greatest volume.
- The ratio of the volume of the box chosen by Isabella to the volume of the box chosen by Kevin is 4:7.
- Kevin did not choose a box with a surface area greater than the surface area of the box chosen by Ladonna.

1. Isabella won _____

2. Joseph won _____

3. Kevin won _____

4. Ladonna won _____

# Data Collection and Analysis
# Red Group

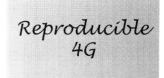

Name: _____   Date: _____

*Plan a Visit to the Capital City*

You are going to plan a place to visit in your state's capital city.
My state's capital city is _____.

1.  Survey your classmates to find out the type of place that they would like to visit.
    The choices are a museum, a historic place, a memorial, or an aquarium.

2.  Prepare a report of what your classmates have chosen. You should include the
    following in your report:
    •   the selections that your classmates made, shown in a frequency table
    •   a circle graph of your data
    •   your recommendation for the place to visit with an explanation as to how
        you analyzed the data to help you decide

3.  Consider what it would cost to visit the place that you chose. You should
    plan to:
    •   brainstorm possible costs
    •   collect the data about cost by researching online the place that
        you have chosen
    •   find the total cost based on the number of students and chaperones
        who will attend

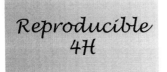

# Data Collection and Analysis
## Blue Group

Name: _____    Date: _____

*Become a Business Consultant*

The local clothing store wants to know more about students' preferences for hats. The owners are interested in learning more about the types of hats that they should keep in stock. You are to collect the data for our classroom and prepare a report to give to the clothing store owners.

1. Discuss the attributes of hats that you would like to know about before you collect data.

2. Make sure to include the data you collect in a frequency table as well as to display the data in an appropriate graph. Include in your report your recommendations with a thorough explanation as to why you made the recommendations that you did.

3. Investigate the prices of hats. Based on the data that you collect, how much do you think that your classmates will spend on hats this year?

# Data Collection and Analysis
## Green Group

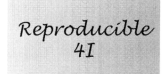

Name: _____     Date: _____

*Make a Fund-Raising Plan for a New Fitness Center*

As the president of the student council at your middle school, you have been asked to make a plan for raising money for a new fitness center at your school.

1.  Collect data about possible fund-raising opportunities. Make sure to include the data you collect as well as graphical representations of the data in your report. You should give a detailed explanation of why you chose the fund-raisers you are recommending. At least one of your graphical representations should be a box-and-whisker plot.

2.  Report on how much money you would like to raise and how you will allocate the monies. Use references, such as catalogs and websites, to estimate the cost of the equipment that you would like to purchase.

3.  Make a plan as to how you will implement your fund-raisers. Include information about how each class in the school will be involved and how you will keep records of how much money is raised.

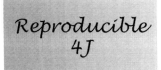

# Quilt Patterns
# Red Group

Name: _____     Date: _____

Look at these quilts.

Quilt 2 shows a total of 2 dotted squares and 13 plain squares.

| Quilt 1 | Quilt 2 | Quilt 3 |

Assume the quilt pattern continues.

- Make a sketch of Quilt 4.

- How many dotted squares will there be in Quilt 6? _____

- How many plain squares will there be in Quilt 6? _____

- How many total squares will there be in Quilt 6? _____

- How many plain squares will there be in the top row of Quilt 7? _____

- How many plain squares will there be in Quilt 10? _____

- Explain your thinking.

# Quilt Patterns
# Blue Group

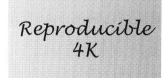

Name: _____ Date: _____

Look at these quilts.

Quilt 2 shows a total of 2 dotted squares and 13 plain squares.

| Quilt 1 | Quilt 2 | Quilt 3 |

Assume the quilt pattern continues.

• How many squares will there be in Quilt 10? _____

• How many plain squares will there be in the top row of Quilt 12? _____

• How many plain squares will there be in Quilt 15? _____

• Explain your thinking.

• How many plain squares will there be in Quilt 40? _____

• Show your work.

• Write an equation for using the number of dotted squares in a quilt to find the number of plain squares.

_____

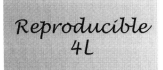

# Quilt Patterns
# Green Group

Name: _____     Date: _____

Look at these quilts.

Quilt 2 shows a total of 2 dotted squares and 13 plain squares.

Quilt 1          Quilt 2                    Quilt 3

- How many squares will there be in Quilt 40? _____

- Show your work.

- Write an equation for using the number of dotted squares in a quilt to find
  the plain squares. _____

- Explain how you can see this equation in the quilt figures.

- If a quilt pattern has 303 plain squares, how many dotted squares does
  it have? _____

- Write an equation for using the number of plain squares in a quilt to find the
  number of dotted squares. _____

- Explain how you can see this equation in the quilt figures.

# The Ice-Cream Shop
# Red Group

Name: _____     Date: _____

Use the graph below to answer the following questions:

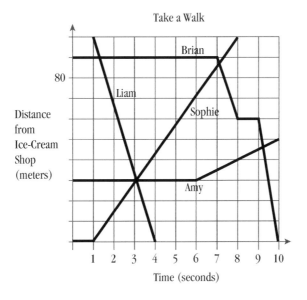

1. Which of the four friends starts out at the ice-cream shop?

2. Which friend is the farthest away from the ice-cream shop when time = 0?

3. How long does it take Brian to get to the ice-cream shop?

4. Who got to the ice-cream shop first: Amy, Liam, or Brian?

5. How far away is Sophie from the ice-cream shop when Brian gets to the ice-cream shop?

6. Write and answer your own question about the graph.

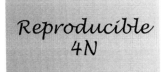
# The Ice-Cream Shop
# Blue Group

Name: _____     Date: _____

Use the graph below to answer the following questions:

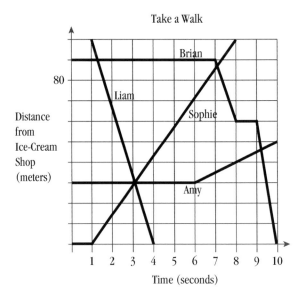

Take a Walk

1. What is Sophie's speed as she walks away from the ice-cream shop?

2. What is Liam's speed as he walks toward the ice-cream shop?

3. Which of the friends never goes to the ice-cream shop?

4. How far is Sophie from the ice-cream shop when Amy starts walking?

5. Whom does Brian meet along his way to the ice-cream shop?

6. Write a story about Liam's trip.

# The Ice-Cream Shop
# Green Group

Name: _____     Date: _____

Use the graph below to answer the following questions:

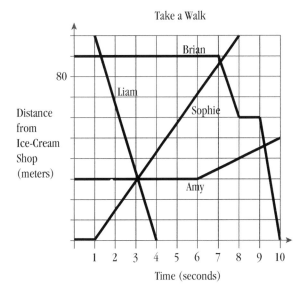

1. What happens after about 3 seconds?

2. Who stayed in one place the longest? _____

   How do you know?

3. Write a verbal description of the story of the four friends and the ice-cream shop.

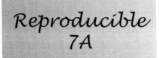

# Project Contract

Name: _____     Date: _____

1. Due date: _____
   The topic for my mathematical project is:


   This is what I want to learn:


   I will use these materials and resources:


   This is what I will create to show what I learned about mathematics:


2. Due date: _____
   This is what I have accomplished so far:


   This is what I still have to do:


3. Due date: _____
   My project is complete. The three most important things I learned about mathematics are:


   The best part of this project was:


   The most challenging part of this project was:

# Project Sheet

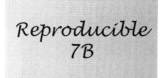

Name: _____     Date: _____

You are about to become an expert on bouncing balls. Pick the ball of your choice and then conduct the following three experiments. Remember that when we measure, it is best to measure three times and average the results.

### Experiment 1

Drop your ball from an agreed-upon height on the meterstick and determine its height after one bounce. Do this three times from the same height and then take an average. Then, drop your ball from various other heights. Relate the initial height and the bounce height.

### Experiment 2

Drop your ball from an agreed-upon height and record its height after the first bounce. Then, drop the ball from the height that it reached after the first bounce. Relate the bounce number and the height it reached after this bounce.

### Experiment 3

Drop your ball from an agreed-upon height and measure the elapsed time until the third bounce. Be patient because measuring the time of the bounce takes practice! Relate the initial height and the time after the third bounce.

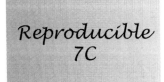

# Menu:
# Symmetry in Art

Name: _____     Date: _____

## Main Course (You must do each one.)

- Make a list of items for a class scavenger hunt that requires your classmates to find different types of symmetry in your school. Be sure to indicate specific types of symmetry for each item on the list.

- Create a symmetrical spinning top that you can share with a younger child. The design should include three line symmetries and a rotational symmetry of 60°.

- Choose one object in nature that has symmetry and study that object in depth. For example, you may choose to study the symmetry in butterflies. Be sure to include discussion of centers of symmetry in your report.

## Side Orders (Complete two.)

- Make a kaleidoscope that makes symmetrical patterns when turned.

- Interview an artist about how he or she uses symmetry in his or her artwork.

- Reread *The Optical Artist,* by Greg Roza (2005), and write your own description of one of the symmetrical pictures in the book.

- Make a slide show of symmetry in nature.

- Choose one of the symmetry websites that have been saved as favorites to explore.

- Find three representations of optical illusions that are interesting examples of different types of symmetry.

## Desserts (Do one or more if you are interested.)

- Read three other books about symmetry and write a review of one of them for your classmates.

- Write a poem about symmetry and visually display this poem in a symmetrical format.

# Think-Tac-Toe:
# Fractions

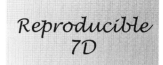

Name: _____    Date: _____

*Choose and complete one activity in each row.*

| | | |
|---|---|---|
| Draw a picture that shows a model of $2\frac{1}{4} \times 1\frac{1}{2}$. Make connections between your drawing and how you use paper and pencil to find the product. Dictate your ideas to a friend. | Your brother divided $6\frac{1}{3}$ by $\frac{1}{2}$ and got the answer $3\frac{1}{6}$. What could you show and tell your brother to help him understand why his answer is wrong? | Write directions for two different ways to find $4\frac{3}{8} - 2\frac{5}{16}$ when you use paper and pencil. |
| Place the numbers $\frac{1}{16}, \frac{3}{16}, \frac{5}{16}, \frac{1}{8}, \frac{3}{8}$, and $\frac{1}{4}$ so that the sum of each side is $\frac{5}{8}$. | Place $+$, $\times$, or $\div$ to make a number sentence that is true. Add parentheses if needed. $$\frac{1}{4} \,\square\, \frac{1}{8} \,\square\, \frac{3}{4} \,\square\, \frac{1}{2} = 1$$ Write two more problems like this one and trade them with a classmate. | Which two numbers should you exchange so that the sum of the numbers on each card is the same? Write two more problems like this one and trade them with a classmate. |
| Make a collage from newspaper ads or articles that include fractions. | Interview a classmate about what he or she knows about fractions. Find out as much as you can in three minutes. Write the teacher a report with suggestions for teaching. | Your friend solved a word problem by multiplying $2\frac{1}{2}$ times $\frac{1}{3}$ and then subtracting the product from 3. Write two interesting word problems that your friend could have solved this way. |

In the card grid cell:

| $\frac{1}{2}$ | $\frac{2}{3}$ | 1 | | $\frac{3}{4}$ | $\frac{2}{3}$ | $\frac{7}{12}$ |
|---|---|---|---|---|---|---|
| $\frac{5}{12}$ | $\frac{1}{4}$ | $\frac{1}{2}$ | | $\frac{1}{12}$ | $\frac{3}{4}$ | $\frac{5}{6}$ |

# RAFT:
## Probability

Name: _____     Date: _____

| Role | Audience | Format | Topic |
|------|----------|--------|-------|
| Meteorologist | Middle school students | PowerPoint presentation | How I use probability on my job |
| Financial advisor | People trying to save money | Song | Why you shouldn't buy lottery tickets |
| Game maker | Game company boss | Game | Game with just the right combination of skill and luck |
| Stockbroker | Clients | Report | Probability of making money in the stock market |
| Sports analyst | Team manager | Convincing argument | Creation of a dream team |
| Fill in your | choice here. | Check with the | teacher for approval. |

# Survey:
# What Matches You?

Name: _____   Date: _____

*Try to find two classmates who match each description. Have them sign their names in the boxes they match. No one may sign more than three boxes on one sheet.*

| | | | | |
|---|---|---|---|---|
| I learn best through hands-on experiences. | I like to solve problems. | I prefer to work alone in mathematics. | I find it helpful to write about my mathematical ideas. | I sometimes get confused when others explain their thinking. |
| I understand fractions better than percents. | I like to measure things. | I use drawings to understand a problem. | I learn best when the teacher writes on the board. | I find a number line helpful when working with integers. |
| I am better at division than multiplication. | I like rotating shapes in my mind. | I need it to be quiet when I work. | I prefer fraction strips to fraction circles. | I prefer to work with others. |
| I know my basic facts well. | I like digital clocks better than face clocks. | I am better at solving equations than graphing them. | I like reading and making maps. | I like learning different ways to solve problems. |
| I like to brainstorm ideas with a group and then follow up alone. | I like logic games and puzzles. | I want rules for solving problems. | I would like to use a calculator all of the time. | I read tables and graphs in the newspaper. |

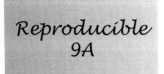

# For the Teacher:
## My Self-Assessment of
## Differentiation Practices

Rate your agreement with each of the following statements.
1—disagree strongly  2—disagree somewhat  3—agree somewhat  4—agree strongly

| | | | | |
|---|---|---|---|---|
| I feel confident in my ability to facilitate the learning of mathematics at my grade level. | 1 | 2 | 3 | 4 |
| I can challenge my most mathematically able students. | 1 | 2 | 3 | 4 |
| I know how to support my least mathematically able students. | 1 | 2 | 3 | 4 |
| I can meet the individual needs of my students in mathematics as well as or better than I can in literacy. | 1 | 2 | 3 | 4 |
| I have enough knowledge of mathematics to support a variety of models, representations, and procedures in my classroom. | 1 | 2 | 3 | 4 |

Rate the likelihood of the following activities occurring within a week of mathematical instruction.
1—very unlikely  2—somewhat unlikely  3—somewhat likely  4— very likely

| | | | | |
|---|---|---|---|---|
| I work with students individually. | 1 | 2 | 3 | 4 |
| Students are grouped by readiness. | 1 | 2 | 3 | 4 |
| Students are grouped by interest. | 1 | 2 | 3 | 4 |
| Students are grouped by learning preferences. | 1 | 2 | 3 | 4 |
| Different students are working with different materials and tasks. | 1 | 2 | 3 | 4 |

Check off each instructional strategy that you have tried in your teaching of mathematics. Give yourself two points for each check mark.

☐ transformation of tasks to make them more open-ended
☐ RAFT
☐ learning station
☐ menu
☐ think-tac-toe
☐ compacting
☐ tiered task

Total score: _____

Scores range from 10 to 47.
Are you comfortable with where you are on this continuum of differentiation?
What next step(s) do you want to take?

# References

Adams, Thomasenia. 2003. "Reading Mathematics: More Than Words Can Say." *The Reading Teacher* 56 (May): 786–95.

Anderson, Lorin, and David Krathwohl, eds. 2001. *Taxonomy for Learning, Teaching, and Assessing: A Revision of Bloom's Taxonomy of Educational Objectives*. New York: Addison-Wesley Longman.

Ansell, Ellen, and Helen Doerr. 2000. "NAEP Findings Regarding Gender: Achievement, Affect, and Instructional Experiences." *Research Results from the Seventh Mathematics Assessment of the National Assessment of Educational Progress*, ed. Edward Silver and Patricia Kenney, 73–106. Reston, VA: National Council of Teachers of Mathematics.

Bley, Nancy, and Carol Thornton. 1995. *Teaching Mathematics to Students with Learning Disabilities*. 3d ed. Austin, TX: Pro-Ed.

Bloom, Benjamin, ed. 1984. *Taxonomy of Educational Objectives: Book 1, Cognitive Domain*. Reading, MA: Addison-Wesley.

Boudah, Daniel, Jean Schumaker, and Donald Deshler. 1997. "Collaborative Instruction: Is It an Effective Option for Inclusion in Secondary Classrooms?" *Learning Disability Quarterly* 20 (Fall): 293–316.

Briggs, Christine, Sally Reis, and Erin Sullivan. 2008. "A National View of Promising Programs and Practices for Culturally, Linguistically, and Ethnically Diverse Gifted and Talented Students." *The Gifted Child Quarterly* 52 (Spring): 131–46.

Burns, Marilyn, and Cathy Humphries. 1991. *A Collection of Math Lessons: From Grades 6 Through 8*. Sausalito, CA: Math Solutions.

Burris, Carol Corbett, and Delia Garrity. 2008. *Detracking for Excellence and Equity*. Alexandria, VA: Association for Supervision and Curriculum Development.

Cahill, Susan, and Sue Mitra. 2008. "Forging Collaborative Relationships to Meet the Demands of Inclusion." *Kappa Delta Pi Record* 44 (Summer): 149–52.

Chipman, Susan, David Krantz, and Rae Silver. 2002. "Mathematics Anxiety and Science Careers Among Able College Women." *Psychological Science* 3: 292–95.

Chiu, Lian-Hwang, and Loren Henry. 1990. "Development and Validation of the Mathematics Anxiety Scale for Children." *Measurement and Evaluation in Counseling and Development* 23 (October): 121–27.

Clement, Rod. 1991. *Counting on Frank*. Milwaukee, WI: G. Stevens Children's Books.

Cole, Karen, Janet Coffey, and Shelley Goldman. 1999. "Using Assessments to Improve Equity in Mathematics: Assessment That Is Open, Explicit, and Accessible Helps All Students Achieve the Goals of Standards-Based Learning." *Educational Leadership* 56 (March): 56–58.

Cole, Robert, ed. *Educating Everybody's Children: Diverse Teaching Strategies for Diverse Learners* Rev. and exp. 2d ed. Alexandria, VA: Association for Supervision and Curriculum Development.

Connolly, Austin. 2008a. *KeyMath 3 Diagnostic Assessment*. Minneapolis: Pearson.

———. 2008b. *KeyMath 3 Essential Resources*. Minneapolis: Pearson.

D'Amico, Joan, and Kate Gallaway. 2008. *Differentiated Instruction for the Middle School Math Teacher: Grades 5–8*. San Francisco: Jossey-Bass.

Dienes, Zoltan. 1960. *Building Up Mathematics*. London: Hutchinson.

Ellett, Kim. 2005. "Making a Million Meaningful." *Mathematics Teaching in the Middle School* 10 (April): 416–23.

Erwin, Jonathan. 2004. *The Classroom of Choice: Giving Students What They Need and Getting What You Want*. Alexandria, VA: Association for Supervision and Curriculum Development.

Enzensberger, Hans Magnus. 1998. *The Number Devil: A Mathematical Adventure*. New York: Henry Holt.

Furner, Joseph, and Mary Lou Duffy. 2002. "Equity for All Students in the New Millennium: Disabling Math Anxiety." *Intervention in School and Clinic* 4 (November): 67–74.

Furner, Joseph, Noorchaya Yahya, and Mary Lou Duffy. 2005. "Teach Mathematics: Strategies to Reach All Students." *Intervention in School and Clinic* 41 (September): 16–23.

Gardner, Howard. 2000. *Intelligence Reframed: Multiple Intelligences for the 21st Century*. New York: Basic.

Gavin, M. Katherine, and Sally Reis. 2000. "Helping Teachers to Encourage Talented Girls in Mathematics." *Gifted Child Today* 26 (Winter): 32–44.

Ginsburg, Herbert. 1997. "Mathematics Learning Disabilities: A View from Developmental Psychology." *Journal of Learning Disabilities* 30 (January–February): 20–33.

Gregg, Jeff, and Diana Underwood Gregg. 2007. "A Context for Integer Computation." *Mathematics Teaching in the Middle School* 13 (August): 46–50.

Gregory, Gayle, and Carolyn Chapman. 2008. *Activities for the Differentiated Classroom: Math, Grades 6–8*. Thousand Oaks, CA: Corwin.

Harrell, Gregory. 2008. "Integrating Mathematics and Social Issues." *Mathematics Teaching in the Middle School* 13 (December/January): 270–75.

Heacox, Diane. 2002. *Differentiating Instruction in the Regular Classroom: How to Reach and Teach All Learners, Grades 3–12*. Minneapolis: Free Spirit.

Hopper, 2000. "Starting Up the Differentiated Classroom." *ASCD Classroom Leadership* 4 (September): 1–3.

Hresko, Wayne, Paul Schlieve, Shelley Herron, Colleen Swain, and Rita Sherbenou. 2002. *Comprehensive Mathematical Abilities Test (CMAT)*. Austin, TX: Pro-Ed.

Jennings, Lenora, and Lori Likis. 2005. "Meeting a Math Achievement Crisis." *Educational Leadership* 62: (March): 65–68.

Jensen, Eric. 2005. *Teaching with the Brain in Mind*. 2d ed. Alexandria, VA: Association for Supervision and Curriculum Development.

Jitenda, Asha. 2002. "Teaching Students Math Problem-Solving Through Graphic Representations." *Teaching Exceptional Children* 34 (March–April): 34–38.

Jones, Eric, and W. Thomas Southern. 2003. "Balancing Perspectives on Mathematics Instruction." *Focus on Exceptional Children* 35 (May): 1–16.

Kenney, Joan, Euthecia Hancewicz, Loretta Heuer, Diana Metsisto, and Cynthia L. Tuttle. 2005. *Literacy Strategies for Improving Mathematics Instruction*. Alexandria, VA: Association for Supervision and Curriculum Development.

Knuth, Eric, and Dominic Peressini. 2001. "Unpacking the Nature of Discourse in Mathematics Classrooms." *Mathematics Teaching in the Middle School* 6 ( January): 320–25.

Lee, Hea-Jin, and Leah Herner-Patnode. 2007. "Teaching Mathematics Vocabulary to Diverse Students." *Intervention and School Clinic* 43 (November): 121–26.

Lubienski, Sarah, and Mack Shelly. 2003. *A Closer Look at U.S. Mathematics Instruction and Achievement: Examinations of Race and SES in a Decade of NAEP Data*. Presented at the annual meeting of the American Educational Research Association, Chicago. ERIC Document No. ED476468. Retrieved July 17, 2004.

Martinie, Sherri, and Jennifer Bay-Williams. 2003. "Investigating Students' Conceptual understanding of Decimals Using Multiple Representations." *Mathematics Teaching in the Middle School* 8 (January): 244–47.

Marzano, Robert, Debra Pickering, and Jane Pollock. 2001. *Classroom Instruction That Works: Research-Based Strategies for Increasing Student Achievement*. Alexandria, VA: Association for Supervision and Curriculum Development.

Maxwell, Vicki, and Marshall Lassak. 2008. "An Experiment in Using Portfolios in the Middle School Classroom." *Mathematics Teaching in the Middle School* 13 (March): 404–9.

Montague, Marjorie. 2006. "Self-Regulation Strategies for Better Math Performance in Middle School." In *Teaching Mathematics to Middle School Students with Learning Difficulties (What Works for Special Needs Learners)*, ed. Marjorie Montague and Asha Jitendra, 89–107. New York: Guilford.

Montague, Marjorie, and Asha Jitendra, eds. 2006. *Teaching Mathematics to Middle School Students with Learning Difficulties (What Works for Special Needs Learners)*. New York: Guilford.

Mullis, Ina, Michael O'Martin, and Pierre Foy. 2005. *IEA's TIMSS 2003 International Report on Achievement in the Mathematics Cognitive Domains: Findings from a Developmental Project*. Boston: Boston College.

Murray, Miki. 2007. *The Differentiated Math Classroom: A Guide for Teachers, K–8*. Portsmouth, NH: Heinemann.

National Clearinghouse for English Language Acquisition. 2007. www.ncela.gwu.edu.

National Council of Teachers of Mathematics (NCTM). 2000. *Principles and Standards for School Mathematics*. Reston, VA: NCTM.

———. 2006. *Curriculum Focal Points for Prekindergarten Through Grade 8 Mathematics: A Quest for Coherence*. Reston, VA: NCTM.

Pierce, Rebecca, and Cheryl Adams. 2005. "Using Tiered Lessons in Mathematics." *Mathematics Teaching in the Middle School* 11 (October): 144–49.

Polya, George. 1945. *How to Solve It: A New Aspect of Mathematical Method*. Princeton, NJ: Princeton University Press.

Ponce, G. A. 2007. "It's All in the Cards: Adding and Subtracting Integers." *Mathematics Teaching in the Middle School* 13 (August): 10–17.

Reeder, Stacy. 2007. "Are We Golden? Investigations with the Golden Ratio." *Mathematics Teaching in the Middle School* 13 (October): 150–55.

Roberts, Sally. 2007. "Not All Manipulatives and Models Are Created Equal." *Mathematics Teaching in the Middle School* 13 (August): 6–9.

Roberts, Sally, and Carla Tayeh. 2007. "It's the Thought That Counts: Reflecting on Problem Solving." *Mathematics Teaching in the Middle School* 12 (December/January): 232–37.

Roberts, Trent M. 2006. "Understanding the Properties of Arithmetic: A Prerequisite for Success in Algebra." *Mathematics Teaching in the Middle School* 12 (August): 22–25.

Ross, John, Ann Hogaboam-Gray, and Ann Rolheiser. 2002. "Student Self-Evaluation in Grade 5–6 Mathematics: Effects on Problem Solving." *Educational Assessment* 8: 43–59.

Rotigel, Jennifer, and Susan Fello. 2004. "Mathematically Gifted Students: How Can We Meet Their Needs?" *Gifted Child Today* 27 (Fall): 46–52.

Roza, Greg. 2005. *The Optical Artist: Exploring Patterns and Symmetry.* New York: Rosen Classroom.

Rubenstein, Rheta. 2007. "Focused Strategies for Middle-Grades Mathematics Vocabulary Development." *Mathematics Teaching in the Middle School* 13 (November): 200–207.

Silver, Harvey, Richard Strong, and Matthew Perini. 2000. *So Each May Learn: Integrating Learning Styles and Multiple Intelligences.* Alexandria, VA: Association for Supervision and Curriculum Development.

Silverstein, Shel. 1974. *Where the Sidewalk Ends: The Poems and Drawings of Shel Silverstein.* New York: Harper and Row.

Smith, Frank. 2002. *The Glass Wall: Why Mathematics Can Seem Difficult.* New York: Teachers College Press.

Sousa, David. 2007. *How the Special Needs Brain Works.* 2d ed. Thousand Oaks, CA: Corwin.

Spielhagen, Frances. 2006. "Closing the Achievement Gap in Math: Considering Eighth Grade Algebra for All Students." *School Psychology Review* 35 (September): 256–370.

Sprenger, Marilee. 2002. *Becoming a "Wiz" at Brain-Based Teaching: How to Make Every Year the Best Year.* Thousand Oaks, CA: Corwin.

———. 2003. *Differentiation Through Learning Styles and Memory.* Thousand Oaks, CA: Corwin.

Stallings, L. Lynn. 2007. "See a Different Mathematics." *Mathematics Teaching in the Middle School* 13: 212–17.

Swanson, H. Lee. 2006. "Math Difficulties: A Selective Meta-Analysis." *Review of Educational Research* 76 (Summer): 249–63.

Tate, William. 1997. "Race-Ethnicity, SES, Gender, and Language Proficiency Trends in Mathematics Achievement: An Update." *Journal for Research in Mathematics Education* 28 (December): 652–79.

Thornton, Carol, and Graham Jones. 1996. "Adapting Instruction for Students with Special Needs K–8." *Journal of Education* 178 (2): 59–69.

Tomlinson, Carol. 1999. *The Differentiated Classroom: Responding to the Needs of All Learners.* Alexandria, VA: Association for Supervision and Curriculum Development.

———. 2003. *Fulfilling the Promise of the Differentiated Classroom: Strategies and Tools for Responsive Teaching.* Alexandria, VA: Association for Supervision and Curriculum Development.

Tomlinson, Carol, Kay Brimijoin, and Lane Narvaez. 2008. *The Differentiated School: Making Revolutionary Changes in Teaching and Learning*. Alexandria, VA: Association for Supervision and Curriculum Development.

Tomlinson, Carol, and Caroline Cunningham Eidson. 2003. *Differentiation in Practice: A Resource Guide for Differentiating Curriculum, Grades K–5*. Alexandria, VA: Association for Supervision and Curriculum Development.

U.S. Census. 2003. *Language Use and English Speaking Ability: 2000.* Retrieved January 11, 2006, from www.census.gov/prod/2003pubs/c2kbr-29.pdf.

Van Luit, Johannes, and Esther Schopman. 2000. "Improving Early Numeracy of Young Children with Special Education Needs." *Remedial and Special Education* 21 ( January/February): 27–40.

Vygotsky, Lev. 1978. *Mind and Society.* Cambridge, MA: Harvard University Press.

Williams, Kathleen. 2004. *Group Mathematics Assessment and Diagnostic Evaluation (GMADE).* Minneapolis: Pearson.

Willis, S., W. Devlin, L. Jacob, B. Powell, D. Tomazos, and K. Treacy. 2007. First Steps® in Mathematics Series. Australia: Pearson Rigby.

Wolfe, Pat. 2001. *Brain Matters: Translating Research into Classroom Practice.* Alexandria, VA: Association for Supervision and Curriculum Development.

Zaslavsky, Claudia. 2002. "Exploring World Cultures in Math Class." *Educational Leadership* 48 (October): 66–69.

# Index